Small Cities Thinking Big

# Small Cities Thinking Big

*Revitalization Lessons
from Augusta, Maine,
and Other Communities*

Michael G. Hall

McFarland & Company, Inc., Publishers
*Jefferson, North Carolina*

ISBN (print) 978-1-4766-8559-5
ISBN (ebook) 978-1-4766-4354-0

LIBRARY OF CONGRESS AND BRITISH LIBRARY
CATALOGUING DATA ARE AVAILABLE

Library of Congress Control Number 2021044613

© 2021 Michael G. Hall. All rights reserved

*No part of this book may be reproduced or transmitted in any form or by any means, electronic or mechanical, including photocopying or recording, or by any information storage and retrieval system, without permission in writing from the publisher.*

Front cover photograph by Dave Dostie

Printed in the United States of America

*McFarland & Company, Inc., Publishers
Box 611, Jefferson, North Carolina 28640
www.mcfarlandpub.com*

For my parents,
Carmela and Patrick Hall

# Table of Contents

*Acknowledgments*   viii
*Introduction*   1

1. Organizing Your House: The Importance of Organizations and Partnerships   13
2. It's All About Distinction: Identifying and Placemaking Your Small Town   33
3. Focus on Aesthetics   47
4. Ignore the Haters: Learn to Trust Your Instincts   63
5. It's the Traffic Count, Stupid   78
6. Marketing Your Small City … the Right Way   94
7. Trickle Down(town) Economics: Why Upper-Floor Development Is Key to Street-Level Retail   112
8. Get a Little Artsy   129
9. Leveraging the Unexpected: A Proactive Approach to Disaster Mitigation   148
10. Avoid the Three Deadly Fallacies of Urban Planning   165
11. Mixing It Up: Celebrating Diversity in America's Small Cities   183

*Conclusion: Not a Moment to Lose*   200
*Chapter Notes*   203
*Bibliography*   212
*Index*   219

# Acknowledgments

This book would not be possible without the participation of everyone involved. I personally want to thank and acknowledge Heather Pouliot, Shawn McLaughlin, Soo Parkhurst, Nancy Smith, Matt Pouliot, Larry Fleury, Cynthia Roodman, Tobias Parkhurst, Jesse Patkus, Andrew LeBlanc and Keith Luke for sharing their guidance and expertise. All are amazing individuals. and I'm very lucky to count them among my friends.

In addition, I want to thank Dave Dostie for allowing me the use of his amazing photos.

Lastly, I want to acknowledge everyone indirectly involved for the strong moral support provided during the writing process. This book is larger than any I have previously written, and I sincerely appreciate the encouragement I've received.

# Introduction

On August 17, 2020, New York City was officially pronounced dead. Just four years shy of its 400th birthday, the City That Never Sleeps fell into a deep coma from which it has yet to awaken. The hollowed-out strip of Fifth Avenue—Manhattan's go-to spot for all things luxury—now sits vacant, its windows boarded up. Times Square, once filled with throngs of tourists, is eerily quiet. The bright lights of Broadway are dimmed.

Longtime residents of the city are quick to remark that all this has happened before. Many still remember the heady days of the 1970s, when the city was on the verge of bankruptcy and denied a bailout. A 1975 article in the *Daily News* captured this sentiment perfectly with the headline: "Ford to City: Drop Dead." Like the past, they proclaim that rumors of the city's demise have been greatly exaggerated. Still, to others, this time feels different. The sickness feels real.

What began as a panic over Covid-19 has turned into an exposé of all things wrong with life in the Big Apple. Murders have skyrocketed, homelessness has spread, racial tensions have flared, and crime has reached decades-high levels. Shootings have surged 82 percent since May 2020 alone.[1] But instead of things getting better, they just keep getting worse. With little hope for change, residents began fleeing *en masse*. Between March 1 and May 1, a total of 420,000 residents fled the city, accounting for roughly 5 percent of the total population. Most of the residents who have fled are those living in the posh neighborhoods of the Upper East Side, the West Village, SoHo, and Brooklyn Heights,[2] and while some have since returned, others are continuing to stay away.

As moving trucks poured into the city, Governor Cuomo, desperate to stop the bleeding, begged them to come back:

"I literally talk to people all day long who are now in their Hamptons house who also lived here, or in their Hudson Valley house or in their Connecticut weekend house, and I say, 'You gotta come back, when are you coming back?'" Cuomo said during a press conference.

"'We'll go to dinner, I'll buy you a drink, come over I'll cook,'" Cuomo said, describing his pleas with wealthy New Yorkers.[3]

As summer months led to clashes against police, as well as widespread looting and violence, these pleas have largely fallen on deaf ears. Covid-19 has shown them not only that they can live elsewhere, but also that they can live better.

No longer confined to an office, many have seen that work can be done more productively from the comfort of their living rooms. The lack of cultural options due to crowd restrictions has also forced them to reevaluate their locales as, without ready access to museums, Broadway plays or fine dining establishments, all they are paying for is overpriced real estate in cramped and crowded conditions.

As days pass, with some prognosticators indicating full recovery for the city is expected to take 10 years or longer, it has become clear that what the pandemic has done is more than just put a dent into the city: It has actually torn the Band-Aid off New York City exceptionalism.

For decades, this myth of exceptionalism has been propped up in the "if I can make it here, I can make it anywhere" trope. However, this trope was only perpetuated as long as people wanted to move there. Well, as 2020 dragged on to 2021, it appeared that people no longer desired to flock to New York. It's too dangerous. The health risks are too great. It's too expensive.

While it would be tempting to lay all of this at the feet of the pandemic, this is actually something that has been happening for quite a while. In fact, during the last three years, roughly 146 people a day have been fleeing the city.[4] This, in itself, is troubling enough for a great city like New York, but as we'll see, these are trends that are being repeated in urban centers nationwide.

## *The Death of the Large American City*

It might seem that the issues raised above are unique to New York; however, New York is just a harbinger for other major cities. As is the case for most trends, New York was simply the first urban center to experience these changes on a mass scale. As the epicenter of the pandemic, it was seen as a symbol of the kinds of flaws that overcrowding can bring, particularly if the structures that supported it, such as readily available access to public transportation and close access to city parks and other amenities, were abruptly halted. Take away these things, and the appeals of city life are less than noteworthy. As noted by Sue Hough (2020), the pandemic has demonstrated:

- The rat race is not all it was cracked up to be.
- Work doesn't need to happen in an office building.
- Losing the daily commute is not a bad thing.
- Focusing life around home reduces expenses.
- Family-centric living has unexpected benefits.
- Social distancing may become permanent.[5]

While New York seems to be getting the brunt of attention regarding demographic decline, eleven of the largest American cities with populations over a million lost people last year as well. According to analysis by Jed Kolko of Indeed.com, the cities of Los Angeles and Chicago saw two of the largest percentage declines. Without immigration gains, seven more large metros, including Miami, Boston, Providence, San Diego, San Francisco, Milwaukee, and New Orleans, would have shrunk.

Throughout much of the 2000s and into the 2010s, America's major cities, including New York, reversed prior decades of population loss as incomes grew and crime fell. Some neighborhoods even surpassed their historic peak populations—for example, New York's Bronx borough, which lost some 20 percent of its residents in the 1970s alone. Newcomers rented out or bought up real estate in the wake of the 2008 financial crisis as urban job creation revved up. But over the past decade, housing creation failed to keep up with job creation: 3.9 new jobs were created in New York City for every one new housing permit.[6]

Even mid-size cities have not been immune to this decline. Fully 48 major metro areas showed peak growth during the first six years of the decade and only one—Tucson, Arizona—realized its highest decade growth in 2018 to 2019.

These trends are also apparent when examining absolute population losses among major metro areas. In 2010 to 2011, only three of the nation's 53 major metro areas—Cleveland, Providence, Rhode Island, and Buffalo, New York—registered population declines. However, that number rose over the course of the decade, with 12 areas sustaining population losses in 2018 to 2019. These include several heartland metro areas such as Cleveland, Pittsburgh, Detroit, and St. Louis, as well as coastal areas like San Jose, California.[7]

While the 2010s, on the whole, will be seen as a positive one for the nation's biggest metropolitan areas, the 2020 census shows an abrupt change as smaller-sized areas and nonmetropolitan territory appear to be gaining ground. The reasons for this are multifaceted and include things like reduced immigration levels, lower fertility rates and lower inbound migration levels, but as the Brookings Institute notes, economics is likely the primary driver: "The late-decade slowdown can be linked to a broader national economic revival, as jobs and housing began to disperse outward after contracting in the immediate aftermath of the Great Recession and housing bust.[8] The study finds that young adults—who are often the most willing and able to relocate— are increasingly drawn to smaller areas including suburban communities and outlier towns. This has resulted in a sharp contraction for many urban counties. And while it's true that recessions, the most recent being the Great Recession, have traditionally halted such movements in the past—which perpetuated a general movement back to larger cities—the pandemic has all but thrown a wrench into traditional models. The allure of densely packed areas has worn thin as the pandemic has continued, making urban communities less desirable among adult Millennials and Gen Z.

So now, as we prepare to enter a new decade, we now find ourselves in uncharted territory. Whereas the last decade brought us urban expansion at unprecedented rates, the 2020s look to push us in a different direction. The era of big cities is over. All hail the rise of the small town!

## *Small Towns Rising*

Unless you live under a rock or simply exist in a portal with no classic rock stations, then chances are you're familiar with the song "Small Town" by John Cougar Mellencamp. This 1985 anthem to small town life celebrates the simplicity of friends, family and community, all wrapped up in a G-D-C chord progression with lyrics like:

> Well I was born in a small town
> And I live in a small town
> Probably die in a small town

Written at a time when small cities were in the midst of a decades-long decline, the song was quite revolutionary for its day, standing in contrast to other songs like Glenn Frey's "You Belong to the City" and the Beastie Boys "No Sleep Till Brooklyn." As Mellencamp recounted in a 2013 *Rolling Stone* article: "I wanted to write a song that said, 'You don't have to live in New York or Los Angeles to live a full life or enjoy your life.' I was never one of those guys that grew up and thought, 'I need to get out of here.' It never dawned on me. I just valued having a family and staying close to friends."[9]

Now, tucked away in his lakeside retreat outside Bloomington, Indiana, it appears Mellencamp is fulfilling the sentiments of his lyrics.

In referencing New York, he states: "I'm too sensitive to live there. I can't see poor people. I can't see the suffering. I can't see the trash on the streets.... I'm not leaving Indiana. I'm going to die here."[10]

The dawn of a new decade promises to endorse this manner of thinking, with the virtues of small town living once again being extolled far and wide. This is especially true as the confines of a formal office space become an increasingly antiquated notion as people grow accustomed to working from home.

Without such constraints to hold them back, small cities and towns now have a means of competing with their larger urban cousins, mainly due to a better quality of life, as demonstrated in an article by *Balance*. Small towns have plenty of great perks of their own to offer, and you may find they're a lot more affordable than a crowded city. Here are some of the reasons why small towns are great, budget-friendly places to live:

- Slower Pace: Far away from the hustle and bustle of a big city, the slower, more relaxed pace of small towns can be a welcome change.
- Fewer Crowds: When you go out on a Saturday night, you won't be waiting in line 45 minutes for a table or fighting to find seats in a crowded movie theater.
- Less Crime: In a small town, it's safer for kids to play outside, for bicyclists to chain their bikes in front of a coffee shop, and for you to leave your car windows cracked when you're parked in your driveway over the summer.
- Lower Cost of Living: Everything from homes to groceries is cheaper in a small town. You can get an entire house for the price of a studio apartment in a large city, and with more mom-and-pop outfits than big corporate chains, the *price of consumer goods* is often lower, too. Not to mention small towns tend to have low property taxes.
- Less Traffic and Pollution: With fewer residents—and towns you can drive across from end-to-end in 10 minutes—commuting is a cinch. You'll save time and gas money, and if you're a runner or cyclist, you'll enjoy not having to jostle for space among heavy traffic.
- Cleaner Air: Another side effect of fewer cars on the road is overall cleaner air, which is great because people in small towns love to enjoy the outdoors. (It's part of that slower pace of living.)
- Close-Knit Community: It's also a great chance to become a "big fish in a small pond," with less competition for jobs and more

opportunity to earn a well-known reputation; you may stand out in your chosen field in a way you never could in an enormous city.[11]

In addition to these reasons, it has been noted that small cities also offer improvements by way of shorter commutes for daily and working needs, as well as fewer stressful stimulators like noise, and foster more opportunities for entrepreneurship.

## A Real Estate Reversal

For decades, it was a commonly held notion that small cities had little to offer and that to advance your career, you needed to place yourself in or within driving distance of a major urban center. As the pandemic showed us, however, this is no longer the case. For better or worse, offices are going the way of the fax machine. Even Twitter recently announced that its workers can telecommute indefinitely. As a result, real estate in small cities is booming. This was summed up in a recent report from Redfin, which documented dramatic spikes in real estate page views in rural and small cities. According to Redfin Lead Economist Taylor Marr, the ongoing pandemic "has shined a bright light on one of the historic downsides of density—the possibility for spread of disease. It will remain to be seen if this shift in demand away from urban metros lasts or is temporary."[12]

Redfin cites that their 2020 first quarter earnings showed a remarkable shift away from larger cities as the pandemic gained hold, already accelerating a population decline resulting from a lack of affordable housing in such places. The onset of remote working and the wariness of close quarters with other people have also contributed to a marked interest in smaller cities, as was noted by Kelman: "Since March 15, searches for homes and towns with population under 50,000 people increased 71%." He added that "more people will leave San Francisco, New York, and even Seattle, some for nearby towns like Sacramento and Tacoma that are close enough to support a weekly office visit, others for a completely remote life in Charleston, Boise, Bozeman, or Madison."[13]

Such data was supported in recent public opinion surveys, including one from Harris Poll, which found that nearly one-third of Americans prefer living in a rural area as a result of the pandemic and that four in 10 are more likely to abandon cities as a result. Such statistics provide a rosier picture for smaller cities as it appears that these trends are not going away anytime soon. Tim Ellis, Senior Data Journalist at Redfin, is quoted as saying, "Based on what we're seeing in the data so far, it looks like the housing market in rural areas and small towns will weather the storm through coronavirus shutdowns better than the big cities."[14]

This opening has led small cities to market themselves to different demographic groups, with smaller cities increasingly appealing to Millennials—those with the largest buying power—by appealing to their love of nature and outdoor spaces; to Gen X by appealing to their love of investment opportunities and simplicity; and to Baby Boomers through their desire to downsize. One such city event went so far as to appeal to everyone at once.

## *Toccoa, Georgia: A Town for Everyone*

The small town of Toccoa (pop. 8,500) is located roughly 90 miles north of Atlanta. Home to Toccoa Falls—a name meaning "beautiful" in the native Cherokee language—it has long been a day-trip destination for metro area Georgians. Now, in light of the Covid-19 pandemic, the city has spied an opening and is beginning to make direct overtures to these visitors in a bid to get them to become permanent residents. One such way is through the use of an excerpt from Eric West, which extolls the virtues of small-town living:

> Are you tired of the hustle and bustle of the city, air pollution bothering you? Are you tired of your children being stuck in classrooms that are too big and the anonymity that goes with living in a city? Perhaps it's time to leave the city and head to a smaller town. There are many advantages of small-town living.[15]

In the excerpt, West breaks down these advantages using a series of questions and answers related to typical tropes of small-town life such as:

> What's the first thing you'll notice?
> No hustle and bustle! Plenty of people walking are common sights. No long lines of traffic on the freeway or bypass. No cars zooming up and down busy roads. You can instantly see the streets are much safer. And of course, car accidents are few and far between.[16]

He then expounds, in similar fashion, upon such things as the abundant green space in small communities, as well as the lack of pollution; the friendly "everybody knows everybody" atmosphere; the small, approachable shops; the personalized attention children receive in local schools; how doctors genuinely know their patients and how basic medical needs are met. After this, he invites the reader to explore other parts of what make small cities so special, including the affordable and older housing stock enjoyed by small town residents and the varied options for working, including remote options. He concludes by stating that:

> Small communities are like traveling back in time to an era where life was less complicated, less stressed, where everyone knew their neighbor, and children could enjoy a game of ball at the park or walk to school without fear for their safety. And it's a lifestyle more and more city dwellers are once again seeking.
>
> So if you are tired of the big city, tired of the crime, the smog, and the lifestyle. Consider moving to a small town where time almost stands still, and you'll get to know your neighbor by their first name. There are many advantages to small town living![17]

What's clever about including promotional material like this on a city website is that it kills two birds at the same time: it promotes small town life in an engaging way and at the same time lessens the apprehension of potential urban fence sitters regarding such a move.

By including this excerpt on their main city website, the City of Toccoa is proclaiming boldly that they no longer intend to be sidelined by larger cities, but rather intend to take a proactive approach to growing their populations without sacrificing their small-town character. Such a what-have-you-got-to-lose approach by small cities was almost unfathomable 10 years ago during the height of the rush to larger metro areas. Given the events of the last year, however, it appears that such aggressive marketing seems to be paying off. This kind of approach is something that will be discussed at greater depth throughout the next chapters.

## *About This Book*

At no other time in the last 100 years have small cities had such an opportunity to capitalize on urban missteps. Even during the midst of the decay and disastrous urban renewal projects in the 1950s and 1960s, small cities were barely a blip on the radar as manufactured suburbs with tract housing were the preferred locale. Now, with offices shuttered and commute times no longer a factor, people are once again eyeing small cities and towns across the country as places where it might be worth settling down. How small cities seize their moments is entirely up to them.

Unlike they were during the rush to the suburbs after World War II, people these days are concerned with more than just safety and yardage these days. Instead, they are concerned with things like authenticity, experiences and culture. These are things that have come to define

## Introduction

Millennials and Gen Z but are also playing an increasingly large role in the lives of Gen Xers and Baby Boomers. Small cities and towns have the opportunity to play to all of them because they offer the fundamental characteristic missing from suburbs—a downtown that acts as the heart of the community.

In this book, we'll define different ways small cities can capitalize upon these opportunities by replicating the experiences of an urban environment within their downtowns. By focusing on things like culture, organization, marketing and proper traffic flow, we'll target the fundamentals that go into revitalizing a small community and at the same time measure the successes—and sometimes failures—by examining what other small cities around the country have done.

To keep the case studies authentic, we will only highlight cities with populations below 150,000 and touch upon all geographic corners of the country. We'll also shy away from using examples of traditional university or tourist towns where students or visitors often overshadow locals. Instead, most of the studies presented will come from small cities that struggled to redefine themselves after years of neglect and abandonment.

In addition, while exploring each topic, we'll have a look at the psychological aspects that go into them and highlight key takeaways to remember when attempting to replicate this for your own city. Some personal reflections from my own experiences as Executive Director for the Augusta Downtown Alliance in Augusta, Maine, as well as expert profiles on various topics related to revitalization from 11 key community players, will also be featured.

**The City of Augusta, Maine, as seen from the air (courtesy Dave Dostie).**

## Why Augusta

It might seem strange at first to compare a small city in New England with other case studies highlighted in this book. After all, Augusta (19,000) is a state capital and enjoys advantages many small and rural communities do not. These include a centralized location that is easily accessed by more than half of Maine's population; a large and steady government bureaucracy who commute in for work; a thriving healthcare system that includes multiple hospital campuses; a state university; the highest retail sales per capita in the state; and a number of museums that draw in tourists. All of these would automatically disqualify the city from being featured in this book, right? After all, this is a work about urbanizing historic downtown areas in small cities. How, then, could a small city with so many advantages not have a thriving downtown? The answer can be summed up in three words: poor urban planning.

Despite its surface advantages, Augusta actually shares more in common with Rust Belt cities in the Midwest than it does with its wealthy coastal neighbors to the east and south. Long an industrial powerhouse, the city once boasted numerous textile mills, including the Bates Manufacturing Edwards Division, a massive complex that covered 17 acres of land on the city's north side, along with a tissue mill, a paper mill, and a meat processing plant, among others. Augusta was, in essence, a center of manufacturing, and like other centers of manufacturing, it suffered the same fate of deindustrialization. Couple that with runaway urban design schemes that gave the center of the city two intimidating rotaries at each entry point, one-way streets, numerous shopping centers miles away from the central core, and haphazard zoning regulations that devalued property in abutting neighborhoods, and you have a perfect recipe for a downtown that, up until 2016, had a vacancy rate as high as 45 percent, which lent the city its nickname "Disgusta."

Fast forward five years, and you have a city firmly on the upswing, with a thriving nightlife, increased pedestrian traffic, a downtown vacancy rate below 20 percent, and an artistic renaissance. Cap it off with a feature cover in *Down East* magazine lauding the city's downtown revitalization and naming it one of the best places to live in Maine.

None of this happened by accident. It was all part of a consistent and coherent revitalization plan that helped bring Augusta back from the brink of characterless strip mall suburbia to one with urban ambiance.

## *The Path Ahead*

Creating an urban experience within a small city is not easy. After all:

> Urban experiences are diverse and dynamic, changing often with advances in technology, shifts in capital investment, and migrations of people. They are shaped by power and wealth, as well as ingenuity and labor. Urbanity is layered with cultural and social histories, and the demands of day-to-day living. Getting from place to place puts a city dweller in contact with a stimulating variety of people and material conditions.[18]

Small cities have not often been at the forefront for much of these things, particularly in the latter half of the twentieth century, where population and job losses, conservatism and a general resistance to change came to define the small-town experience. This wasn't always the case, however. Go back a century, and you'll find that small cities were just as urban as their larger counterparts. For with industrialization came a walkable and compact city center with a mix of retail and residences, a place in which jobs were in abundance and attracted a diverse array of cultures and income levels. As a consequence, small cities were often bastions of cultural richness as they experimented with trending architectural styles, funded libraries and art displays, and played host to opera houses, movie theaters and performing arts venues. As Ocjeo, Kosta and Mann (2020) report, the concept of examining smallness and urbanity is nothing new, for in the 1920s, husband-and-wife sociologists Robert and Helen Lynd did just that.

One of the cities they chose for their studies was Muncie, Indiana, which at that time had a population of 35,000 and was considered the quintessential Midwestern community. An industrial city with roots in farming, this city, which they called "Middletown" to highlight its averageness, was undergoing serious changes by the turn of the century, with gasworks, steel mills and glass manufacturing ruling the day. As a result, the once-agrarian community was undergoing growing pains from pollution to congestion:

> In short, an industrial economy and culture was reshaping work, family life, education, leisure, and the community itself. Like in large cities, people from smaller nearby communities began moving there, while "potential leaders" (37) left for even greater opportunities in larger cities (most likely Indianapolis and Chicago).[19]

While "Middletown" did not have the same influx of African American or even foreign immigration that larger cities like Indianapolis, Chicago or Cleveland had experienced, it did, in fact, see inbound migration from the surrounding region. Because of this, serious strains were placed upon the community's resources, making it an ideal place to study. The resulting statistical, archival and observational data produced by Lynd and Lynd not only provided a "total-situation picture" (1929:6) of American community life but also proved a landmark work in what would amount to the first-ever comprehensive study of small town urbanity. Such a study would later be repeated in the 1930s by other anthropologists and sociologists such as W. Lloyd Warner, who led a team of 30 researchers to Newburyport, MA (pop. 17,000). This East Coast city—which Warner aptly named "Yankee City"—was even smaller than Muncie but had seen some influx in population due to the increasing popularity of the automobile.

> Warner's field research lasted longer than Lynd and Lynd's, and his output was even more prolific, resulting in five volumes that touched on such topics as social class and status systems and the symbolic order in the realms of social, ethnic, religious, and business relations (Warner 1963; Warner and Low 1947; Warner and Lunt 1941; Warner and Srole 1945). Yankee City's size gave Warner the chance to explore these issues by studying a community as a whole. Heavily empirical, Warner's in-depth taxonomies were criticized at the time (see Opler 1942; Pfautz and Duncan 1950; Thernstrom 1965), but his methodological choice to examine phenomena across a range of institutions has been praised as influential [Baba 2009].[20]

As these studies highlighted, a city's smallness had very little to do with how urban a place was, as the basic elements for urbanity were present in most population centers regardless of size.

Today, these elements still exist. One just needs to bring them back to the surface to refine them. While this book can't promise all the answers, it can, in fact, serve as a guide to fostering that growth. The path forward for replicating an urban experience in a small city doesn't need to be complicated. It just needs to be right.

# 1

# Organizing Your House

*The Importance of Organizations and Partnerships*

So, you want to bring a dose of urban vitality to your small community but don't know quite what to do or how to get started? Sure, you know the basics of what makes a great city: walkability, entertainment, culture, etc., but do you know how to get there? Well, as it turns out, there's a whole array of organizations out there that can help with that, many of which can provide the necessary paths to getting started. These include nonprofit, community and governmental entities that base their means on helping cities learn how to develop the proper steps to advance their goals.

This chapter will explore a few of these organizations and how they can help guide a community on the paths towards revitalization. Before, we delve into some of these programs, however, let's look at the importance of organizing through action.

## Organizing Around the Ten Key Principles

The successful revitalization of a community isn't something that can be accomplished with just the flick of a wrist. It's a lengthy process that runs more like a marathon than a sprint and involves quite a bit of forethought and planning. This makes sense with any serious undertaking but is especially pertinent when it comes to small cities, which often operate on a philosophy of community buy-in when it comes to development rather than through blanket mandate.

To effectively accomplish the goals of revitalizing your community and making it more urban-friendly, there are 10 general principles a community should follow to establish an effective movement. Eight of these are generally accepted notions as espoused by Edward T. McMahon of the New Hampshire Municipal Association, while the last two are ones I've added from my personal experience. All of them will be summarized here but will be discussed more in later chapters.

While not every community will display these characteristics right from the start, it's important to note that each should eventually be fostered and adopted in order to get the most out of community partnerships.

Highlighted below are the 10 important principles, followed by a brief description of each:

1. Have a vision for the future
2. Inventory assets
3. Build plans on the enhancement of existing assets
4. Use education and incentives, not just regulation
5. Pick and choose among development projects
6. Cooperate with neighbors for mutual benefit
7. Pay attention to community aesthetics
8. Have strong leaders and committed citizens[1]
9. Support, but regulate, community buy-in
10. Align yourself with a program that plays to all of the above

## Have a Vision for the Future

Abraham Lincoln used to say that "the best way to predict the future is to create it yourself." Communities can do this by establishing a vision for themselves. This can be done through focus meetings or "visioning sessions" so to speak, where representatives from the community—ideally from different backgrounds—can come together in common cause and discuss what they'd like to see accomplished. This is best done with an experienced facilitator who can readily take the suggestions presented and formulate a coherent path forward.

## Inventory Assets

Creating a vision for the future begins with inventorying a community's assets: natural, architectural, human, educational, economic, recreational, scenic, etc. Successful communities then build their plans—whether a land-use plan, a tourism plan, or an economic development plan—around the enhancement of their existing assets.

## Build Plans on the Enhancement of Existing Assets

After communities have inventoried their assets, they shape their futures around them. Whether focusing on a land-use plan, a tourism plan or an economic development plan, savvy communities build on what they already have.[2] If, for example, your community is known for its museums, think like an outsider and develop plans to promote them by weighing in about what appeals to an artistic crowd.

## Use Education and Incentives, Not Just Regulation

Regulation is great and has its place in revitalization, but it only goes so far when making changes. The last thing you want to do in a small community is anger businesses or developers who might not see the value in particular ordinances. This is why it's so important to inform and incentivize with regards to regulation so that people will know why the regulations are being employed and will have the motivation to support them.

Here in Augusta, for example, we have a sign ordinance and incentivized the changing of non-historic signs by providing a grant to help with the costs.

## Pick and Choose Among Development Projects

Not all development is good development. Just because you have the opportunity to build something doesn't necessarily mean it should be built. Examine projects with a magnifying glass and determine what the long-range benefits will be. If such developments don't meet with your goals, then don't be afraid to say no.

## Cooperate with Neighbors for Mutual Benefit

Successful communities know that today's world requires cooperation for mutual benefit. They know that the real competition today is between regions. They also understand that very few small towns have the resources, by themselves, to attract tourists or to compete with larger communities. Regional cooperation does not mean giving up your autonomy. It simply recognizes that problems like air pollution, water pollution, traffic congestion and loss of green space do not respect jurisdictional boundaries. Regional problems require regional solutions.[3]

Here in Augusta, for example, it is common to work with our neighboring cities, Hallowell and Gardiner, on promoting the whole of

Kennebec County, rather than just a part of it. For what benefits one town will undoubtedly benefit the whole area.

## Pay Attention to Community Aesthetics

Mark Twain once said: "We take stock of a city like we take stock of a man. The clothes or appearance are the externals by which we judge." In other words, looks are important.

As we'll discuss in a later chapter, the amount of attention you pay to gussying up the look of your community is the same amount of attention people will pay when passing through your community. Don't be afraid to focus on the little things before thinking big, because it's the little things that will often make the biggest difference.

## Have Strong Leaders and Committed Citizens

This is an obvious one: successful communities have strong leaders and committed citizens. A small number of committed people can make a big difference in a community. Sometime these people are longtime residents upset with how unmanaged growth has changed what they love about their hometown, while at other times, they are the ones driving the changes. Fostering leadership is important in developing a coherent strategy forward.

## Support, but Regulate, Community Buy-in

Community buy-in is wonderful and should be supported through flash polls, surveys and meetings, but there needs to be a point when such buy-in is regulated and finessed. Trying to please everyone will get you nowhere, so it's important to narrow down the best ideas and continue a path forward with those that are most engaged.

## Align Yourself with a Program That Plays to All of the Above

No ideas are truly unique, and there are many paths forward through programs that will advise your community on best practices, depending upon the level of revitalization where you happen to be. Think about joining one of these organizations and adapting their model to your community. It can make a big difference in sustaining your city's revitalization efforts.

Remember, in the end, while it's possible to tackle three or four of these principles at a time, it's nearly impossible to work with all of them at once. Certain steps must be completed before moving on to others, and it's not uncommon in the early stages for organizations to lay the groundwork over the course of a couple of years. A thorough job in the early stages of organizing is much better than a sloppy outcome.

## Getting to Know the Stages of Revitalization

Before doing anything else with your city, you need to know the current stage of your revitalization. Revitalization comes in stages, and these stages are hardly uniform in their size or results. This is especially pertinent when organizing your community around a strategic plan

**Members of the Augusta Downtown Alliance take a tour of downtown businesses and properties during the summer of 2019 (author's collection).**

forward, as your current stage might be well ahead of others and not require as many of the steps outlined above.

Generally speaking, there are three main stages of revitalization that occur over the lifetime of a community: infancy, middle, and mature stages, with varying degrees of sub-phases in between. These stages play a role in the kinds of businesses and developments that are established and often dictate how well they can thrive. We'll go through each of the stages in depth below.

## 1.1 Infancy Stage

The infancy stage is where most communities begin. In this bottom-of-the-barrel stage, a downtown community is basically holding on by its fingertips for dear life. Any semblance of anchor retail has long ago made its exit, and the only businesses left include pawn shops, discount stores, and adult-themed businesses. Long gone are the days when the streets were thronged with crowds or traffic, and the whole district remains deserted past 5 p.m.

Typically, in this stage, the vacancy rate hovers at 40 percent or more, and the downtown has acquired a dangerous reputation amongst the public.

## 1.2 Mid-infancy Stage

In this stage, the downtown has started to improve slowly. A local community organization has formed, and the groundwork for general aesthetic improvements has been laid with things like sign ordinances, historic districts and improvement grants being introduced. At this point, the vacancy rate will begin to fall slightly as excitement over the fact that things might actually be turning a corner draws in business enthusiasts into some of the stores. These enthusiasts are often first-time business owners from the area and can border on being hobbyists, interested in opening very niche businesses catering to small audiences. No anchor stores have moved in at this point, and new businesses, which include second-hand and thrift shops, remain scattered from one another. At this point, some residential development is likely to occur on a small scale, providing downtown with its first residents, mainly retirees.

## 1.3 Late-infancy Stage

During the late-infancy stage, a city has continued to make improvements to the street, mainly in the form of artwork and aesthetics. More buildings are cleaned up, and community organizations begin to come into their own. At this point, mom-and-pop restaurants begin to move in. The general downtown is still catering towards a 9–5 crowd at this point, but some new residences have been added, and artists and young singles begin to move in. The general population is now only ⅔ retiree or 50+, and there is hope that a nightlife could one day take shape. The general outlook of the greater community is that it is still unconvinced during this stage, but optimism begins to grow amongst those closely involved.

## 2.1 Early Middle Stage

During the early middle stage, things are starting to speed up. Community organizations have shifted from design to infrastructure work, and things like traffic patterns and walkability begin to be studied. Experienced restaurant owners begin to move in at this point, and for the first time, restaurants begin to outnumber retail spots.

In this stage, the downtown area begins to draw in more nightlife, as the first bars are opened up and large-scale residential development begins because of the introduction of economic incentives. This is the stage where hobbyists, thrift shops and second-hand stores begin to exit as rent increases and disruptions with residential and neighboring remodels begin to occur. It's thus not unusual to see a temporary increase in vacancy rates in this stage.

## 2.2 Middle Stage

Things continue to blossom by the middle stage. Young professionals now dominate the streetscape, and more residences are announced by developers. Major infrastructure changes have been made to increase walkability and slow traffic, and downtown once again regains an anchor location. The first signature events begin to take shape from community organizations, and long-time business owners from different areas of the city begin to take note. Vacancy rates drop exponentially.

Growing pains occur in this stage, particularly with parking, as those unaccustomed to walking long distances in your downtown must retrain themselves to the new normal. At this point, downtown has taken on a nightlife and activity peaks past 5 p.m.

## 2.3 Late Middle Stage

At this stage, your downtown is unrecognizable from just a few years ago. Most of the eyesores that dominated the downtown for decades have been remodeled and almost all absentee landlords have sold out. While there are still pockets of vacancy that exist along the edges of your district, almost all new retail and restaurants have now clustered around your anchor giving you a solid shopping and dining area. Early businesses in the downtown that have managed to hold on through the changes are not just surviving any longer—but are thriving—as daytime traffic catches up with nighttime traffic. This is the point at which your downtown is no longer referred to as "revitalizing" but rather as "up and coming" or "the next thing."

## 3.1 Mature Stage

You've done it. You've reached the place where everyone wants to be, and your community is a hit. The vacancy rate is below 10 percent, and the quality of new businesses coming in just keeps getting better. Regional and out-of-state developers have taken note of your success and make plans to capitalize off it. The street is now a full-fledged neighborhood with businesses that cater to the daily needs of the residents who live there, and more families begin to dominate the street.

By now, you're past the point of laying the groundwork for infrastructure improvements and are instead the driving force behind them. More emphasis on bike lanes, entertainment, alternate forms of transportation, and accessibility to both nature walks and parks begins to increasingly dominate your community organization's discussions.

Street art has become bold and daring, and you are finally seeing visitors outnumber locals in public places. At this point, you are ready to put on large-scale signature events that can draw in big numbers, as your downtown is no longer an embarrassment to the city, but rather a point of pride.

The final holdouts of absentee landlords sell off their properties due to the irresistibly inflated prices, along with some early investors who cash in.

## 4.1 Stage Realization

While each of these stages presents special opportunities, no stage is 100 percent guaranteed without putting in the work. Even those places that have reached the mature stage need to put in the work to keep it at that level so as not to go stale or become complacent. The worst thing you can do is have a downtown that has "made it" but no longer attempts to keep challenging itself, as this is the surest way to being passed over and finding your downtown back in the infancy stage.

Volunteers with Central Church paint a merchant's door during an organizational cleanup day (author's collection).

This is why being organized and fostering the right partnerships are instrumental, not just for your development but also for your survival.

## *Main Street America: Taking Action the Right Way*

When organizing a revitalization effort for your small city, there's no better organization to partner with than Main Street America. This organization has experienced countless successes over its history and provides one of the quickest paths for turning around a derelict community.

Begun in 1977 as an offshoot of the National Trust, the Main Street movement grew out of recognition that a community is only as strong as its core. In an era when many people had given up hope about the commercial and cultural viability of downtown, and when suburbs, shopping malls, and big box retailers were dominating the American landscape, this seemed like an unlikely proposition. But over the last four decades, the Main Street movement has proved that downtowns are the heart of our communities, and that a community is only as strong as its core.[4]

A part of the National Trust, Main Street has helped over 2,000 communities across the country bring economic vitality back downtown, while celebrating their historic character and bringing communities together.[5]

As Ed McMahon, Chair of the National Main Street Center Board of Directors was fond of quoting: "Downtown is important because it's the heart and soul of any community." If you don't have a healthy downtown, you simply don't have a healthy town.[6]

While emphasis on saving and renovating a city's built heritage is a major part of the program, perhaps the biggest thing about Main Street is their emphasis on grassroots movements to achieve change. As we all know, grassroots movements are key to many successful political campaigns as it drums up enthusiasm for a particular candidate. For small communities undergoing revitalization, what Main Street provides is no different, as they lay out an essential roadmap of transformation through a patented Four Points Approach. This Four Point Approach includes Economic Vitality, Design, Promotion, and Organization. As they definite it:

> ECONOMIC VITALITY focuses on capital, incentives, and other economic and financial tools to assist new and existing businesses, catalyze property development, and create a supportive environment for entrepreneurs and innovators that drive local economies.
>
> DESIGN supports a community's transformation by enhancing the physical and visual assets that set the commercial district apart.
>
> PROMOTION positions the downtown or commercial district as the center of the community and hub of economic activity, while creating a positive image that showcases a community's unique characteristics.
>
> ORGANIZATION involves creating a strong foundation for a sustainable revitalization effort, including cultivating partnerships, community involvement, and resources for the district.[7]

Even more importantly, Main Street provides a resource for those communities it serves, providing grant opportunities, sources of information through blogs and discussion panels, field services which focus on development and team training, and a direct connection with 860 other accredited programs.

Their requirement of ⅓-⅓-⅓—meaning that ⅓ of funding is to come directly from the city, while ⅓ is to come from fundraising from events and ⅓ from events—also contributes to further community partnerships as it forces city leaders, businesses and other nonprofit organizations to become invested in the health of the downtown.

As Main Street surmises in their mission statement:

> We believe that everyone deserves access to a vibrant neighborhood—a place that has a thriving local economy, is rich in character, and features inviting public spaces that make residents and visitors feel that they belong. Yet, we know that many Americans, whether in small towns or big cities, miss out on these benefits. Our collective mission is to make this right.[8]

## *Wheeling: A Main Street Success Story*

While countless cities have experienced success through the Main Street program, one small city's success was so remarkable that they earned the coveted Great American Main Street Award, earning national recognition for their achievements.

Located in the far northern tip of the state, Wheeling (pop. 29,000) was West Virginia's original capital before it settled on the more centrally located city of Charleston. Becoming an industrial giant in the late nineteenth century in its own right, Wheeling was once home to a thriving steel company, Wheeling Steel & Iron, which led to a whole host of building by wealthy Wheeling Steel & Iron Company industrialists who beautified the downtown area.

With the onset of the Great Depression and World War II, Wheeling's fortunes began to decline. Such decline only increased with significant divestment from the downtown in the 1980s and '90s as retailers fled to suburban shopping malls.

When Wheeling Heritage formed in 2015, as an accredited member of the Main Street program, they found themselves in dire straits, with vacancy rates at 32 percent.[9] In a mere four years, however, their downtown area completely transformed, with new businesses and investment moving into the area.

Now with a vacancy rate that stands at 15 percent and 124 buildings that have seen improvements or rehabilitation, the downtown area has blossomed into a shopping, dining and entertainment district anchored by the Capitol Theater. In addition, while there were no multi-family, market-rate apartments in 2015, there are now 100 new multi-family, market-rate units in Wheeling's historic downtown.

Wheeling Heritage has also worked to cultivate a strong small business community. From launching a live community crowd-funding event for new business ideas called Show of Hands, to bringing an international entrepreneur training program to assist new business owners, Wheeling Heritage has been creative in their approach to community-based economic development. These programs have yielded positive results. Over the past three years, their downtown has added 37 net new businesses.

Such a quick effort with turnaround led Wheeling to be chosen for the Great American Main Street Award, in which accredited cities are evaluated on the:

- Overall strength of the Main Street program and documented success in creating an exciting place to live, work, play and visit;
- Demonstrated impact aligning with the Main Street Approach;
- Commitment to historic preservation;
- Active involvement of the public and private sectors;
- Model partnerships, including inclusive engagement of community members and local stakeholders in the downtown revitalization process[10]

"We've been successful because we are cognizant of the ever-changing nature of our community. While we've taken great strides, our work isn't done," said Alex Weld, Project and Outreach Manager at Wheeling Heritage, who oversees Wheeling's Main Street program. "We continuously evaluate and adapt our programming to address pressing needs in the community, which we feel is the best way to help Wheeling continue to flourish."[11]

Wheeling's success in the Main Street program is a prime example of how partnering with an organization like Main Street can guide a community in their revitalization efforts. This guidance can be seen in the resource and support network that an organization like Main Street can provide.

As West Virginia Governor Jim Justice opined:

> Wheeling Heritage has worked to revitalize its downtown, preserve its historic character and make the city an exciting place to be. The effort, and the fantastic results, can be done only when the business community, the civic leaders and the public pull together.[12]

## *Finding the Heart and Soul of Your Community*

Yet another organization that has proved helpful is Community Heart & Soul, which focuses on a more community-wide and -driven revitalization. A subsidiary of the Orton Family Foundation, Community Heart & Soul utilizes a more collaborative approach to revitalization, directly encouraging community participation in the process.

As described, Community Heart & Soul is a four-phase, step-by-step process. Developed and field-tested for more than a decade in partnership with small cities and towns (populations less than 50,000), Community Heart & Soul has evolved into a proven method for bringing the community together to chart a course forward. For most communities, completing the four phases takes about two years. But the completion of the Community Heart & Soul model is really just the beginning. It launches a new way of doing business that nurtures a more vibrant community far into the future.[13]

The Community Heart & Soul's four phases, as outlined by the Community Heart & Soul website (2020), are: Imagine, Connect, Plan and Act. We will present each phase in full below.

## Phase 1: Imagine

In the Imagine phase, three core principles are invoked. These include:

- Involving Everyone—especially from those whose voices are often missing or overlooked.
- Focusing on What Matters Most—common themes that become the foundation for sound decision-making emerge from residents' shared stories.
- Playing the Long Game—Heart & Soul equips communities with the skills and tools that change how towns view themselves, how they govern, and how they make decisions.[14]

## Phase 2: Connect

In the Connect phase, Heart & Soul discovers what residents love about where they live, and identifies common hopes and aspirations. This is accomplished by:

- Gathering stories and input from the community.
- Creating Heart & Soul Statements that reflect the observations and aspirations of the entire community.[15]

## Phase 3: Plan

In the Plan phase, communities decide which ideas best reflect what matters most and create a plan that ensures action, both now and long term, by:

- Prioritizing action ideas to determine what is important to the community.

- Developing an Action Plan guided by Heart & Soul Statements that captures prioritized ideas.
- Revisiting Community Network Analysis to ensure as many people as possible are included in decision-making, aiming for broad and meaningful participation in developing and evaluating options.[16]

## Phase 4: Act

The final phase is all about changing the way the community takes action by putting resident engagement at the center of decision-making. This is done through:

- Adoption of Heart & Soul Statements by city council; incorporation into comprehensive and other plans.
- Forming a Stewardship Team to coordinate with community partners to make actions happen.
- Continuing to apply the principles of Community Heart & Soul in future community endeavors.
- Celebrating your accomplishments![17]

Whereas the Main Street program is 100 percent locally sourced with requirements for a structured board made up of a paid executive director, along with merchants, developers, city leaders, and interested parties as board members, Community Heart & Soul is led by experienced "coaches" who move into a community to share their expertise on revitalization efforts and lead the way through meetings. Coaches are assisted in their efforts by "champions," who are volunteer based and live in the cities where the program is ongoing; "trustees," who run the organization; "staff," who work for the organization as experts in their field; and "partners," who support the organization through sponsorship. In this way, Community Heart & Soul practices more of a resources-oriented approach to revitalization, in which experts are brought on to facilitate rather than direct the needs of the community. From there, local leaders are identified who can continue the work to make sure goals are completed

While the Main Street program accomplishes many of the same things as Community Heart & Soul, such as encouraging branding and protecting the built heritage of a city, they differ in certain ways. For one, the Main Street program is seen as a permanent, ongoing program that continues to operate well after accreditation is conferred. Community Heart & Soul, however, is temporary, and meant to engage a community so long as the process is occurring. Once all tasks and goals are set, they leave it up to the leaders themselves to continue through the process. It is for this reason that these programs are essentially noncompetitive with one another and why it's not at all uncommon for small cities with Main Street programs, like Biddeford (see Chapter 3), to have gone through Community Heart & Soul programming as well.

## Other Partnership Programs for Organizations

While Main Street America and Community Heart & Soul are two of the best-known programs when it comes to revitalization efforts, they are hardly the only routes a community can take when organizing a concerted movement to develop their downtown areas.

Among such alternatives are community development corporations, or CDCs. These not-for-profit organizations are incorporated to provide programs, offer services and engage in other activities that promote and support community development. CDCs usually serve a geographic location such as a neighborhood or a town and often focus their attention on serving lower-income residents or struggling neighborhoods. They can be involved in a variety of activities including economic development, education, community organizing and real estate development but are most often associated with the development of affordable housing.

Formed out of the Economic Opportunity Act of 1964, CDCs run the gamut from large, well-established organizations, to community groups meeting in church basements. Following a bottom-up approach, CDCs are set up and run by community members or local groups like churches and civic associations. In fact, a key feature of CDCs is the inclusion of community representatives in their governing/advisory boards. While it's difficult to enforce because CDCs act independently, the rule of thumb is at least one third of the board is composed of local residents.

While most CDCs are located in larger cities, there are indeed cases where smaller communities have utilized them as well. One example is OneHolyoke CDC, which runs out of Holyoke, Massachusetts (pop. 40,000). Operating under a board of directors, OneHolyoke tackled downtown revitalization and "has rehabilitated the historic Hadley Mills Townhouses in the Flats and the Library Park Condominiums in downtown Holyoke, and has replaced blighted, empty lots with attractive, newly constructed two-family homes sold to qualified low-to-moderate-income buyers—working families who are committed to their neighborhoods and our community, and who contribute to Holyoke's real estate tax rolls."[18]

Yet another resource a community can utilize is Americorps VISTA, which can provide the volunteers to implement the work needed to launch an organization.

Created by Lyndon Johnson in 1965, Americorps VISTA (Volunteer in Service to America) was formed as part of the War on Poverty, in response to Kennedy's Peace Corps Initiative. Defined under the Domestic Volunteer Service Act (DVSA) of 1973, AmeriCorps VISTA's sole responsibility is to supplement efforts to fight poverty in low-income communities by engaging Americans from all walks of life in a year of full-time service. VISTA members support the program's purpose through three primary objectives: (1) encouraging volunteer service at the local level, (2) generating the commitment of private sector resources, and (3) strengthening local agencies and organizations that serve low-income communities.

Working with either existing nonprofits or public entities, such as city governments, Americorps VISTA provides communities with volunteers who help tackle economic development solutions. Some of the benefits for serving AmeriCorps Vista include:

- Student loan deferment
- Skills and training
- Living allowance
- Limited health benefit options
- Education Award upon completion of service to help pay for college, graduate school, or vocational training, or to repay student loans
- Career opportunities with leading employers from the private, public and nonprofit sectors[19]

Today, there are approximately 5,000 VISTA members serving in over 900 projects throughout the nation.[20] Many of these individuals are recruited to specifically help downtown organizations, particularly in smaller communities, where resources for hiring are limited. An example of this can be found in the community of Nampa, Idaho (pop. 82,000), which advertised the following position in order to launch a Main Street program:

> The VISTA volunteer will work with City of Nampa staff, Downtown Nampa Association and community volunteers to implement the four-point Main Street strategy and help Nampa move toward becoming a certified Main Street community. Project Goals are twofold: (1) To build capacity for community organizations to serve low-income populations and for businesses to

provide jobs through development of a nonprofit organization to implement the Main Street Program; and (2) To develop new jobs and support retention of current businesses in Nampa by creating an economically vibrant downtown.

We aim to build capacity and create an economically vibrant downtown through the following activities: (1) Create a new non-profit organization to implement the Main Street model in Downtown Nampa and help Nampa become a certified Main Street community; (2) Create new partnerships between the Main Street organization and stakeholder organizations in the community including those who serve low-income populations; (3) Work closely with the Downtown Nampa Business Association board and committees to support downtown revitalization; and (4) Develop a volunteer recruitment, training, tracking and rewards program to support the Main Street program.

Member Duties: (1) Create a new nonprofit organization to implement the Main Street model. (2) Create new partnerships between the Main Street organization and stakeholder organizations in the community. (3) Report monthly to the Downtown Nampa Business Association Board of Directors and work with each of the four Main Street Committees. (4) Develop a volunteer recruitment, training, tracking and incentives program to support the Main Street model. (5) Work with the Nampa Public Library to provide skill development services which will be available to low-income populations such as computer classes and job search skills. (6) Market new job opportunities created by downtown businesses to the residents in surrounding neighborhoods. (7) Identify resources for training to enhance the workforce skills of current and new downtown employees. (8) Develop baseline data and prepare semi-annual reports to measure metrics identified by the national Main Street program.[21]

Job advertisements like this are a regular part of the AmeriCorps program, and coordinators often serve a full year in their positions.

## *Matt Pouliot and the Role of Organization in Revitalization*

Whether it's civil service, real estate, nonprofit leadership or general election campaigns, Senator Matt Pouliot has been organizing in one way or another for most of his life. In this manner, he's kind of an expert on the subject of organization and its effects on revitalization efforts.

Purchasing his first home at the age of 20, Matt unwittingly entered his first foray into politics after having a run in with Codes. "My plan was to live in one of the apartments and rent out the other. I wanted to actually add a third apartment to it to get extra income, but when I went to Codes, they said it wasn't permitted and that I needed variance," he said. "This is how I got into the Board of Zoning appeals."

Serving on the board for six months, Matt later went to Mayor Katz and requested an appointment to the Planning Board. From there, he learned a great deal about urban regulations before being approached once again to organize.

"Roger was terming out as mayor in Augusta and asked me to run his campaign for state office," he said. "I helped him with it and he ended up winning. Two years later, while I was visiting Heather [his wife] in New York, I got a call from him and he asked me to run, myself. I didn't really know what to say. I had been on the planning board, but this was a big leap. I thought 'I'm not really a politician.' My superlative in high school was 'Teacher's Pest.'"

Matthew Pouliot has been a major player in state politics over the last decade and has been a driving force behind Augusta's downtown revitalization (courtesy Dave Dostie).

Knocking on a lot of doors, Matt won his election for state representative and was sworn in three days shy of his 25th birthday. At the same time Matt was whetting his appetite with civil and state politics, he was also gearing up for a career in real estate.

"I started doing real estate in college and finally passed my license exam in 2010. I began working for Chris Vallee part-time, and kept my day job at Hammond Lumber. In November of that year, though, I made the decision that would change my life by going off on my own full-time."

After working for Re/Max for several years, Matt eventually opened his own real estate firm in 2020, setting up his office in downtown Augusta, where he had worked with members of the Augusta Downtown Alliance in attempting a renaissance.

"I actually got involved with downtown because of Larry Fleury," he recounts. "Larry knew I had experience with the planning board and approached me about getting involved in an organized effort. This was actually before the Augusta Downtown Alliance was even the Augusta Downtown Alliance. Back then, it was really just a group of people who wanted to make things better. This was the capital city and back then everything was just dead. It was awful. I really wanted to be a part of the change for our community and wanted to step up. This was a tangible way for me to make a difference."

Describing these early organizational efforts, Matt said, "We started to formalize our plans for downtown over spaghetti dinners at Larry's. We ended up growing from there. After a while, Maine Downtown Center gave us the framework for how to legitimize our efforts, and turn it into something more formal."

Regarding his feelings about these early efforts Matt says: "I really look back fondly over those years of organization. Maine is a small state and Augusta is a small city. I don't think it would be possible to have this level of community involvement in a city the size of New York, or even a city the size of Baton Rouge. This is a place you can make a real difference," he said. "Augusta really is a great city and we had all of the infrastructure in place to organize a concerted effort. Now," he continues, "it appears we have finally turned a corner. Millennials are moving here and they're increasingly interested in becoming involved."

Matt's time in both politics and organization has given him a lot to reflect upon regarding what makes a successful city.

"To me, the core of what makes a successful city is whether there is a sense of community among those who live there and whether they have a desire to collaborate and grow together. From a practical side, organization is key. You need a healthy group of volunteers and a supportive local government. Real estate also plays a role as you need to keep things affordable so people can live there."[22]

## *Key Takeaways*

When organizing a revitalization effort, it's important to remember these key takeaways:

- Successful revitalization requires the formation of partnerships to achieve the desired results.
- Partnerships are established through the formation of an organization.
- An organization needs to abide by 10 key principles when revitalizing a community.

- An organization should be cognizant of what they want as a community and what stage of revitalization that they are in.
- There are several established programs which exist to help organizations become further developed and turn their plans into actions.

## *Conclusion*

> "There is no power for change greater than a community discovering what it cares about."—Margaret J. Wheatley

Replicating an urban environment in your small community takes effort, and no movement in history was ever sustained without a solid organization behind it. Without the foundation that an organization can provide, attempts at anything substantial with regards to revitalization increase the risk of becoming self-serving causes that completely lose sight of their goals.

By organizing under a strategic vision and partnering with a program dedicated to supporting that vision, your chances of achieving success not only increase because of the structure provided but also increase because of the buy-in that it generates from the community.

As will be a major theme in this book, no decent revitalization effort is made without genuine authenticity, and authenticity can only come from a community-initiated approach. How you choose to enhance that approach, whether through partnering with the Main Street program, engaging with Community Heart & Soul, or forming a CDC, is entirely up to you, but it's important to remember that revitalization is not a one-and-done mission. There is no point at which you can just sit back and relax. If you want to keep things going, you have to keep putting in the effort, and the best way to keep those efforts afloat is by forming an organization.

# 2

# It's All About Distinction

*Identifying and Placemaking
Your Small Town*

Identity and placemaking are concepts that are well-ingrained in the human psyche. Since birth, we have been bombarded with images ranging from logos to landmarks that represent everything from sports teams to corporations, and yes, even cities.

Think about it. What comes to mind when you think about Philadelphia? Chances are that it's the Liberty Bell. What about Los Angeles? Likely, it's the Hollywood Sign. New York City? The Statue of Liberty. Orlando? Theme parks. These tropes have been with us for so long that we barely stop to think about where they come from. When we do, however, it becomes clear that these images were no accident, but rather a part of sustained placemaking concepts that marketing firms seized upon long ago to bring tourism dollars to their cities. So, what of our smaller communities, you might ask? With less-developed infrastructure and populations, can they develop their own identities? As it turns out, they absolutely can. It's just about digging deep enough to find out what makes you distinct.

In this chapter, we'll examine how certain small cities around the country not only have crafted identities for themselves, but also have actually found ways to market them to the public. Before we do so, however, let's first explore the psychological connections between place and identity.

## *The Psychology Behind Identity and Placemaking*

Identity is a powerful construct in the human psyche. From the first moment we are born, our identities are shaped by the people and places that surround us. Small cities work in much the same way.

An interior view of Old Fort Western, as seen from the reflection of a flatboat after a rainstorm. Built in 1754, Old Fort Western remains the oldest wooden fort in North America and is an enduring symbol of Augusta (courtesy Dave Dostie).

In her book, *The Power of Place: Urban Landscapes as Public History*, Dolores Hayden writes that "Identity is intimately tied to memory: both our personal memories (where we have come from and where we have dwelt) and the collective or social memories interconnected with the histories of our families, neighbors, fellow workers, and ethnic communities"[1] Her theories support the notion that identity is not only inextricably tied to the everyday interactions we as a community share together daily, but also to the past actions of those who came before us. Take New England, for example. What comes to mind when I mention this region? Chances are that it's lighthouses, lobsters, rocky beaches and sailboats. While this image is a stereotype, of course, and doesn't speak for many of the inland communities, it nevertheless is an immediate identifier that speaks to the unifying aspect of the region because of its history as a maritime powerhouse.

Similarly, think of the American South. What comes to mind? Chances are it's live oaks, humidity, NASCAR, columned plantations, soul food and yes.... Confederate flags. Again, a lot of this is stereotype, but it speaks both to the identity people assume from those who live there and to the actual identity of its residents, who are surrounded by these things.

Like the examples cited above, collective memories can form a strong part of the identity of a place, affecting everything from the particular symbolism used to the prevailing attitudes of its residents. As Edward Relph writes in *Place and Placelessness*:

> ... experience of place can range in scale from part of a room to an entire continent, but at all scales places are whole entities, syntheses of natural and man-made objects, activities and functions, and meanings given by intentions. Out of these components the identity of a particular place is moulded, but they do not define this identity—it is the special quality of insideness and the experience of being inside that sets places apart in space.[2]

With deep-rooted traditions and populations that are less transient than their more urban counterparts, small cities often present the perfect backdrop for placemaking. An example of this was highlighted by Karen Good while recounting a trip to the small city of Rutland, Massachusetts (pop. 7,900).

In her work, she reflects upon the sudden transition of bland suburbia, with its endless array of car lots, strip malls and fast-food chains to wooded areas, modest homes, and small businesses, with only the occasional business chain. As she drives further into the community, she describes how the scattered pattern of businesses and houses suddenly gave way to a cohesive rhythm and pattern of tree-lined lots that continued all the way up the hill to the center of town. She then recounts how, in the heart of the community, there stood a fire station along with a Community Hall, which looked frozen in time. There she would meet up with two members of the Mast Planning Community, Mike Sullivan and Dick Williams, who would take them on a tour of the city.

> The two longtime residents briefly described their town, a place each of them had grown to love. Pride was evident in their voices as they spoke. Each building or plot of land had a story and was tied to people who they knew. They were aware of local happenings (e.g., the plan for the new library, a newly arrived baby, who had bought the old farm outside of the town center). It appeared there was a large collective knowledge of history and culture in this community.[3]

Mike and Dick took the time to highlight the landscape, the architecture, and the local history of the area. They explained the significance of various war monuments and were well-versed in town lore. They described that the hills in the community once served as a major draw for travelers, as it was rumored that their height enabled health benefits due to their good air, clean water and unobtrusive surroundings. They then pointed out the locations of past community buildings:

Across the street from the Hall stood a small-time, local gas station. At the far end of a second linear common stood a historic fire station with a historic graveyard on an adjoining lot. The first meetinghouse was once on the site of the fire station; now a marker records its former presence. The sun streamed down from a cloudless blue sky, lighting the two long linear greens that lay at the center of the town. Our tour was over and it was time to head home.[4]

As recounted by Good, the people of Rutland were deep-rooted in their history, which added to their sense of place in the world. This rootedness of identity was physicalized during their tour and included things like architectural symbols and monuments, but also contained more abstract and hard-to-define concepts such as a collective commitment to their environment and their way of life. Their knowledge and comfort of place thus made it easy to market their distinctions to newcomers, leaving a lasting impression upon Good's group.

Below, we'll examine several cases of how cities attempt to identify themselves both publicly and privately.

## *Redefining the Country Landscape: Owen County's Quilt Trail*

Sometimes the assets a small community has are pretty glaring. Take, for example, Coeur d'Alene, Idaho (pop. 52,000). Blessed with an abundance of natural beauty in the form of majestic mountains on the north shore of Lake Coeur d'Alene, it has successfully established its identity as an outdoor sportsman's dream. From skiing in winter to water sports in summer to hiking in the fall, there's no shortage of recreational activities to be had. This has led to the establishment in the city of several resorts catering to these interests.

In other communities, however, the assets aren't so obvious. Consider Owenton, Kentucky (pop. 1300) and the surrounding area of Owen County.

Located in the heart of the Golden Triangle, as defined by Lexington, Louisville and Cincinnati, modern-day Owen County first began attracting settlers sometime around the early 1800s. These settlers were different from the horse traders that tended to flock to Lexington, or the river merchants that tended to flock to Louisville, as they were largely farmers, hailing from the tobacco regions of Virginia and the Carolinas. It was these settlers that would ultimately lay the foundations for Owen County's role in the tobacco trade and help transform it into one of the most productive tobacco regions in the Commonwealth.

Cut off from much of the Bluegrass by steep hills and winding roads, and blocked on three sides by rivers, Owen County seemed to miss out on the gradual transition to industrialization that swept through Kentucky's larger cities in the latter part of the nineteenth century. The promise and later reneging of a railroad, as well as the depreciation of tobacco prices, further hindered this growth.

Today, Owen County remains a place largely isolated from the rest of the state. Bypassed by the main interstates that define the Golden Triangle (I-64, I-71 and I-75), most of the county requires back roads travel to see. As a result, much of the infrastructure has remained relatively intact and bears many of the scars of its nineteenth century past. As former Owen County Judge Executive Carolyn Keith put it, "It really hasn't changed all that much."[5]

Fraught with rampant poverty and seeking to attract more visitors to the area, an idea was formulated to draw more people in: why not establish colorful patterns on the many tobacco barns surrounding Owenton? Thus, the Owen County Quilt Trail was born.

Conceptualized as the brainchild of the Owen County Vision Project and Owen 20/20, a survey that highlighted a group of long-term goals for the community, the project ultimately materialized under partnership from extension homemakers, resident farm wives and quilt enthusiasts who worked diligently to raise funds for the first few squares. As Judy Hetterman, the Owen County Extension Agent for Family and Consumer Sciences explained: "We started this trail back in 2008 with just five squares, after that, interest grew and we had a flood of people asking how they could get those patterns hung on their barns."[6]

Currently numbering around one hundred squares, the Quilt Trail stretches out over 140 miles and takes roughly six hours to complete by car. Today, it is largely credited by the extension office with having saved many of the endangered tobacco barns dotting the county landscape.

"The Quilt Trail is important because it has rejuvenated two of our county's most enduring traditions, tobacco farming and quilting," said Hetterman. "It's really allowed us to preserve our heritage in a positive and lasting way."[7]

In addition, it has brought a lot of attention to the county, particularly after the U.S. Open Sporting Clay Championship hosted by the Elk Creek Hunt Club in 2009. "We began to receive a lot of calls from people that wanted to know more about them after the competition. Many of them were from out of state and were very supportive of the idea."[8] Such support was even expressed in Iowa, where a couple, who had attended the event, had called the extension office for the purposes of ordering a square for their own homestead. "It was definitely a sign that we were attracting outside attention," she explained. "But unfortunately, we had to tell them that we were a local organization geared solely towards the beautification of Owen County."

Priced at around $500 for the larger patterns and $100 for the smaller ones, the vast majority of squares displayed are hand painted by the extension homemakers themselves, with a great deal of input from the farmers and barn owners. "The great thing about these patterns is that there's a lot of input from the owners. Many of our squares are highly personalized, often from the patterns found on old family quilts," said Hetterman.[9]

In some cases, such personalization has been expressed through name and owner characterization. One farmer, for example, who was originally hesitant about adorning his barn with a quilt square but changed his tune after finding a pattern associated with his surname Jacob, while yet another sought to showcase his unique disposition through a square called "Farm Friendliness." Still others chose to highlight memories of loved ones choosing patterns like "Grandmother's Flower Garden," in honor of the numerous flowers found on the farm's garden, or the "Double Wedding Ring," and "Toss the Bouquet" in honor of their committed relationship to their partner/spouse. "It's all very personal. In some rarer cases, we'll even have the farmers request to paint the squares, themselves," said Hetterman.[10]

This venture has had such success in garnering interest that it can now be found featured on garages, outbuildings and even yard signs, in addition to the traditional tobacco barns. It has also spawned a similar, yet newer project featuring scenes of tobacco harvesting. This latest undertaking, appropriately called the Agricultural Heritage Trail, will display different hand painted designs showcasing the different stages surrounding tobacco production and harvesting.

For a closer look at some of the quilt patterns showcased along the Trail, the Owen County Cooperative Extension sells a bound pamphlet entitled the "Owen County Quilt Trail," complete with brief descriptions of the owners and their chosen designs. Still, the best way to see these magnificent squares is to make a visit to the county and see them up close and personal. You'll know when you've arrived after the first wave of color hits you.

## *The Conch Republic: Seceding Where Others Failed*[11]

Even the most popular spots can have trouble establishing an identity at times. This was certainly the case with Key West, Florida (pop. 24,000) in the early 1980s, when a glut in tourism led the tiny city to attempt one of the most daring PR stunts in U.S. history: secession from the United States.

Born out of a serious protest movement, the disunion of Key West from the United States arose out of a roadblock set up by federal authorities on Highway 1 in 1982 to combat the drug trade. The roadblock, which was established on the mainland side of the peninsula, caused massive traffic jams, effectively isolating Key residents from the outside world. As the islands' tourism began to suffer, the City Council filed an injunction with federal authorities, but to no avail. Thus, with the situation growing increasingly worse by the day, local authorities decided to take matters into their own hands.

Gathering in Mallory Square with other prominent members of the City Council, Key West Mayor Dennis Wardlow read off a list of grievances and declared the birth of a new nation—the Conch Republic. After breaking a loaf of stale Cuban bread over a naval officer's head, he promptly surrendered and applied for a billion dollars in foreign aid from the United Nations. All of this took place in the matter of a minute!

This little act of defiance made widespread headlines, bringing attention not only to the island itself but also to its grievances, and the roadblock was quickly lifted. But this was hardly the end as periodic acts of "rebellion" continued over the next two decades, including in 1995 and 2006.

While the acts of defiance were born of serious grievances, they nevertheless gave the inhabitants of the island something they had long been craving: an identifiable hook by which they could lure tourists. Today, when entering the Keys, you can purchase specially made Conch Republic merchandise.

Still, despite the creation of such merchandise, which includes a flag, a constitution, a military, a passport, a vehicle registration and a currency, the greatest legacy the Conch Republic has given the people of Key West is the Conch Republic Independence Celebration, a ten-day spectacle you have to see to believe.

Since 1983, the people of Key West have been commemorating their secession annually. Kicking off in late April on the Friday before the anniversary of secession, this "anything goes" festival features a party, a flag raising ceremony, a military reception and a conch shell-blowing contest, complete with prizes, music and food. And that's just the first day!

In the ten days that follow, activities almost too numerous to name go on nonstop from sunrise to sunset. These include a miniature golf tournament, a royals' ball, a naval parade, a battle reenactment of the Conch Republic's past triumphs, the "world's longest parade," a music festival and a red ribbon bed race, where participants motorize their mattresses and race down Duval Street. The hedonistic festival concludes the following Sunday, leaving its participants in a hangover-induced coma that can only be described as legendary.

The party draws tens of thousands of visitors to the Keys each year, making it one of the largest and most outlandish festivals in the state. Just remember to be respectful of the local culture when you're down there, for they may seem all frivolous and laid back, but parties are taken quite seriously. Key West is after all, "THE WORLD'S FIRST FIFTH WORLD NATION, A SOVEREIGN STATE OF MIND SEEKING ONLY TO BRING MORE HUMOR, WARMTH, AND RESPECT TO A WORLD IN SORE NEED OF ALL THREE."

## *Conquistadors, Cajuns and Crawfish: How Pensacola Embraced a Geographic Heritage*

Heritage is a tricky subject to tackle. When examining one aspect of heritage, one inevitably leaves out another. This can be especially knotty for cities that have traditionally served as melting pots for various cultures, which brings us to the small Gulf Coast city of Pensacola, Florida (pop. 53,000).

A former colonial capital, Pensacola was already 286 years old by the time Florida became a state in 1845. Throughout its lengthy history, this tiny spit of sand by Pensacola Bay has seen near-consistent migrations of Spaniards, Cajun fishermen, Southern planters, Northern transplants and U. S. Navy servicemen. Finding a single unifier that could appeal to these disparate groups was tough, which was why a shared geographic heritage was settled upon that would reflect the entire melting pot and its history. So it was that city leaders came to embrace the Fiesta of Five Flags.

As Florida's first ever celebration geared solely towards the promotion of heritage, this Pensacola party takes place each June for a period of ten days. As the festival's name suggests, the event is in celebration of the five flags that have flown over the city, including that of Spain, France, Britain, the Confederacy, and the United States, but its reality is so much more, as it's since become a general celebration of Gulf Coast identity.

Begun in 1950 as a ploy to increase interest in the region, the fiesta is one of only a handful of parties highlighting the state's history. This is accomplished through a variety of events beginning with a kickoff celebration, in Pensacola's Historic Seville Quarter, that features live music, food, drinks and colorful decorations leading up to a Gasparilla-like surrender of the city to Don Tristan de Luna, the city's foremost conquistador. Throughout the week, more events occur, including a boat parade on Pensacola Bay, in which local craft deck out in their fanciest bling, as well as a tongue-in-cheek reenactment of the original De Luna landing, a sand-sculpture-building contest and a downtown float parade.

Like their Mardi Gras-crazed neighbors to the west, Pensacola honors many of their socialites and community activists through a series of balls held during the celebration. One of these is the Fiesta All-Krewe Ball, geared mainly to participants in the festival. It features live music, dancing, a best-dressed krewe costume contest and, most importantly of all, the presentation of krewe royalty. Following this is the DeLuna Coronation Ball, perhaps the most important symbolic event of the fiesta. It is here that the new king and queen, in representation of the actual Spanish monarchy, are crowned. They will be formally honored in next year's celebration.

Today, the Five Flags Fiesta draws thousands to the region and is a great way to get acquainted with some local history, all while taking in the historic charm of the city's historic Seville Quarter.

## *Augusta and the Schizophrenic Capital City Complex: A Reflection*

Not every identity is singular and not every city needs to market it that way. Take a look at Augusta, for example. Ask any Mainer to sum up a single identifying symbol for the City of Augusta and you're likely to hear "the Statehouse." Ask a native Augustan, however, and you're likely to hear everything ranging from "Old Fort Western" or "sturgeon" to "the Kennebec River." So why such divergent thoughts among the general public and the full-time community? It all comes down to perception.

Like most state capitals, Augusta has a schizophrenic personality. A home to bureaucrats, legislators and lobbyists of all sorts commuting in each day, it's also home to a relatively stable population whose families have been here for generations. These two groups coexist in the same place but experience two different realities—one rooted in office work and the other rooted in tradition. This form of schizophrenia is inherent in many other capital cities including the likes of Atlanta—home to the Georgia state capitol building but also home to Coca Cola, CNN, Civil Rights and *Gone with the Wind*. The same goes for Austin—home to the Texas Governor but also to South by Southwest, microbreweries and liberal politics—or even Tallahassee, home to the Florida legislature but also to Florida State, FAMU, and tailgating parties.

An evening shot of the dome above the Maine State House during a full moon. Augusta became Maine's state capital in 1827, and much of the city's identity revolves around this aspect (courtesy Dave Dostie).

There are approximately 24 state capitals with populations under 150,000. Many, like their larger counterparts mentioned above, are fortunate enough to have a solid identity to build around, but much like these counterparts, they often have far more going for them than their governmental status. Just like Augusta, which highlights outdoor parks, historic streetscapes, and museums, it's okay to have multiple identities because of all of these things are part of what makes it a distinct place worth visiting. Augustans can therefore be proud of being a state capital and simultaneously be proud of having the oldest wooden fort in the country or one of the cleanest rivers in Maine. These things are part of the authentic fabric of the community and can easily resonate with outsiders.

## 2. It's All About Distinction

When first visiting the city back in 2015, I was struck by how deeply Augusta's status as a capital— from its plethora of office workers and legislators frequenting bars and restaurants to its amalgamation of hotels offering extended stays—permeated the community. I was also struck, however, by the general nonchalance of the full-time residents who were just as proud to show off their fort, their history and their landscape. To them, one thing was not necessarily better than the other and all played a role in what it meant to be an Augustan. This notion is best represented on the city's flag and seal, which features Old Fort Western, the State House and the river.

Augusta represents an example of how a small community, particularly a capital city, doesn't always have to fit the mold by identifying with just one aspect of its heritage. It can embrace a whole host of things and still know what it is at the end of the day.

## *Larry Fleury and Establishing an Identity*

Larry Fleury has been working on reinvigorating a downtown identity for over 30 years. Having grown up in downtown Augusta, he spent much of his youth hanging out with friends in the district.

"Back then, downtown was like our shopping mall. Everything was

**Larry Fleury was a founding member of the Augusta Downtown Alliance, as well as a former city councilor (courtesy Dave Dostie).**

here. We had a record shop, a pet shop, and a jewelry shop," he said. "It was the place to see and be seen in the city. It was the heart and soul of Augusta. Even so," he concedes, "it had already started to fade with the malls being built up on Western Avenue."

Beginning his professional work downtown in the late 1980s, he recalls a downtown that was mere shell of its former self. "A lot of retail had begun emptying out at that point," he says. "That's when I began to get involved with revitalization."

A founding member of the Heart of Augusta, the predecessor of what would later become the Augusta Downtown Alliance, Larry served as Board President and opened an office in the center of the street. Later, in 1990, he decided to run for city council. "Downtown needed representation," he explained.

Working with the council, as well as with the associate developer for the city, they hired the firm Hyatt Palma to develop a strategy to move forward.

"The plan included all the basics [for revitalization] and had all the precepts of what we would later do with the Augusta Downtown Alliance. It basically told us to start simply and reshape our identity," he said. "We concentrated a lot of our efforts on changing the sidewalks and street lights," he said. "They were in poor shape and gave off a bad impression. We also went to work cleaning up storefronts and getting them ready for retail. We knew we had to make changes because the #1 thing you need to do to revitalize a community is to change people's perception by forming an identity that things are happening."

Recognizing the successes his group has accomplished, he is proud of the groundwork they laid for future efforts. "We had a lot of success for the 12 years we were active and it seems to have paid off," he said. "The identity of downtown is now completely changed. The younger generation is hanging out here once again and that's all due to identity. They appreciate the historic character of the buildings and recognize this as an area with great restaurants and art."

In reflecting upon the general identity of the Augusta area, Larry states that they always tried to find ways to tie in what was going on with their revitalization work with the city's contributing features.

"Augusta as a whole has multiple identities," he said. "First and foremost, we're a capital city and although a lot of people around here shy away from that, it's a pretty special thing. There are only 50 of them, after all. We're more than just a capital, though," he continued. "We have the Old Fort, and we're both a river and a valley city. All of these things played an important role in helping us move forward with our plans."

When it comes to communities just starting out on the path of revitalization, Larry offers this advice: "Start small and get organized. Identify what needs to be done so you can put it into action. Finding a symbol to unite behind is great, but the look and feel and cleanliness of a community is all part of establishing an identity. For only when people see that you're organized and have a professional look can you give them something to rally behind and root for."[12]

## Key Takeaways About Identity and Placemaking

When it comes to establishing an identity for your community it's important to remember:

1. Distinction and placemaking can only be found when an identity is formed.
2. A small city's identity can often be rooted in tradition, whether it be geography, heritage or culture.
3. It's possible to embrace multiple identities at once.

## Conclusion

> "We know that where community exists it confers upon its members identity, a sense of belonging and a measure of security.... Communities are the ground level generators and preservers of values and ethical systems."
> —John Gardener

Just as the case studies above show, the formation of a small city's identity is almost always rooted in tradition, whether it is geography, heritage or culture. This doesn't mean, however, that it's monolithic.

We've already proved, in cases like Augusta, that small cities— capital cities in particular—have identities that are multifaceted and can't be pinned down to just a single notion. So, what of the other three examples, then? All of them found distinction because of their singular embrace of one aspect of their traditions, right?

Well, not exactly.

Take the example of Key West's "secession." Many underlying factors were considered when forming this identity: isolation from the roadblocks erected by the Federal Government, feelings of disenfranchisement, and a high cost of living. Combine that with a tradition of *laissez faire* attitudes celebrating otherness, and you have the perfect recipe for a communal identity born from protest.

Similarly, look at the case of Owenton; a place of tobacco farmers long forgotten by the bigger surrounding cities, it demands attention by expressing that it is more than just a community tied to the land, but one rich in the history of crafting, artistry and design.

All large cities have identities that can be embraced, marketed and packaged. This is something small cities can learn to do as well. Small cities, after all, like humans, are more than just extensions of their traditions: they are entities composed of a whole host of traits that help them form a larger community. Discovering what makes them that way is one of the most important steps to take in the process of replicating an urban experience.

# 3

# Focus on Aesthetics

Building a community is a lot like running a marathon. It's not speed that matters, but endurance, as making it to the finish line is the ultimate goal. This is not to say that it's impossible to make large strides in the race. As has been proved by multiple cities, large strides are indeed possible, but if you're starting from the ground up, you need to be in it for the long haul. After all, most small cities faced decades of neglect and population losses, and these sorts of trends are not something that can be remedied overnight.

In this chapter, we'll explore the marathon that is small-city revitalization by focusing on the incremental steps certain cities have taken, with particular attention to the role of aesthetics. Many of these steps are common-sense notions and have been borrowed from larger urban areas but have been adapted to fit the needs of a small community. As we'll demonstrate, it's always important to think big and keep your eye on your ultimate goals, but rushing too fast and glossing over the basics of good design and curb appeal are the quickest ways to lose steam.

## *The Science Behind Aesthetics*

As human beings, we are predisposed to prefer beauty and even to seek it actively. We typically perceive it to indicate quality and superiority, and this phenomenon is known as the beauty premium. Interestingly, the inherent bias for beauty is found even in infants, as they prefer attractive faces over unattractive ones.[1] As creatures with five core senses, we inherently want things that look, taste, feel, sound and smell right. Our affinity for beauty is deeply rooted and is reflected in all aspects of our behavior, including consumption.

Marketers recognize that aesthetics is ubiquitous and carefully consider it during product development and promotion. We make decisions based on our automatic responses to aesthetics every day. We choose one phone case over another at the mall because of its color or choose someone on a dating website because of his or her pleasant appearance. Our affinity for beauty is reflected in our actions and is frequently instinctive. Aesthetic considerations are pervasive and are an integral part of our lives, including our consumption. In this highly competitive market environment, there is an increased parity in the functionality of products, which means that each product functions as expected. However, consumer choices are also swayed by the aesthetics of particular products and services.

The concept of aesthetics is fascinating due to its omnipresence and its almost automatic effects. Aesthetics play a vital role in our lives and are significant in our decision-making processes.[2] Think for a second about your own experience when walking past a bakery or a restaurant pumping out sweet or savory smells through their vents. Chances are you're likely to think about your hunger and make a stop. In fact, so ingrained is beauty in our DNA that there is an intelligence and moral equivalency that comes into play when we interact with each other:

> [B]eautiful children are rated as more intelligent than unattractive children, even when their grades are the same (Clifford & Walster, 1973). Similarly, employees with above-average physical attractiveness enjoy the beauty premium regarding higher salaries (Hamermesh & Biddle, 1994), and people demonstrate more willingness to help attractive people than unattractive people [Andreoni and Petrie, 2008].[3]

In addition, studies have shown that employers tend to show preference for those with attractive features and personalities during the hiring process, even going so far as to give the edge to better looking candidates even their skillsets might not match those of other candidates.

As living and breathing organisms in their own right, cities too are judged by humans on their aesthetic values. When driving down the road of a strange and unfamiliar place, for example, our focus tends to be on our personal well-being, which, as we mentioned in an earlier chapter, is driven by instincts. Such instincts are reinforced through our experiences directly related to our comfort level. Foot traffic, shaded trees and well-maintained storefronts are all going to relax our anxiety and therefore increase our likelihood to stay in an area—while unkempt sidewalks, weeded-out parks, and unpleasant odors are all likely to prevent us from exploring the area by raising our danger inhibitors. As Mari Peltonen notes:

In addition to visual features, the city is associated with smells, flavours and soundscapes characteristic of it. This way, various food cultures and urban technologies become part of a multisensory urban experience.... Aesthetic values pertaining to cities are also affected by cognitive, ethical and ecological values. What we find pleasant or aesthetically interesting always reflects, to a certain degree, our knowledge of the subject or phenomenon in question, and whether we otherwise consider it desirable.[4]

Like a residential home, proper aesthetics can be achieved through attention to design and curb appeal. Such curb appeal, with regards to an urban environment, can be broken down into four distinct categories, which include:

- Streetscapes—the sensory elements that enhance the nature of the street (signs, lighting, etc.)
- Greenscapes—the greenery in public gathering spaces (trees, flowers, etc.)
- Townscapes—the general look of the urban landscape (buildings, pocket parks, etc.)
- Soundscapes—the general auditory environment of the area

All these things play a role in determining the success of a revitalizing downtown and are critical to achieving investment from both consumers and business developers. No one, after all, wants to spend time in a place that makes them feel uneasy, so why should we expect anything different in our small cities? By starting small and focusing on the aesthetics, we open the path to creating an environment that is welcoming for all.

## *A Sign for Every Kind: Guidelines from San Marcos, Texas*

When it comes to tailoring the aesthetics of your small community, one of the first things you should tackle is your streetscape, and the best way to go about doing so is through a sign ordinance. As the chief identifiers of businesses, signs are the most impactful visual element of your urban center and can play a leading role in one's decision to spend money there.

By regulating the type, size, and location of signs in a municipality (as well as the process for erecting new signs), a sign ordinance can help preserve or create community character and stop visually distracting sign competition between businesses. A municipality may adopt a sign ordinance as a part of the zoning ordinance or as a stand-alone ordinance.[5] The National Park Service recommends the following when designing and constructing new signs for historic buildings:

- signs should be viewed as part of an overall graphics system for the building.
- new signs should respect the size, scale and design of the historic building.
- sign placement is important: new signs should not obscure significant features of the historic building. (Signs above a storefront should fit within the historic signboard, for example.)
- new signs should also respect neighboring buildings. They should not shadow or overpower adjacent structures.
- sign materials should be compatible with those of the historic building.
- new signs should be attached to the building carefully, both to prevent damage to historic fabric, and to ensure the safety of pedestrians.[6]

This is something the small city of San Marcos, Texas (pop. 63,000), sought to do as part of their Vision San Marcos Comprehensive Plan back in 2018. To gain a better understanding of how they applied these standards to their own ordinance, I'm including the full guidelines listed below:

**Article 2: Sign Guidelines**
　**Division 1: OVERARCHING SIGN GUIDELINES IN CD-5 AND CD-5D**

　　**Section A.2.1.1 Purpose**
　　This section provides general design guidelines for signs. Balancing the functional requirements for signs with the objectives for the overall character of the area is a key sign design consideration. A sign is seen as serving two functions: first, to attract attention; and second, to convey information, essentially identifying the business or services offered. Orderly sign location and design should be applied to make fewer and smaller signs more effective. If a sign is mounted on a building with a well-designed facade, the building front alone can serve much of the attention-getting function. The sign can then focus on conveying information in a well-conceived manner. Similarly, for a free-standing sign, landscaping and other site amenities can help to give identity to the businesses located on the site. In this respect, each sign should be considered with the overall composition of the building and the site in mind. Signs should be in scale with their structure and integrated with surrounding buildings.

## 3. Focus on Aesthetics

A. Consider a sign in the context of the overall building and site design.
B. Design a sign to be in scale with its setting.
C. Design a sign to highlight architectural features of the building.
D. Design a sign to convey visual interest to pedestrians.
E. Avoid damaging or obscuring architectural details or features when installing signs on historic structures.

### Section A.2.1.2 Guidelines

**A. Historic Signs in CD-5D.** Historic signs within CD-5D contribute to the character of downtown. They also have individual value, apart from the buildings to which they are attached. Historic signs of all types should be retained and restored whenever possible. This is especially important when they are a significant part of a building's history or design.

1. Consider history, context and design when determining whether to retain a historic sign.

**B. Sign Character in CD-5 and CD-5D.** A sign should be in character with the materials, colors and details of the building and its site. The integration of an attached sign with the building or building facade is important and should be a key factor in its design and installation. Signs also should be visually interesting and clearly legible. Signs that appear to be custom-designed and fabricated, and that convey visual interest in the urban setting are preferred. Those that are scaled to the pedestrian are especially encouraged. A sign should also reflect the overall context of the building and surrounding area.

1. A sign should be subordinate to the overall building composition.
2. Use sign materials that are compatible with the architectural character and materials of the building.
3. A sign should not obscure character-defining features of a building.

**C. Sign Illumination in CD-5D**

1. Illumination should occur in a manner that keeps it subordinate to the overall building and its site as well as the neighborhood, while accomplishing the functional needs of the business. Minimize surface glare and manage light spill such that glare is not created on adjoining properties.
2. Where allowed, an external light source should be shielded to direct the light and minimize glare.
3. External Illumination, Tube Lighting, Halo Lighting, and Direct Illumination shall be designed to be in character with, and subordinate to, the building facade.

### Section A.2.1.3 Specific Sign Types

**A. Awning or Canopy Sign.** An awning or canopy sign may be placed on either the vertical valance flap, the top, the sloped portion, or on a side panel of the awning or canopy.

1. Use an awning or canopy sign in areas with high pedestrian use.

2. Use an awning or canopy sign when other sign types would obscure architectural details.

  **B. Projecting Sign.** A projecting sign is attached perpendicular to the wall of a building or structure.
  1. Design a bracket for a projecting sign to complement the sign composition.
  2. Locate a projecting sign to relate to the building façade and entries.

  **C. Sandwich Board Sign.** A sandwich board is a portable sign designed in an A-frame or other fashion, and having back-to back sign faces.
  1. Locate a sandwich board to maintain a clear circulation path on the sidewalk. A minimum of 4 feet in clearance is required.
  2. Design the sandwich board to be durable and have a stable base.

  **D. Wall Sign.** A wall sign is a sign that is attached flat against the facade of the building consisting of individual cut letters applied directly to the building, or painted directly on the surface of the building.
  1. Place a wall sign to be flat against the building facade.
  2. Place wall signs to integrate with and not obscure building details and elements.

  **E. Directory Sign.** A tenant panel or directory sign displays the tenant name and location for a building containing multiple tenants.
  1. Use a directory sign to consolidate small individual signs on a larger building.
  2. Locate a directory sign at the street level entrance to upper floor businesses or on facades facing entrances to alleys, rear lanes and parking lots for business way finding purposes.

  **F. Pole and Monument Signs.** A monument sign is a sign that is erected on a solid base placed directly on the ground and constructed of a solid material. A pole mounted sign is generally mounted on one or two simple poles.
  1. A pole or monument sign may be considered where it has been used traditionally and the building or activity is set back from the street or public right-of-way.
  2. A pole or monument sign may be considered on a historic property or within a historic district when it is demonstrated that no other option is appropriate.
  3. Design a pole or monument sign to be in character and proportionate with its structure and site.
  4. Design a monument sign to incorporate a sturdy supporting base that is at least 75 percent of the width of the sign face at its widest point. Appropriate base materials include, but are not limited to brick, stone, masonry and concrete.[7]

As you can see from the above model, guidelines for a sign ordinance don't have to be overly complicated. They can be achieved by simply defining the types of signage that exist, with recommendations that any new signage adhere to the principle of enhancing the architectural features of an area. While some ordinances go overboard with trying to cram too much information in, the City of San Marcos actually does a pretty good job with making it user-friendly.

## The Importance of Trees

Whether we realize it or not, our personalities are molded through the kinds of stimuli we come into contact with each day. These stimuli can affect our moods, our habits, and most importantly, our anxiety levels.

As mentioned earlier, our anxiety level is often the motivating cause for whether we choose to spend time in a location. This is why natural greenscapes like trees play such an important role in developing a sustainable urban environment. Not only do they provide shade and oxygen, but also, they play a role in reducing anxiety. Two studies examined this phenomenon.

In the first, 585 young adult Japanese participants reported on their moods after walking for 15 minutes, either in an urban setting or in a forest. The forests and urban centers were in 52 different locations around the country and about a dozen participants walked in each area. In comparison to those who walked in urban centers, the participants who walked in the forest were shown to be less irritable, depressed and fatigued and emerged overall less anxious and with more vigor. The

Having an ordinance to encourage proper signage can go a long way towards giving your downtown a more cohesive look. Here we see an example of a bracketed sign in front of a downtown barbershop (author's collection).

psychological benefits of walking through forests are very significant, and forest environments are expected to have very important roles in promoting mental health in the future," the authors write. Indeed, various other studies suggest that the practice of "forest bathing"—deliberately spending time among the woods—can help us deal with the stresses and strains of urban living.[8]

In a similar study, participants in Poland were asked to spend 15 minutes gazing either at either a forested landscape in winter or at an urban area devoid of trees. The trees in the forest had straight trunks and no greenery due to the cold and there was no other shrubbery present. Meanwhile the urban landscape consisted solely of roads and buildings. The participants were then asked to fill out questionnaires related to their moods and emotions. It was discovered that those who viewed the forested landscape were more likely to report significantly better moods, more positive emotions, more vigor, and a greater sense of personal restoration afterwards than those who gazed at the urban scene.

As researchers from both studies noted both outcomes are likely due to the effects that trees have on our brains, as it showed people in proximity to trees as having better "amygdala integrity"— meaning, a brain structure better able to handle stressors.[9]

Many of America's earliest urban planners recognized the importance of proper greenscapes, which is how both Philadelphia's and Savannah's famous tree-lined squares were born. Today, this way of design is making a comeback, particularly in smaller communities seeking to revitalize their downtowns.

Flowerpots, such as the one above, enhance the aesthetics of a street by providing splashes of color along the pavement. These particular pots are placed each year along Water Street through a program called Water Street Gardens (author's collection).

## Greenscaping Duluth and Edmonds

For many of America's small cities, shade trees were often a part of the urban landscape being incorporated in both downtowns and neighborhoods alike. Unfortunately, the ravages of Dutch Elm disease, along with everyday urban stressors, eradicated many of the older trees lining our historic inner cores, leaving barren, sterile streetscapes. This is the predicament in which Duluth, Minnesota (pop. 86,000) found itself when revisiting the topic.

Recognizing the calming effects that trees have on the human psyche, and nostalgic for the era when downtown streets were shade-covered, the Greater Downtown Council launched an initiative to restore 40 trees to the area in the mid–2000s.

"A lot of the trees have died over the years as a result of the harsh urban environment. The soil also gets polluted with salt, or the trees get hit by cars," Greater Downtown Council President Kristi Stokes said.[10] Launching the Adopt-a-Tree program, the Greater Downtown Council approached area businesses for $500 donations to sponsor a tree and receive a brick with their name on it.

City Gardener Tom Kasper said a lot of the problems were soil- and design-related but said he believes the downtown council's plan will address both concerns. For instance, he said, the plan includes "structured soil," which is a rougher grade that holds up much better. Kasper also suggested planting maples or lindens. With Duluth's well-publicized budgetary problems, the city hasn't replaced a boulevard tree in five years, he said.[11]

Endorsed by the mayor, the program was brought about in phases, the first phase involving the planting of 18 trees. The second phase, occurring a year later saw another 10 trees planted in downtown streets and continued on until all 40 trees were replaced. As was stated in their program:

> If you've ever wanted to make a difference in the appearance of your central business district; if you've ever wished you could make a lasting contribution to the downtown; if you have wanted to honor or memorialize a beloved family member or friend, you can do it through the Greater Downtown Council's Adopt-A-Tree program.
>
> For just $500, you can sponsor a tree, and receive recognition in a permanently etched brick on the sidewalk near the tree.[12]

Like Duluth, the city of Edmonds, Washington (pop. 42,000) also launched a greenscaping initiative that involved private partnership, albeit much earlier.

Launched in 1922, and begun in earnest in the 1970s, the City of Edmonds Beautification Program involved a city-private partnership through the Floretum Garden Club. Growing from a few small flower beds and a handful of baskets, the initiative has since taken off, boasting 186 flower beds and over 138 flower baskets adorning the core of their downtown. As outlined by their website:

**Flower Program/City Beautification by the numbers:**
- Supported by the Edmonds Floretum Garden Club for 97 years (they still assist with planting)
- 138 flower baskets maintained (and 186 individual flower beds)
- 22,000 plants grown in our greenhouse each year (20–30 percent grown from seed)

Baskets are available to adopt for $100.00 per season (June through September) and corner parks for $250.00 per season (through early November).[13]

Market Square Park is an example of a pocket park concept brought to life. The work of Augusta Downtown Alliance volunteers, University of Maine at Augusta students, and city officials, the park occupies the site of a former bus stop and has since become a shady reprieve for picnickers (author's collection).

## Cheyenne Experiments with Pocket Parks

Pocket parks are a trend that took off in cities in the late 2000s and early 2010s. Originally called vest pocket parks, a term first used in the 1960s, pocket parks are urban open spaces on a small scale, usually no more than ¼ acre, providing an inviting environment for surrounding community members. Meeting a variety of needs and functions, many parks include small event spaces, play areas for children, spaces for relaxing or meeting friends, or taking lunch breaks, etc. Successful "pocket parks" have four key qualities: they are accessible; they allow people to engage in activities; they are comfortable spaces and have a good image; and finally, they are sociable places where people meet each other and take people to when they come to visit.[14]

Often designed in unsightly areas, pocket parks generally differentiate themselves from city parks both by size as well as function, as they are generally tailored to meet the needs of a specific area rather than the city as a whole. Many are funded through grants and organized through community programs, as was the case with the most recent pocket park opened in Cheyenne, Wyoming (pop. 64,000).

Developed through a partnership with the Cheyenne Downtown Development Authority (DDA) and two downtown merchants, Cheyenne's pocket park was designed to accommodate seasonal patrons in an unused alley for the summer months. The surrounding space was chosen both for the prominent parking as well as for the vibrant art murals that surround it.

"We had the idea to use our parking lot for something more than just parking because it's such a beautiful space with the vibrant murals. This seemed like the perfect time to make it happen, and thanks to the DDA, it has," Paramount Cafe owner Renee Jelinek said.

In addition to the collaboration with business owners, the DDA had the support of Cheyenne Mayor Marian Orr and the City of Cheyenne, Wyoming–Government Parking Division, to bring the park idea to fruition. "We are proud to support our small businesses and hope that the addition of this pocket park encourages the public to enjoy our downtown and everything it has to offer while being able to follow the social distancing guidelines," Mayor Orr said.[15]

Featuring picnic tables with plants, the entrance to the park is free and is the perfect solution for Covid-19 guidelines as it allows for communal gatherings in a socially distanced setting.

"It's a weird time and so that ability to be able to gather as a community while maintaining those socially distant guidelines and following those rules, it's a great way to kind of do that and foster that community togetherness," Cheyenne DDA Marketing and Events Director Haylee Chenchar said.[16]

As demonstrated through Cheyenne's most recent addition, pocket parks can be created in a grassroots manner, involving either city or community partnership. In this way they can be quickly installed and adapted to fit a particular area. More importantly, they can enhance the look and feel of the general townscape by making formerly underutilized spots into oases for community engagement.

## *Soundscaping: The Case of Van Wert*

The impact that Covid-19 played upon the psyche of Americans cannot be overstated. From lockdowns to residential quarantines to restrictions on gatherings, the disease had a devastating impact upon downtown businesses and raised the anxieties of many. This is something the small city of Van Wert, Ohio (10,000), sought to allay when reopening by introducing the concept of soundscaping to their community.

Focusing on the importance of positive stimuli in reducing anxiety, Main Street Van Wert took a unique route by lessening fear through sound by installing speakers in their downtown that could play music. Mitch Price, Executive Director of Main Street Van Wert, said that early on in his position it was always one of his goals to illuminate downtown with the sound of music.

"I think it adds a lot to the downtown," said Price. "There's a lot of studies that show that having speakers downtown makes people happier, it makes them spend a little bit more money, and it puts people in a better mood."[17]

Working with Streetscape Speakers, the group installed a series of wireless speakers through several blocks, with the intent of pumping family-friendly music into their downtown.

"The speakers are wireless, so we had to put an antenna on our building that bounces signal to them, but they can also bounce signal to each other too," said Price. "We can add to it, as well. If we got funds next year or the following year, we could keep adding to it. That's the plan. We can buy as we go."[18]

The City of Van Wert and Van Wert County chipped in to give Main Street Van Wert some funding for the speaker system, which can also be utilized for public events and emergencies. Avangrid Renewables also provided funding toward the speaker, said Price.

"When we have parades again, this will be super nice," explained

Price, who noted that people will be able to hear parade announcements more easily now. The system also came with a wireless microphone. "It's great for emergencies as well. Heaven forbid if we have any, we can alarm people. We can also put promotions or commercials on there. We can honor our supporting partners with it. There's a lot of stuff that we can do."

Currently, the music is being played downtown from 8:00 a.m. to 10:00 p.m. and is on a family-friendly station that permits the use of copyrighted music.

"I think this will give people another positive for downtown," said Price. "What we're trying to do as a whole—a City and County—through the downtown, I think it just adds to it. It's another tool in the tool shed and adds to the experience of downtown."[19]

While Van Wert's experiment in soundscaping is a relatively new addition to the urban environment, the concept has actually been with us for quite a while. Go into any store or mall around Christmas time, for example, and you're likely to hear Christmas music. This is not done because of the Holiday season, but rather to remind people to shop, and it floods people's subconsciouses with images of family gatherings and gift giving. The same tactics are often used by ice cream trucks in the summer, which can flood a neighborhood with the familiar songs used in carnivals and fairs to invoke a sense of excitement to consumers.

## Jesse Patkus and the Role of Aesthetics in Downtown Development

Jesse Patkus is a long-time Augusta resident and downtown building owner who has been involved with improving downtown since 2011. An architect for a Portland-based firm which specializes in constructing residential and vacation homes, Jesse sits on the board of the Historic District Review Board and began his involvement with downtown improvement while still a student at the University of Maine's Architecture Program. In discussing downtown, he says:

> Things like signs are a big deal for me because of the way they enhance the elements of a building. For me, consistency is key. Natural elements or natural looking elements can go a long way to complimenting a historic district, but it doesn't always have to be the same. I think there is indeed room for a variety of styles including bracketed and flat signs since historically downtowns were pretty eclectic. What ties them together, is consistency of height and scale. If you look at most historic buildings there's a distinct ribbon line that lend themselves as pretty solid places for the placement of things like bracketed signs.

> In terms of sign style, I think natural or natural-looking signs work best. If you utilize the materials around you, you're likely to enhance the features of a particular building. This doesn't mean, however, that that's the only way to achieve a decent look. On the contrary, things like neon signs can lend themselves really well to a place like a diner, and backlit signs can work in certain instances, particularly if scale and height are respected. The only thing I don't think could ever work are changeable signs with moving images. These kinds of signs you're likely to see on the outskirts of a downtown in places like strip malls and are inconsistent with the timeless quality of a downtown area. Development for development's sake does not equate place making and I think it's important for any downtown to recognize that when attempting to tackle a project.

An avid member of the Steering Committee, which predated the formation of the Augusta Downtown Alliance, Jesse worked on a variety of projects related to aesthetics that included green space initiatives and cultural events like an art walk. It was his work on a community gathering space, however, that he looks upon as being among his biggest accomplishments, as it helped change the face downtown:

> One of the projects I'm most proud of being a part of during my stint on the Augusta Downtown Alliance was Market Square Park. Where the park sits now was formerly a bus stop that had fallen into serious disrepair and neglect. It had really grimy bathrooms and a large conical tree in the center and was built over the old remains of Capitol Theater which had burned down in the 80s. The city had long supported moving the bus stop to another area of town and turning the area into a green space for the community, and I worked a lot with Dan Nichols from the city in trying to make that happen.

Having already launched the popular Light on Water art walk, Jesse spotted an opportunity for community buy-in on the park by incorporating a vote on elements that the public wanted to see included.

> Working with Dan and the university students, we came up with some ideas for how it might look and then asked for those in attendance to give us their feedback. We then incorporated that feedback into one cool design that I put together graphically to present to city leaders.

In describing the changes, he recounts:

> One of the first things we called for was taking down the huge tree in the middle. It had been used as a Christmas tree by the city and was way too big for the downtown area. We then worked on bench placement and concert space.

On reflecting on the park as it is now, Jesse states:

> There are definitely things looking back on it I would've done differently. I would've probably placed the benches in different areas than where they are now. Right now, when entering the park, we have these benches in front of

### 3. Focus on Aesthetics

**Developer Richard Parkhurst added planters with a self-watering irrigation system to enhance the look of his corner building in downtown Augusta (author's collection).**

the fountain that look and act like barriers. It doesn't really have that open, inviting feel you want for a park like that. I'd also reposition all the benches to face the Olde Federal Building rather than the concert area. The thought at the time was that there would be a lot more music when we placed them. Unfortunately, the park is too small to host huge crowds so what we have now are benches that are essentially facing a wall. It's not really something we could've predicted at the time, but it's always kind of bothered me. To be fair though, hindsight is 20/20 and a park is something you really have to live in and feel around in order to do it right. Still, I'm pretty happy with the way it turned out overall. It's a vast improvement over what was there, and it really marked a turning point for downtown revitalization. It also marked the beginning of a partnership between the Augusta Downtown Alliance and the City. Many people come up and comment on how beautiful the park is and I love watching people use it. It was a little thing that made a big difference for downtown.[20]

## Key Takeaways on Aesthetics

The following takeaways are important to recall when discussing ways to improve aesthetics:

1. Aesthetics are an important first step to improving the success of a small city's revitalization.
2. Aesthetics can play a role in reducing anxiety.
3. Aesthetics can be broken down into categories of streetscaping, greenscaping, townscaping and soundscaping.
4. Aesthetics can either be led by the city or through grassroots efforts.
5. Aesthetics can be adapted to tackle different situations.

## *Conclusion*

> "Aesthetic matters are fundamental for the harmonious development of both society and the individual."—Friedrich Schiller

Whether we want to admit it or not, we humans are prone to judge books by their covers. This inherent instinct is something we are taught from birth and adapt through experience. When something does not look right, then it does not feel right. This is why aesthetics matter.

Focusing on community enhancements through what we visually encounter every day is more than just putting lipstick on a pig. It's actually one of the first steps we can take to making things better. When you clean up visual clutter, you're not just getting rid of the clutter, you're actually sending out a signal that things are different and that standards will be applied.

By incorporating things like sign ordinances, or by adding things like pocket parks, trees, flowers or soothing sounds, you can help both improve the image of your community and at the same time reduce the anxieties of visitors. All these things can be accomplished through cost-effective measures and will go a long way to improving the chances of long-term sustainability.

Cities are living, breathing entities, after all, and just as a child needs nurturing and grooming to grow, so to do our communities. This is something larger cities have recognized over the years and something that our smaller towns can adapt from them.

A true urban experience requires participation from all levels, particularly from first-time visitors, and a good aesthetics program will help enhance those experiences. The next time you head to your community's city center, stop, take a walk, and make notes of what can be improved; it will make all the difference.

# 4

# Ignore the Haters

*Learn to Trust Your Instincts*

No one ever tells you how contentious small-town revitalization can actually be. Most people who sign up for a job with the task of changing things recognize that at some point things can get heated. Very few realize just how personal the attacks can get, however, particularly when those changes affect the way things have been for years, or even decades. As former President Barack Obama often stated in his presidential campaign: "Change is never easy, but always possible." To make it possible, one has to do two things: believe in your own wisdom and carry on no matter what. This is why learning to trust your instincts and ignore the crowds is so important.

In this chapter, we'll explore how a few cities did just that, even when it meant potential job losses or unpopularity with the business community.

## Trust Your Instincts: A Personal Reflection

When first traveling into a city, one can tell right away what is or isn't working. It's not rocket science and doesn't require a degree in urban planning. I myself had no such degree but could tell from the moment I entered downtown Augusta that something was not right.

It was late November 2015, and the icy Maine landscape was brown and barren. When my future boss picked me up at the airport for an in-person interview, we drove through two neighboring communities on the way into Augusta. Each city was uniform, tidy and cute in appearance. More importantly, they had traffic. They were lovely places, and in listening to my future boss, I knew Augusta had even more potential. You can imagine my surprise then when we descended the hill to the desolation that was Water Street.

Boarded-up windows, empty streets and sparse vehicular traffic were what greeted us when we finally exited the car. It only got worse after 5 p.m.

Although Augusta's central business district was nearly twice as large as those of the other towns, it was easy to tell from the outset what was different. The buildings were mishmash in style and loomed ominously over the streetscape like something out of a J.G. Ballard novel. The street was devoid of vehicular traffic, and the majority of first-floor retail spaces were far too large for typical mom-and-pop retail.

Later, when meeting in a local pub with the rest of the board of directors, I was asked what my initial impressions were and what I thought they could do differently. My response was simply that I thought they had a beautiful, historic downtown with lots of potential, but that (1) a lack of a sign ordinance prohibited a cohesive look to the community, (2) they needed to fine absentee landlords for code violations, and (3) they need to establish historic district standards to regulate building additions. At that point, I hadn't even begun to crack the real surface of our issues, which included one-way traffic, and a co-dependent emphasis on downtown office workers, which held local business owners hostage to a 9 a.m. to 5 p.m. crowd. Still, what I said was true and from the looks on a few of the faces at the table, I could tell it was not what they wanted to hear. Many, at that time, preferred that I emphasize growing large-scale events that could bring more people to the street. When pressed on the issue, however, I replied bluntly that it was too early for events to take place on that kind of scale and that even if such events were successful, they would do little to improve their fortunes. Despite their arguments to the contrary, I calmly explained that what they had to tackle first and foremost was an image problem. Fix the image, and people will come. Needless to say, I did little to endear myself to this portion of the table. They wanted a large event, and they were convinced that this was the only acceptable path forward. I stood my ground, and even though I was a mere stranger to their community, I did not give an inch when it came to presenting them with the proper path forward.

When, two weeks later, I received a call announcing that I had gotten the position, I knew I had done the right thing by standing strong. Although I had no degree in small-town revitalization, my past experiences from living in an emerging downtown district, along with my degree in historic preservation and my brief run-in with those two cities to Augusta's south, told my gut everything that was wrong and needed to change in Augusta. In sum, I trusted my instincts because my observations in life led me to those conclusions.

## Understanding the Psychology Behind Instinct

Good leadership is not something that people are born with, but rather something that people grow into. In fact, there is some very basic science that backs up the distinguishing characteristics between what makes a good leader and the average individual. This typically revolves around trusting your gut.

Human behavioral science believes that from the moment you're born, your mind absorbs all experiences like a sponge. When faced with decisions, these experiences flood your mind and allow you to make decisions quickly. This was backed up more recently by a study conducted by neuroscientist Antonio Damasio of the University of Southern California. In the study, Damasio tells us that it is important to pay attention to "*somatic markers*." Originating in the insula (the island in the brain responsible for social emotions like pride or guilt) and the amygdala (which cues our response to threats), they send messages that something just feels right—or it doesn't. The more you pay attention to the outcome of trusting your intuition in combination with facts, the better your future decision-making can become.[1]

To test his theory, Damasio performed an experiment called the Iowa Gambling Task. In it, subjects could choose between different decks of cards to win cash. Among the choices includes two "good" decks, which turned up consistent profits and two others that contained riskier cards.

> Though it took about 50 cards to make a decision to switch decks and 80 cards to explain why, the subjects' skin was also being monitored for response to stress. The physical reaction showed that after drawing just 10 risky cards, the body was already displaying signs of anxiety, which meant that their feelings were firing signals faster than rational thought.[2]

Damasio concluded that those winning more cash were quicker to pick up on which decks were good compared to the bad one, and that there were automatic internal reactions long before consciousness could make the decision before them. In other words, those that were more successful in this experiment were those that acted on good instinct.

## When to Trust Your Instincts

Not all instincts are created equal, and there are times when your gut can very well betray you. Many leaders have actually suffered because they zeroed in purely on instinct and not enough on other factors such as education, experience, data and intuition. An article by

Forbes highlighted this fact, by breaking down the six dangers one faces when focusing too much on instinct and not enough on other factors. The six revelations are highlighted below:

1. **Just because it's comfortable doesn't make it right.** Because something has worked in the past doesn't mean it will work in the future. Technology changes in a blink. Business has transformed overnight. And so have the expectations of today's employees. If you want to be a great leader, you must consistently strive for improvement—because success only lives in the present.

2. **Data shouldn't be ignored.** We might all be bombarded by the latest research and findings that supposedly inform us on how we should improve our leadership skills. It can seem overwhelming at times, but it shouldn't be ignored. Research on employee perceptions, magnetic cultures, and preferred leadership traits might not change who you are, but it may give you insight into who you could become.

3. **There's always an exception.** We've heard many leaders say, "I understand people." And while that may be true, we never want to clump all people into the same category and assume we know everyone's intentions, goals, or frustrations. Your intuition may be spot-on with the majority of people. But never forget that there is always an exception, and if you truly want to be a great leader, you need to do your research, get feedback, and only make one assumption—that your approach doesn't work for absolutely everyone.

4. **You overlook the basics.** Intuition can lead to brilliant ideas, fresh approaches, and outstanding results. Nevertheless, it's important to realize that your job as a leader is to inspire greatness in others. And, as much as the world is changing, humankind doesn't change so drastically. In fact, *O.C. Tanner Institute's 2018 Global Culture study* discovered that the company cultures people find most appealing are those who focus six, very human, areas of excellence—the provide a sense of purpose, opportunity, success, appreciation, well-being, and leadership. These are basic human desires. If your intuition leads you away from the basics, you may be making a dangerous decision.

5. **You trust your gut too much.** We've all been in situations in which the data tells us one thing, but intuition tells us the opposite. These decisions can be tough. As humans, we want to feel "right" about our decisions. But it's important to understand

that feeling right about a decision doesn't always make that decision right. Learn how to separate the two.

6. **You don't trust your intuition enough.** Contrary to the point above, it's important to acknowledge how you feel about a leadership decision. If data tells you one thing and you somehow feel a decision contradicts your sense of morality, doesn't fit with your values, or challenges your character, it's time to take a step back, pause, and keep hunting for options.[3]

Like the observations made by Forbes, Damasio's experiment highlighted that good instincts are not purely reactionary but come from a combination of awareness of one's surroundings coupled with knowledge from past experiences. If a certain pattern emerges, it therefore stands to reason that it will be repeated.

So just how do we discover this pattern, and can we apply it to small town revitalization?

## *Applying Your Instinct*

In his landmark book, *Sources of Power*, Gary Klein details four kinds of information that humans process when making an instinctual decision: Relevant Cues, Expectancies, Plausible Goals and Typical Actions. While these are more often than not applied to people, they can very well be applied to a particular place as well.

Relevant cues are those we witness with our senses. What does a place look like? What does it smell like?

Expectancies are what we determine based on these cues. Am I safe? Am I in danger?

Plausible Goals inform us of actions we can take based on the first two points of information processed. Should I stay? Should I leave?

Typical Actions further define plausible goals with realistic outcomes. Should I get in my car and drive away? Should I stick around and explore?

To further hammer this home, let's imagine for a second that it is summer and that you are going for a leisurely drive to the coast. On the way, you happen upon a small downtown area. The shops are busy, and the sidewalks are packed with people. If you were in no particular hurry, what would your instinct tell you to do? Likely, because of all the people, you would immediately feel that it was safe. Your instincts would tell you that there are likely good restaurants and interesting retail stores and that this is a place worth spending some time. Chances are you'd probably get out of the car and explore it.

Now, imagine, you enter a downtown, and no one is there. You see boarded-up windows, a smattering of vacancies, and unkempt sidewalks. What would you do? Likely because of the lack of people, you'd feel uneasy. Because of this, and the other cues you have picked up on, your instincts would tell you that this place is not a good location to be and that you should probably drive away.

In both these scenarios, your actions either to stay and explore or to leave and drive away are more than appropriate as they are gut responses to the patterns you have noticed your whole life (i.e., places that draw in more people are desirable, while those that are desolate heighten the sense of danger).

As was stated earlier, I was able to correctly deduce upon my initial visit to Augusta that throwing or pursuing a large event in downtown would be premature due to the lack of regular traffic and the general public's perceptions that the area was dangerous. What was needed first was to fix those perceptions by cleaning up the area's physical image. Events should be secondary.

To sum things up, your initial instincts about a place are rarely wrong. You know already what makes a welcoming and inviting place

Cushnoc Brewing Company opened in 2017 as the brainchild of partners Tobias Parkhurst, Casey Hynes, James Bass, and Chris Geerlings. The brewery was a major leap of faith for the partners and has since become a staple in the Maine brewery business (author's collection).

just by drawing upon your experiences. Trust those initial instincts and use data and education to forge a path forward.

## *Discovering the Heart and Soul of Biddeford, Maine*

The small city of Biddeford, Maine (pop. 21,277), is an anomaly for the oldest state (by residents' age) in the Union. Hugging the southeastern coast, and located conveniently between Portland and Portsmouth, it has become a virtual mecca for those under 30 seeking a place to live, particularly in the last decade. Such a youthful shift has helped spawn art, restaurants, retail and capital for a city whose reputation was anything but youth-oriented a few years back. So, what changed? The singular vision of one man: David Leckey.

While it might seem strange to those unfamiliar with coastal New England, the states of Maine, New Hampshire and Massachusetts share quite a bit in common with their Rust Belt counterparts in the Midwest. As one of the first bastions of industrialization, they were leaders in innovation, particularly in the textile industry. This, of course, changed in the late twentieth century, as industry shifted south for cheaper opportunities, leaving former mill towns like Biddeford to rot. By the end of the 2000s, there was little socioeconomic difference between Biddeford and Detroit, as rising unemployment coupled with a declining tax base led to a crisis of direction: "The city did not need a short-term, band-aid solution list or lackluster plan," says Daniel Stevenson, who previously served as Biddeford's economic development director. "We needed solutions."[4]

At the heart of Biddeford's problems was a municipal waste incinerator. The behemoth disposal system occupied eight acres of downtown riverfront and was among the largest of such systems in the state. The rancid fumes it emitted, along with the unsightly nature of the incinerator, dissuaded many outsiders from moving to Biddeford or investing in the community, and it became clear that something needed to be done. Unfortunately, in a town strapped for cash and steady employment, the incinerator proved hard to shut down: it was one of the largest employers and taxpayers in the city. That's when Stevenson approached outside help in the form of David Leckey.

Leckey, executive director of the Orton Family Foundation based in Vermont, introduced Biddeford to the Community Heart & Soul program, which used a participatory two-year process that included financial assistance and training to create a master plan for the community.

Going through the Community Heart & Soul process from 2008–10, it was found that residents of the city strongly expressed a desire for a different kind of downtown that was both family-friendly and retail-heavy. These values were linked to a goal of developing a model for compatible businesses that would support these visions.

Though the master plan faced some stiff headwinds from the city council, it was ultimately approved by voters who decided to trust the instincts of Leckey in the promise of a better city center. Residents voted on all outcomes listed in the master plan and the city of Biddeford and Casella reached a $6.65 million deal in August 2011 to shut down the Maine Energy Recovery Co. incinerator—finally resolving a quarter-century of complaints about the smell and truck traffic created by the facility.[5] The city acquired the property and razed it, opening the acreage up for development.

The partnership with the foundation was a "game changer," says Mr. Stevenson, who made his comments in an email interview. "The City is better off today with over $100 million in new private-sector mixed use investments and millions in downtown public infrastructure improvements including the RiverWalk...."[6]

Stevenson goes on to cite that prior to completing Heart & Soul, only 400,000 square feet of 1.6 million square feet of mill space was being used. After going through the revitalization, only 400,000 square feet is vacant. The rest is filled with restaurants, shops, retail stores, art studios and apartments. In addition, a hotel is being constructed, and Biddeford turned one of the factories into a museum.[7]

Leckey's visionary guidance helped the people of Biddeford see beyond their industrial past by promoting an adapted reuse of these relics for future generations. By going against the prevailing thought that any industry was better than no industry, the city was able to more than recoup the loss in tax revenue, and because of the deal allotted, which moved the incinerator to a nearby community, they were able to keep many of their citizens employed. Today, the partnership forged between the city and Leckey is no longer considered controversial, but one of the best decisions they could've pursued.

What Leckey's instincts told him is what many Biddeford residents had always known—that small towns are not just about jobs, but the people who live there. Leckey's instincts helped him achieve this vision. "After all," Leckey says, "you don't live in an economy, you live in a community. Build your community first."[8]

## Olathe, Kansas: A Redirection of Priorities

Change is a difficult thing to navigate, particularly in small communities where tradition runs strong. It's especially true in the Midwest, where suspicion of anything new runs high. This is something city officials are currently navigating in the small city of Olathe, Kansas (population 125,000+).

Located a mere 22 miles outside of Kansas City, it would seem downtown Olathe is in an ideal spot to capitalize on growth. Its larger counterpart witnessed phenomenal growth in residents from 2018 to 2019, being listed among the top metro areas for residential expansion, with almost 17,000 new residents moving there,[9] but this boom has failed to take hold in their city center.

With a quaint downtown of low-rise commercial buildings, downtown Olathe looks like something out of a Norman Rockwell painting. Unfortunately for the residents of that city, that's about all it has going for it at the moment.

Inundated with law offices and government agencies, Olathe's city center has fallen into the trap that many such county seats and state capitals fell into during the era of urban renewal—an overreliance on office workers to support and sustain growth. As we've seen in previous chapters, such reliance has fostered a culture of 9 a.m.–5 p.m. living, with very little activity occurring after dark. One resident, Pamela Hall, who grew up in Olathe, lamented the current state of downtown recalling the good old days when things were vital: "I remember when we had shops and a theater and restaurants and all sorts of things to do downtown for people on Fridays and Saturdays," Hall said. "I mean it was packed."[10]

Now, changes are afoot, as sweeping new developments were announced in 2019, with a new courthouse, a new city square, a new, modern library featuring mixed-use office and retail, and the biggest change of all—a new residential development.

Developed by the Indianapolis-based company Milhaus, one four-story apartment building will take the place of the old library at 201 E. Park St, while the other will take over a city-owned public parking lot at the southwest corner of East Santa Fe and North Chestnut Streets. The two will add 240 residences to the downtown area.

The development is coming about as a result of the forward thinking of city leaders who aggressively marketed the area to private developers. The city sold the land to Milhaus for $10.[11] The announced development was just what city officials were hoping to attract, as they finally see a chance to reinvigorate the downtown area with life.

"Downtown Olathe has a vibrant atmosphere during the work week but lacks any Class A apartments to bring vibrancy after business hours and on weekends," said John McGurk, with Milhaus. "We believe with its proximity to jobs and the historic center of town, both our residents and the downtown neighborhood will greatly benefit."[12]

Still, not all business owners are happy, as they see this development as a threat to their popular Old Settlers Festival, which occurs annually in downtown.

Featuring arts and crafts, concerts, food trucks, and games, among other things, the festival draws in an estimated 200,000 people to the downtown area and is an annual boon for small businesses located there. The new development proposed by Milhous is perceived as a threat to this event, however, as its construction over the parking lot of the old library will eliminate 137 public parking spaces, conceivably making it more difficult for tourists to gather. That sentiment is most apparent among members of the Old Settlers group, who worry that their festival will no longer have a home.

"This is going to affect Old Settlers in a big way," said Sheila Newbanks, owner of Silvers Jewelry and a member of Old Settlers, which organizes the festival. "But Old Settlers is just a small part of the entertainment we bring to the downtown. And the arts and crafts vendors pay sales tax that goes to the city. Thousands of people come, and they have to go somewhere to eat and stay somewhere. We bring a lot of money to the city."

While acknowledging the concerns of business owners and seeking out solutions to address arising issues such as parking, many in the Olathe City Council have wisely stayed the course and trusted their instincts. The 240 market-rate residences not only promise to bring in a lot of sustained capital to a community that has struggled for years to reinvent itself, but also promises to reinvigorate the landscape of downtown from one that's office-oriented to one that's residential-driven.

"It's exciting to think about development coming to downtown Olathe that's not government-driven," planning commission member Ryan Nelson said at the meeting. "The challenge is we often think of downtown Olathe like how it was in the 1980s. ... I think we need to acknowledge this is a challenging shift. There's going to be a lot of adjustment. But I think for us to advance our downtown, you have to have a vision different from the past. Because what we've been doing since the '80s isn't advancing our downtown."[13]

As of right now, the development is underway, a testament to the fortitude that city leadership had by trusting their instincts and data over the objections of others so that downtown Olathe could finally become a place to live, work and play.

## Tobias Parkhurst and Investing in Instinct

Tobias Parkhurst is a literal jack of all trades. A Central Maine native, Tobias earned his B. A, at the University of Hartford and for 10 years traveled the world as a professional skateboarder. In 2008, Tobias returned to Maine and is now the President of Oakes & Parkhurst Glass. Since 2009, he's bought and refurbished five historic buildings in Augusta's downtown which has been an integral part of the revitalization efforts for this city. Tobias is both the landlord and a partner for two successful businesses on Water St., including Cushnoc Brewing Co. which opened in 2017, and State Lunch which opened in 2020. In addition to these robust roles, Tobias serves on the Augusta Board of Trade, the Colonial Theater Board, the Harold Alfond Institute for Business Innovation Advisory Council, and the Augusta Parking District. As past Chair for the Augusta Downtown Alliance, Tobias shared a little bit about his instinctual drives.

**Tobias Parkhurst was the first building owner to develop market-rate housing in downtown Augusta. His success in this venture sparked interest from others, launching a housing boom in the area (courtesy Dave Dostie).**

"To me, instinct is when experience and action come together. If you've only ever experienced one community, then you're likely going to experience its limitations. Once you travel, however, you get to know how other places work. When you finally discover this and want to bring it back to your l city, it takes courage," he said. "Courage is especially important in places like Augusta, where it can often feel like moving an immovable object. You have to be willing to have the courage and take the risk by saying 'Yes, Augusta can be better.'"

Reflecting on his early experience with downtown, Tobias said it all began when a building went up for sale on Water Street.

My dad wanted my brother to go after it. He flat out told me "no, it's not for you," so that was all the motivation I needed. I did the math and it added up so I went ahead and bought it. I designed two apartments, one for myself and one for another tenant. I didn't really even renovate it that much. I decided to put the other unit out there for $1k and to my shock it immediately rented. Since then, I acquired more buildings downtown, but I have always kept them anywhere from 2–4 bedrooms.

Tobias took this way of thinking into business with him when he founded Cushnoc Brewing Co. with his partners.

Some people say we got lucky with how successful Cushnoc has been, but it really involved a lot of hard work. We were successful because we saw a hole

The building the Downtown Diner now occupies was one of the first projects undertaken by local community leader Tobias Parkhurst. Painted in red, it was one of the first mixed use developments undertaken in downtown (author's collection).

in the market and went for it, and we went in to it not depending on the success of those around us, but focused instead on our own success. These were the instincts that drove us.

Regarding his role in the development of the community, he states:

> I really don't see myself a developer. I just like taking a bad building and making it cool. When I was designing apartments, I always figured if no one wanted to live in them, then I would. I think those with bad instincts are the ones who don't see the whole picture or ignore the possibility of something more. Take Augusta, for example. I didn't choose this place. It just happened to be where my business was located. And while there's been lots of cool stuff that's happened, it's all happened organically. I feel like my success in this town is because I'm not the big guy with a ton of money driving everything, and people can get behind that. Those areas you see where it's forced on people [revitalization], you're not inclined to get behind because it becomes bleeding edge, and not cutting edge, and that's a mistake because that's where gentrification starts. I have no desire to be that big guy. I'm pragmatic about my place in the world.[14]

## *A Personal Recommendation on Instincts: Key Takeways*

One of the primary reasons top leaders are able to make tough decisions is because they have learned to trust their intuitive instincts. Bill Gates says, "Often you have to rely on intuition."[15]

Good instincts are not something you're born with, however, but rather something you pick up from personal experience. Learning when and how to act on them can be tricky, particularly in smaller cities, but if you're willing to do the work you will be rewarded in the knowledge that what you've done is right.

The facts are great, and we need them, but sometimes it boils down to what we feel in our guts. Facts are the "math" of decision-making; intuition is the "art."[16]

During my time as Executive Director for the Augusta Downtown Alliance, I have developed a process by which to examine my own instinctual drive when it comes to important decision-making. This includes:

1. Take a step back to look at the bigger picture.
2. Jot down what's working in other similar-sized communities.
3. Examine whether those things could translate well in Augusta.
4. Look into the alternatives.
5. Reflect on the consequences of a decision either way.

6. Gather the data to support a decision.
7. Make a decision and don't ever look back.

None of this is done lightly, and no decision is taken without the "math" to support it.

Over the course of my time, I have battled a lot with people about these decisions. From putting my foot down on certain events to pushing the boundaries of new artwork to promoting the switch to two-way traffic, nothing has ever come easy. Two-way was a particularly hard-fought battle as the community was comfortable with the one-way system they had had in place for over three quarters of a century. As was pointed out in an earlier chapter, however, what might have been comfortable was not working.

I knew going into it that the decision to take a stand on the traffic pattern would be a tough one. The traffic study our organization had pushed for was tonally neutral and reflected the unpopular reality that some parking spaces would be lost. There were also notes that crosswalks would need to be changed, increasing the costs of the project. Still, the hard math of more cars turning onto the street was supported, and that was all that mattered.

For the next nine months, I went to the city council no fewer than a dozen times arguing the need for a change and organizing advocates who agreed to speak on our behalf. The research pored over was intricate, and my nights and weekends became filled with fact-finding.

While the resistance to our stand was stiff, with some threatening to leave the downtown, and certain people in the community threatening a general boycott if a change were to occur, our organization stayed steadfast and dug in on our position. We knew that two-way proved effective in other communities and that it was the right thing to do.

## *Conclusion*

> "I have been and still am a seeker, but I have ceased to question stars and books; I have begun to listen to the teaching my blood whispers to me."—Hermann Hesse

To truly replicate an urban experience in a small city, one needs first to determine what urban elements the small city is missing and then act upon them. This is what defines instincts.

Instincts are a funny thing and can cast a lot of self-doubt, particularly when big decisions need to be made. No one ever said taking a stand is easy, especially in a small city where traditions and relationships run deep, but to progress, such stands are necessary.

Any person in charge of revitalizing a community's city center instinctively knows what to do if they really take a step back and examine the situation at hand. Through experience they know what makes a successful city versus a failing one. The trick is acting on this knowledge and trusting these feelings.

# 5

# It's the Traffic Count, Stupid

Almost everyone is familiar with the adage "it's the economy, stupid." Coined by James Carville in 1992, the phrase has been used in presidential elections as a way to tie the strength of the economy to the person in power. If the incumbent has a strong economy, the wisdom goes, then the incumbent will be reelected. If not, the incumbent will lose. Well, the same can be said for your downtowns and traffic counts. Have high foot and vehicular traffic counts, then the health of your business district will be assured. Have lousy traffic counts, then you will struggle.

Now, there are a number of ways leaders in small communities have tried to accomplish this, but there is really only *one way* that has proved to be effective.

## *No Two Ways About It, One-Ways Are a Bad Idea*

When it comes to revitalizing your small town's city center, there is no quicker path to success than by increasing your traffic flow. While it's true that art adds character, and events bring people, they are all mere Band-Aids for the silver bullet that is traffic. Get your traffic counts (pedestrian as well as vehicular) up, and the people will come, followed in quick succession by residents and businesses. But how do you do this, you might ask? The answer is surprisingly simple: convert your Main Street to two-way traffic.

Two-ways not only increase vehicular traffic counts but also lead to more foot traffic and less vacancy. But don't just take my word for it. Look at the examples that follow. In this chapter we'll have a look at the hard data surrounding one-ways followed by case studies of small cities that successfully made the conversion.

Before we delve into why one-way streets are a bad idea, let's look back into the not-too-distant past to learn why they were implemented

## 5. It's the Traffic Count, Stupid

This logo was developed by Heather Pouliot, Chair of the Augusta Downtown Alliance during the transition of Water Street from one-way to two-way traffic. It was used on all official communications (author's collection).

to begin with. After all, one-ways didn't just happen overnight: they were part of a long restructuring of traffic patterns.

### *The Great Fallacy: A History of One-Ways*

Go into any center city in North America, and you're likely to come across a one-way street. These little bits of geographic annoyance, which have been confusing Americans for well over a century, can all be laid at the feet of one man: William Phelps Eno.

First conceptualized by Eno in 1900 in his paper, "Reform in Our Street Traffic Urgently Needed," the first one-way streets appeared in New York and Boston in 1908 and later in Buenos Aires in 1910.[1] Eno was personally inspired by a traffic jam he had witnessed in Manhattan back in 1887. Reflecting on that traffic jam, Eno later wrote, "There were only about a dozen horses and carriages involved, and all that was needed was a little order to keep the traffic moving. Yet nobody knew exactly what to do; neither the drivers nor the police knew anything about the control of traffic."[2]

While Eno's ideas on traffic were slow to take off, the rising popularity of the automobile brought them back to the forefront by the 1940s. Dubbed by the press as "The Father of Traffic Safety,"[3] Eno's solutions involved such things as the introduction of rotaries, traffic lights and, most notoriously, the conversion of two-way streets into one-ways. In the post-war world, this only made sense.

A frenzied building boom, brought on by generous bank loans and cheap construction, inspired millions of Americans to stake a claim in the suburbs. Such a rush to what was previously countryside drained the cities of millions of dollars in tax revenue, leading to a vicious circumstance where previously well-funded cities were saddled with less money and more infrastructure upkeep. To alleviate this burden city governments readily embraced the radical idea of converting their streets into one-ways.

Not to be outdone, small cities soon began to adapt these principles to their own needs, as well. Egged on by city planners from the Eno Center for Transportation, smaller and smaller cities adopted the mantra as a way to alleviate their own congestion.

Here in Augusta, these changes came earlier than they did to most towns, having been adopted by the city council in 1945. As was stated in the *Kennebec Journal* at the time, then-mayor Sanford Fogg, Jr., announced the plan to convert both Water Street and the parallel Commercial Street to one-way traffic, in opposite directions from each other. He said it had been worked out by then-police Chief Vernard W. Dudley. The goal of the change, according to a May 29, 1945, *Kennebec Journal* report, was to speed up traffic. Fogg was quoted in that day's paper as saying the police chief believed the change in traffic flow "will clear Water Street faster and I think we should give it a trial." Fogg concluded with "we'll see how it goes."[4] Little did he know how well it would work.

## *A One-Way Exodus*

In terms of clearing up traffic congestion, one-ways were a godsend. Previously clogged streets were able to clear traffic in ways previously unimaginable. The unidirectional flows combined with synchronized lights cut down on traffic time and made rush hour for office workers a breeze. Unfortunately, a whole host of new issues emerged that cancelled out these gains.

In the decades to follow, center cities all over the country began to notice a steady shift to the suburbs. The longstanding notion to seek out the greatest speed by which commuter motorists can flee from work only accelerated the downtown deterioration process. The sad results were streets congested with fast-moving automobiles and barren of lively pedestrian, cultural, or commercial activity. As downtown workers continued the flight to the suburbs, providers of goods and services soon followed.[5]

Small businesses, which had been the focal point of downtowns for more than two centuries, were replicated in the suburbs in automobile-friendly strip malls. Soon, even offices relocated to the suburbs, with downtowns all across America serving no other purpose than as pass-throughs for rushing motorists.

By the mid–1980s, the four Ds—deindustrialization, deinstitutionalization, depopulation, and drugs—had given downtowns a dangerous reputation, with even small cities like Augusta suffering from decline.

While it might seem overly simplistic to lay all urban historical woes on a change in traffic flow, it starts to make more sense if you look at it in the form of an allegory. For as with a virus like HIV, death is often not caused by the virus itself, but rather by the underlying complications it awakens. For, just like the HIV virus, one-ways supplanted the established order, in this case the usual traffic pattern, setting off a host of underlying symptoms that were already permeating under the surface (i.e., a rise in suburban growth, a dwindling amount of city capital, the establishment of freeways, etc.). Thus, by increasing the speed by which motorists fled city centers, the virus that was one-way conversions hastened the demise of downtowns by making them more susceptible to the changes already in motion.

## The Science Behind Traffic Patterns

So, other than allowing for a quick exit from downtown, what makes one-way traffic patterns so bad? The answers can be found in the following categories as one-ways lead to:

- A reduction in storefront visibility
- A decrease in foot traffic
- Confusion for new motorists
- An increased chance for collisions
- An increase in crime
- Systemic inequalities

We'll have a closer look at each.

### Reduction in Storefront Visibility

Storefront visibility is an essential prerequisite for "impulse" purchases and stops at smaller stores, even if the motorist plans to return later on foot to shop. Studies show that visibility is optimized when drivers go at speeds of 18–25 mph, but when speeds are in excess of 29 mph, as they are with most vehicles on one-way thoroughfares, visibility is severely decreased.[6] This lack of visibility is exacerbated at intersections as the closer sides of streets are almost completely blocked from view as one approach an intersection.

Two-way streets, by comparison, slow traffic down as lights are no longer synchronized, giving drivers more time to stop and take in their surroundings. Furthermore, two-ways draw the eye to the closer side of the street, increasing storefront visibility by 50 percent. Even critics of two-ways agree on this point: "Specialty stores that rely on impulse sales and depend on high margins per sale do better on two-way streets, since only half their potential customers would see them on a one-way couplet."[7]

### Decreased Foot Traffic

Any Main Street retailer will tell you the importance of foot traffic for business. This all has to do with the kinds of businesses typically found within the district. For rather than location points, which are often automobile-oriented and chosen for their ease of access to the Interstate (think Walmart, hotel chains, or shopping centers), downtowns are destination points. You don't just stumble upon them; you have to want to go to them. Because of this, it's important to grab as much business as you can. Unfortunately, one-ways do nothing to help retailers in this regard, as higher speeds and reduced visibility diminish the chances for a pedestrianized culture to develop. Furthermore, studies have shown that pedestrians also prefer crossing two-way streets, as drivers tend to travel more slowly on them, and vehicular conflicts are more predictable.

### Confusing for New Motorists

One-ways are confusing! Think about it: More than 95 percent of the streets on which you drive every day are two-way thoroughfares. As a result, motorists traveling on one-ways are often easily confused.

Visitors driving in a two-way grid network, however, can easily approach their destination from any direction. A one-way network may prevent drivers from approaching their destinations from the most logical direction as they are forced to loop around parallel streets to get to their intended destinations. This uncertainty can intimidate drivers and, in some cases, make them hesitant to return.

### Increased Chances for Collisions

When it comes to reducing collisions, the case for two-ways vs. one-ways is a little more mixed. While it's true that one-ways have historically been shown to reduce collisions with their unidirectional flow—Baltimore experienced a 10–15 percent reduction upon its conversion to one-ways in 1950[8]—modern research tends to support the opposite point of view. For, contrary to popular belief, one-ways often prove more hazardous to motorists, as speed limits are often ignored. One study from Louisville showed that before the conversion of First Street in Louisville, Kentucky to two-way traffic, First Street stood out as the most dangerous street in terms of traffic collisions. Following its conversion, however, auto collisions decreased there by 60 percent.[9]

## Increased Crime

It might seem like a stretch, but one-way streets have been shown to be linked with increased crime rates. The reasons for this are varied and are likely bound with the other symptoms outlined, including faster speeds, decreased visibility, etc., but the fact of the matter remains that reduced speeds result in more awareness of one's surroundings.

In the same Louisville, Kentucky, study outlined above, the crime rate was shown to have decreased following a downtown street's conversion to two-way traffic. While Louisville experienced a five percent jump in crime during the post-conversion study period (2011 to 2013), as well as the period before conversion (2008 to 2010), a disproportionate amount of crime occurred on multi-lane one-way streets (according to police records). Yet nearly three years after the conversions took place, crime had decreased by jaw-dropping 23 percent on the converted streets. Auto theft alone decreased by almost a third on the converted streets, even as it climbed by 36 percent on the nearby one-way streets. At the same time, there was a 42-percent reduction in robberies on the converted streets.[10]

## Exacerbates Systemic Inequality

By and large, downtown areas are disproportionately poorer and more racially diverse than their suburban counterparts. One-way streets, with increased vehicular speeds, along with their penchant for reduced pedestrian culture, exacerbate inequality for minority communities as they inhibit investment. This lack of investment will make an area less attractive for better, affordable housing as well as for local job offerings, forcing residents within their boundaries to seek out opportunities away from their communities. Two-ways thus help equalize these downtown areas with the suburbs by fostering more of a "neighborhood" feel for those that live there.

## New Albany, Indiana: A Case Study

New Albany (pop. 37,000) is typical of many Midwestern boom towns. Built along the northern banks of the Ohio River in 1813, the city flourished during the heyday of the steamship industry, ultimately becoming an industrial powerhouse. At its peak, the city was the largest and wealthiest in the state, with many of the richest residents building elaborate mansions along Main Street. However, deindustrialization, followed by two natural disasters, crippled the city's growth in the twentieth century, relegating it to a mere suburb of the much larger Louisville, Kentucky, located to its south. By the end of the twentieth century, its central commercial district was a mere shadow of its former self, with almost a century between the present and its glory days.

In contemplating this loss of stature, New Albany Mayor Jeff Gahan focused particular attention on the impact that one-way conversions played on Spring Street. "There's no question that New Albany is a jewel," he said. "But I always thought that Spring Street was, sort of, off. And I didn't know what it was."[11]

This feeling of "offness" was reflected in the odd changes as one neared the interstate:

> As the road approached downtown at the Vincennes Street intersection, the design of Spring Street changed. It became a one-way street heading west, with eastbound traffic moved a block south to Market Street—a common practice referred to as one-way pairing. Once in downtown, parking lanes were removed and driving lanes expanded. Finally, on the west side of downtown, the houses, businesses, sidewalks and street trees that make up the urban fabric disappeared, as the roadway prepped drivers to enter I-64.[12]

Then, in 2014, the city decided to do something about it. "The backdrop was the toll," Gahan said, looking back. "We knew we had too much capacity on our roads, and with all of this excess capacity, we were going to turn our downtown into a drag strip. People were going to cut across Clarksville and blow through New Albany to get on the no-toll bridge. We knew that we needed to make a change."[13]

After reviewing studies on two-way conversions, Gahan and other city leaders hired Jeff Speck, a leading two-way proponent and engineer, who had done similar work for other Midwestern cities. As Speck stated: "I was hired by New Albany to redesign their downtown street network in the face of a very real threat: the new tolling regime planned for crossing the Ohio River into Louisville was going to cause a lot of cut-through traffic to inundate New Albany, the site of the one free bridge," he explained. "They understood that their one-ways attracted speeding, and also had a sense that their considerable excess capacity—which I demonstrated to them—was quickly going to fill up with new car trips if they did not constrain them to hold roughly the current volume."[14] What resulted was the largest switch to a downtown road network anywhere in the country.

Completed in 2017 at a cost of $1.475 million, aided with $2.8 million in federal funds,[15] the switch not only converted the flow of traffic but also incorporated street repaving, new signs, signal modifications, crosswalks, landscaping, markings, and other improvements to the downtown area.

In the summer of 2019, Police Chief William Todd Bailey reported, in an open letter to the public, that New Albany's gamble paid off. In the letter he cites:

- Accidents involving pedestrians were down.
- Speeding was reduced.
- Motor vehicle crashes were down, especially injury crashes, compared to previous years.

"It has been our observation that the new designs allow for motor vehicles, bicycles, and pedestrians to all interact in a much smoother manner," Bailey says. "Additionally, due to the new design, when we experience a problem, we are provided with more options to redirect traffic. The design has also facilitated a better response from police and fire as those options have multiplied."[16]

What New Albany accomplished in such a short amount of time was nothing short of impressive. While the much larger city of Louisville dithered on large-scale conversions, preferring instead not to interrupt the flow of interstate traffic, New Albany chose to buck the trend and limit the effects of thruway traffic into their city center. The result was a revitalized commercial corridor with more attractive streetscapes, a thriving pedestrian culture and safer speeds.

## DAVENPORT, IOWA: AN EXPERIMENT IN TWO-WAY

Back in 2015, the merchants of Davenport, Iowa (pop. 100,000) were understandably anxious when plans were announced that Harrison Street was closing for repair work. Coming off a particularly bad summer for retail sales, the announcement of a four-month sanitation project was the last thing any of the merchants wanted to hear.

"Shut up," said Andrew Spyrow, a downtown Davenport resident, upon learning how long all four southbound lanes of Harrison Street would remain closed. "It's going to be a nightmare."[17]

The angst naturally spread to retailers, as people publicly announced their intent to avoid the area at all costs.

To help accommodate the new traffic flow, city officials opened up neighboring Brady Street to two-way traffic, something that hadn't been done for 42 years. Naturally, there was trepidation as residents nervously speculated about how many collisions would occur due to the confusion and how many residents would end up in the morgue by stepping out and looking only one way instead of two. Speeding was already a major issue down the one-way thoroughfare, as traffic sped quickly up the hill towards the light.

But things quickly changed as apprehension gave way to optimism over the course of the next two weeks, particularly for business owners who began noticing an immediate uptick in sales. "I am not mad about it. I am not mad at all," said Kelvin Anderson, an employee at Flamin' Hot JJ's Fish and Chicken. "I like it, because it's helping us pick up our business. We're catching all the traffic coming from Illinois coming up this way, and all the traffic going to Illinois the other way, so it works out pretty good," he said.[18]

Another retailer also reported on positive effects. "If you haven't gone down Brady Street yet, please go down Brady Street hill. It's wonderful. It's the way it's supposed to be," said Kelly Wallace, owner of The Estate Sale Shop. Wallace said her business decreased significantly during the first weekend as drivers avoided the area, but she supports the switch to two-way and says it's bringing new faces into the shop.

"They'd been driving by, wanting to come in, and that two-way on Brady allowed them to turn right on 14th Street, down Brady Street into our place. So that worked for us, we're very happy about that," said Wallace.[19]

Many like Anderson and Wallace began to wonder whether the switch could even be made permanent.

While the positive effects of two-way proved a surprise to residents and merchants alike, they were hardly a surprise to people like Jeff Speck, who, in 2008, drafted a comprehensive plan for downtown revitalization with just such a conversion topping his list. Turns out, he was right once again.

## *Augusta, Maine: A Reflection*

As a river city, Augusta, Maine (population 19,000) suffered from many of the same ills as New Albany and Davenport. Founded in 1754, the city thrived on industry. At one point, the city housed 32 mills, employing almost a quarter of the population. Deindustrialization and haphazard urban planning helped stymie growth, however, particularly

## 5. It's the Traffic Count, Stupid

Seniors from Cony High School's class of 2020 drive southbound down Water Street a year after the thoroughfare transitioned to two-way traffic. The transition represented a fundamental shift for Augusta after 75 years of one-way flow (courtesy Dave Dostie).

along its commercial district on Water Street. When the central section of that street—the very heart of the retail district—converted to one-way traffic in 1945, the first nail in the coffin was hammered in. What followed was a half century of decline.

### A Broken System

By the time I took over as Executive Director for the Augusta Downtown Alliance in 2016, the damage done by one-ways was more than apparent. The downtown vacancy rate stood at a whopping 45 percent, and the one-way traffic system had created an almost hostage-like situation in which office workers crowded businesses during the mornings and afternoon but left the street a virtual ghost town past 5 p.m. While I did my best to attract new business into the area, I kept bumping into the same situation over and over again: our traffic patterns were just too low to warrant investment. Then, in 2017, everything changed. The city agreed to fund a traffic study and look into conversion.

Hiring Maine Traffic Resources, the consultants studied traffic patterns for a period of two weeks. What they discovered was a huge discrepancy in the form of traffic flow: "The Water Street and Commercial Street one-way system carries significantly less traffic than either the State Street or Bangor Street/Riverside north-south routes. This is likely due to the fact that motorists not destined towards the downtown or to the Calumet Bridge avoid the area given the downtown nature."[20]

In addition, they discovered major discrepancies in traffic flow between the parts of Water Street that were two-way versus the single section that was one-way. Their general consensus found that converting the 800-ft. stretch of Water Street back to two-way would not only be feasible, but also beneficial in the long term (despite a loss of 12 parking spots). The Alliance thus threw its full weight behind the measure over the course of 2018 and lobbied the city to get behind the move.

While a good number of merchants, developers and residents supported conversion, the general community did not. Concerns about a loss in parking, as well as pedestrian safety, collisions, and winter maintenance, were paramount, dominating online forums for months. Despite a large educational campaign on the issue which hoped to debunk these concerns by showing results from other communities, the mantra remained: "Well, two-way may work there, but this is Augusta." As it turned out, however, Augusta wasn't so special.

## Positive Results

In the year between the city's vote to convert and its final implementation in 2019, downtown Augusta saw no fewer than four major developers announce new projects for the street. In addition, three new businesses opened up. This continued to increase following conversion, with three more major developments announced, followed by an additional three businesses opening, bringing the vacancy rate in 2020 below 25 percent for the first time in over a decade. While no traffic study has been conducted since conversion, merchants have commented that the streets and the sidewalks appear fuller since the switch has been made.

As for the doom-and-gloom prophesiers who foresaw collisions and pedestrian calamities, no accidents were reported in the first six months of conversion, and winter maintenance actually became more efficient with snow plowing and removal being conducted in the same shift. Even the initial loss of parking spaces (a big concern for several business owners) was mitigated following the reconstruction of neighboring Commercial Street. Above all, however, traffic increased, and slower speeds prevailed.

"The whole idea of this new traffic pattern was to have more people in the downtown traveling at slower speeds," Police Chief Jared Mills said. "I believe the intended consequences are coming to fruition."[21] Local business owner Tobias Parkhurst, a partner in Cushnoc Brewery, went on to state in the months following conversion that he was glad it happened: "I'm a believer and glad we did it, and (I'm) proud of the way the city and the downtown community handled it," he said. "It was a controversial thing, but it never got nasty. And it's working now, and we look good." Parkhurst went onto state that every month in 2019 Cushnoc saw more business than it did during the same month in 2018.[22]

## Other Ways to Increase Traffic

While two-way conversions are often the quickest way to foster an increase in foot and vehicular traffic, they are by no means the only way. In some circumstances, a street might not even lend itself to a two-way conversion, particularly if it is narrow or houses emergency operating services like fire stations, which rely on ease of speed. If this is the case, small cities can turn to one of three alternative modes: rotaries, pedestrian malls, and bump outs.

### Roundabouts

Roundabouts, or "rotaries" for all you New England readers, are circular intersections that allow for counterclockwise traffic flow around a center island. Their design is relatively simple: Vehicles entering rotaries yield to already circling traffic.

While less common in smaller cities, roundabouts can provide lasting benefits and value in many ways. They are an excellent choice to complement transportation objectives—including Complete Streets, multimodal networks, and corridor access management—without compromising the ability to keep people and freight. Furthermore, the FHWA Office of Safety identified roundabouts as a "Proven Safety Countermeasure" because of their ability to substantially reduce the types of crashes that result in injury or loss of life.

While roundabouts provide a way to reduce traffic speeds to the optimum 15–25 mph range, their sheer size often makes them impractical for the central portions of downtowns. Like Augusta, which has two on its entry points into the downtown, they do little to decrease speed once navigation is completed.

PEDESTRIAN MALLS

I could write a whole book on why pedestrian malls are a terrible idea (more on this in Chapter 10). They take away parking, block access to delivery trucks, reduce storefront exposure, etc. The list goes on.

First emerging as a trend in the 1960s, pedestrian malls were seen as a way to compete with suburban shopping centers by closing off streets to vehicles. At their height, there were over 200 of them. Unfortunately, like one-ways, pedestrian malls had unforeseen circumstances, which led to high vacancies, empty streets, and vagrancy. Today, less than 15 percent of them remain.

Still, there are certain circumstances where they can work. Examples of thriving pedestrian malls can be found in Burlington, Vermont (pop. 43,000), St. Augustine, Florida (pop. 15,000), as well as Charlottesville, Virginia (pop. 48,000). These communities, however, fit very specific criteria, and any attempt at implementing them should be taken with extreme caution.

BUMP OUTS

Bump outs are the most cost-effective way to achieve most of the benefits of two-way traffic. Essentially a curb extension that brings sidewalks out onto the streets, bump outs can help reduce speed while fostering a pedestrian culture. Cities like Grand Forks, North Dakota (pop. 53,000) experienced great success with temporary bump outs generating increases in foot traffic.

Unfortunately, bump outs also have their drawbacks. They can be hindrances for winter maintenance operations and can negatively affect the ability of such vehicles as buses and fire trucks to make turns. If going this route on your one-way street, it's best to copy the model from Grand Forks and try them on a temporary basis.

## *Keith Luke and the Benefits of Two-Way Traffic*

Keith Luke has been involved in municipal economic development for over 20 years. Beginning his career in Topsham, Maine, he played a leading role in the redevelopment of the historic Pejepscot paper mill, which led to the establishment of a brewery and mixed-use office space. From there, he went on to Windham and Westbrook, before eventually taking up his current position in Augusta in 2013.

"Out of all the places I've worked, I've been in Augusta the longest," Keith said. "I feel like I'm really vested in this community and I'll say that

## 5. It's the Traffic Count, Stupid

**Keith Luke was an early proponent of two-way traffic in the City of Augusta and helped play a role in its transition (courtesy Keith Luke).**

of all the places I've worked, it's Augusta that makes more and better use of financial programs than any other community in the state, particularly with regards to TIFS [tax increment financing]. It's also one of the most welcoming places I've ever lived in. It's friendly, open minded, and compared to other small towns shows no opposition to New Mainers [immigrants]."

As both a municipal employee, and a downtown resident, Keith had a unique vantage point when it came to the two-way traffic conversion: "We always had a lot of internal support for it," he said. "But there was a lot of apprehension internally about its implementation. It was seen as a controversial decision and required local business people to get behind it in order to make it happen. When it finally did, things changed really fast. It was like putting Augusta from 1st to 3rd gear."

Though the change has only been implemented for a year, Keith already stresses the positives. "We went in this thinking about long-term dividends, but it's the short term dividends that have really been paid off. We now have the lowest vacancy in 30 years, and you have to go back to the '70s or early '80s to find the level of activity that exists here now."

While reminiscing about the process to get it passed, he cites the importance played by unexpected speakers, like Casey Hynes, a co-owner of Cushnoc Brewing Co., who used humor to come out in support for the change. "When it comes to persuading the city council to make a major decision like two-way, you have to have a champion who doesn't work for the city either in a full-time or adjunct role. Instead you need grassroots speakers. The council instead loves to hear from someone unexpected. In addition, you want to do your research and be prepared," he said.

"In my research, I spoke to a half dozen communities who had gone through the switch to two-way and out of all of those whom I had spoken to, none of them even remembered the process because it had become so thoroughly accepted. That's not to say there wasn't any. There most certainly was, but like most things that works, it becomes second nature after the fact."

When facing initial opposition to the switch, Keith said he wasn't surprised. "Augusta's opposition to this change was pretty textbook for small towns," he said. "Yea, there were comments in the paper and online, but they never spilled over to the council level. I think that's the most important thing—and a lesson that councilors should remember: 'don't live in fear of online critics because they never manifest at meetings.'"

He recounts: "When I was in Westbrook, there was a controversial decision we had to make about closing the library. Two to three hundred people loudly complained online against the closure, and we prepped our meeting for the hordes of people. Altogether less than 10 showed up—none of the complainers by the way."

In the end, Keith is thrilled with the results of the change: "I think even in spite of the pandemic, the switch has been a success. I can't see us thriving this much without it. Augusta did the right thing."[23]

## Key Takeaways About Traffic

1. The health of your business district is paramount to revitalization efforts.
2. A successful business district needs both foot and vehicular traffic.
3. One-ways inhibit growth in both areas.
4. Two-ways increase traffic volume, while fostering pedestrian culture.
5. Small towns can serve as models for other communities.

## Conclusion

> "Dictatorships are one-way streets. Democracy boasts two-way traffic"—Alberto Moravia

There is simply no getting around the benefits that two-way traffic conversions can bring to your small-town revitalization efforts. From reduced speeds to decreases in vacancy to increased storefront visibility, the overwhelming success of two-way traffic speaks for itself.

Cities large and small that have made the conversion from one-way to two-way traffic have all witnessed the benefits of such conversion. All have reported an increase in property values, and all have reported an increase in outside development. By returning to the natural order of traffic, these cities have essentially turned back the clock and set themselves on the path to success, ensuring a rise in both vehicular motorists and pedestrians.

Here in Augusta, conversion of our one-way street back to two-way was no easy task, but it's proving well worth the effort. Conversion has not only achieved the desired result evident in the studies of communities of similar size, but also has garnered statewide attention for its innovative efforts. As the first city in the state to make the switch, Augusta's success in this endeavor exemplifies the ways small towns could play a leading role in revitalization.

# 6

# Marketing Your Small City ... the Right Way

In the first chapter, we identified the importance of developing distinction through identity as a first step to placemaking. But how do you leverage placemaking for growth? It's simple: through branding and marketing.

When most of us think of marketing, we think of a product—one that could be bought and sold and is commodified based upon a unique and special quality. These qualities are espoused in such a manner as to make you think a specific product is so wonderful that no other product of a similar nature can compete. Think about some of the everyday products we use and the qualities espoused: "It isn't clean unless it's *Clorox* clean" or "The absorbent quicker picker upper—Bounty" or, lastly, Energizer batteries—"They keep going and going and going...."

On the surface, these common items are little different than other cleaning solutions, paper towels and batteries, but clever marketers have capitalized on an "otherness" to set them apart. This otherness is highlighted and celebrated

Logos are an important aspect for messaging. The logo of the Augusta Downtown Alliance utilizes the colors from the first three buildings painted downtown, while incorporating different fonts to make it lively and recognizable (author's collection).

in commercial ads and ingrained in the heads of its audience through images, songs and colors.

Like everyday items in stores, your city is a product that can be sold to the public based upon the notion of otherness. Think about some of the common taglines, you're no doubt familiar with from two larger communities: "The City that Never Sleeps" and "What Happens in Vegas Stays in Vegas." Both evoke a sense of uniqueness, as you'll likely have experiences you wouldn't otherwise have anywhere else.

Small cities can do this too.

In this chapter we'll explore how small cities can effectively brand themselves and market themselves to the public—*the right way.*

## The Psychology of Branding and Marketing

According to the Applied Psychology Department at the University of Southern California, there are five core dimensions that go into a successful branding and marketing campaign. These dimensions play a role in the personality of your brand and include sincerity, excitement, competence, sophistication, and ruggedness.[1] Let's break some of these down:

- Sincerity—is the act of being genuine or true to oneself.
- Excitement—is the act of being spirited and daring.
- Competence—is the act of being responsible and dependable.
- Sophistication—is the act of being glamorous and charming.
- Ruggedness—is the act of being tough and strong.

These core dimensions form the heart and soul of one's brand identity, allowing for a narrowing of factors that play into the personality. For example, take a look at Ford's iconic campaign "Built Ford Tough." Their branding clearly settled on the dimension of "ruggedness" to show off the power of their best-selling F-150. To do this, they show images of their truck in atypical driving situations such as dirt roads, water-laden fields and rocky mountainscapes so that consumers can see just how versatile the vehicle is in all sorts of environments.

Similarly, think of the now-memorable Grey Poupon mustard ad from the 1990s. Their core dimension was focused on sophistication, and they attempted to market it that way by showing two limos approaching one another to exchange mustard. In this way, they could let consumers know that their product was more than just ordinary mustard and carried an air of refinement.

Such dimensions are just the beginning of forming a brand identity, however, as proper coloring, crafted language, a sense of belonging, and experience shaping help mold brand personality. Coloring for example gives a visual context to a particular feeling or mood, while a sense of belonging evokes an "us" vs. "them" mentality. Crafted language is used to add descriptors that can promote the right sensations within a person, while experience shaping is managed by creating an environment in the physical realm which supports brand identity.

When considering the elements above, take a look at two popular brands, Apple and Starbucks, and how both utilize each concept. With Apple, for example, you can see that their logo is black and white, featuring a silhouette of an apple with a bite out of it. The colors evoke a sense of modernity and timelessness, while their "think different" tagline, crafts an "us vs. them" mentality to show that users of Apple products are special. They then drive their brand home by creating a physical environment of sterile white walls and floors, with extreme minimalism to better show off their products and bring them to the forefront. Their staff members are labeled as "geniuses" to evoke a sense of superiority in the consumer's minds, while at the same time building staff loyalty and retention.

Now take Starbucks. Their logo features the colors green and white, which speak to their commitment to fair trade and environmentally friendly practices. The image of a double tailed mermaid in the middle also evokes sensations by drawing a connection between the image and the founders' hometown of Seattle. As Starbucks recounts on their website:

> In case you're wondering, there are two big connections between Starbucks and the seafaring world. (1) Our hometown of Seattle is a port city. We're right on Puget Sound and we feel this very strong connection to the water. (2) Coffee often travels long distances across the water to get to us. Even today, it arrives at the port in big container ships.[2]

To drive their brand home, the interior of Starbucks shops creates an atmosphere that is completely coffee centric. Rich hues of browns often fill their cafes and can be seen on walls, furniture and countertops. The words "Fair Trade" are often stamped across their products and their work staff are referred to as "partners" or "baristas" to bestow a sense of importance to their employees. In addition, their customer loyalty rewards program allows frequent users to feel a sense of achievement and belonging by reaching a "superior" status.

The success of both these brands in crafting marketing strategies, which speak to the whims of their consumers, have paid off in big ways, particularly with regards to consumer loyalty. Both have earned the #1 spot in their categories according to the most recent customer loyalty engagement index.³

## The Right Way to Get Started in Branding Your Community

Branding a small city is a lot like branding a business. To do it right, you need to follow the same core dimensions and concepts outlined above. This is what sets off successful small cities like Hershey, Pennsylvania (pop. 14,000), which has tied itself to the chocolate produced there by its namesake company, from unsuccessful cities like Flint, Michigan (pop. 96,000), which is known more for its wide array of problems with poverty and water treatment issues than anything else.

In one of his sessions on marketing a community, Roger Brooks of Destination Development International mentioned "activity" as being the chief driving force behind a person's desire to go somewhere, with "location" being the second. He asks specifically whether a person has ever gone somewhere simply because it was the gateway to somewhere else or offered something for everyone. As he states, "97% of community-based marketing is ineffective. The reason is that we filter out everything that isn't directly relevant to us."⁴

To drive home the message about narrowing your tourism marketing to a niche, Brooks presents 10 things to know about branding your small town. I have included the full list below with summarized notes from Small Biz Survival founder Becky McCrary:

**1. Don't get hung up on logos and slogans.**
They are not brands. They are just marketing messages that support your brand. Logos and slogans are 2 percent of marketing, but 98 percent of local attention goes to them, Brooks said. You don't choose Ford over Chevy because of their logo or slogan.

**2. A brand is a perception.**
A brand is what people think of you, not what you say you are, Brooks said. We create them through visual cues, people and attitudes, word of mouth, publicity, and social media. Negative perceptions can require a repositioning or rebranding effort. Good brands evoke emotion. They make a statement. They **sell** a feeling, not a place or a product. Brands are all WHY, not WHAT or WHERE.

**3. Successful brands have a narrow focus.**
If I can take out your town's name and plug in any other town,

it fails, Brooks said. You're not doing anything wrong; you're just saying the same thing everyone else is saying. You must jettison the generic. You cannot be all things to all people. Promote your primary lure. Memberships kill attempts to specialize tourism marketing.

Here are some of those "everyone uses them" words and phrases to delete from your marketing:

- explore
- discover
- outdoor recreation
- so much to do
- four-season destination
- historic downtown
- center of it all
- best kept secret
- close to it all
- playground

I'm sure you can think of many more.

Don't just market what you have, market what will close the sale, Brooks said.

**4. Narrow focus so much that your name becomes synonymous with your brand.**

Brooks listed off destinations that have succeeded at this: Napa Valley for wine, Las Vegas for adult fun.

**5. Brands are built on product, not just marketing.**

People are looking for things to do, not just things to look at, Brooks said. That's why it's so hard to market your history in tourism. You have to find ways to make people involved in the experience of that history. Brands are always experiential. Tourism organizations sell cities, towns and counties before experiences. Economic development groups sell infrastructure and land before opportunities. These are mistakes according to Brooks. Avoid hiring any branding company that does not talk about product, he said.

**6. Never, ever use focus groups.**

They are never the way to build a brand, Brooks said. Cute and/or clever seldom work in tourism marketing. Never do branding by public consent. Period. When lots of people get involved, that carefully crafted narrow niche gets spread out into making everyone happy. Build your brand by feasibility, not local sentiment. Top-down branding efforts fail 98 percent of the time, Brooks said.

**7. You never "roll out" your brand until you can "deliver on the promise."**

If you market your community for a niche you really don't deliver on, you are setting up for upset visitors, Brooks said. Brands are earned, good or bad. Communities have used transitional brands to talk about what they are becoming.

**8. Great brands always start with a plan.**

Brooks outlined a simple plan:

- What do you want to be known for?
- What do you need to own the brand?
- How will you tell the world?
- What goes on the to do list?

**9. Build your brand by feasibility, not local sentiment.**

Brooks said to start with an assessment. Where you are today? Then, ask the locals, where do you want to go as a community? When someone mentions your community in 10 years, what do you want them to mention? Next, do the research. Which of all the ideas make the most sense? Answer these key questions about feasibility:

- Is this something the markets we are hoping to attract can't get or do closer to home?
- Can the community buy into it over time?
- Can the private sector invest in it?
- How much will it cost, and when will we see return?
- Does it have legs? Can we start with a niche, then add extensions to the brand?
- Can we make it obvious and pervasive throughout the city?
- Will it extend our seasons?
- Do we have tireless champions for this cause?
- Is it experiential? Things to do, not things to look at.

Only when the concept is proved feasible does Brooks recommend developing an action plan. The strategies, goals and objectives should fill no more than 10 pages. An action plan is a to do list. Each item on the plan should include:

- the recommendation—what is to be done
- who's in charge
- what it will cost
- the source of funds

- when it must be completed
- the rationale—give the reason

10. **Don't let local politics kill your branding efforts.**
    Brooks listed three killers of branding efforts:
    - local politics, especially "membership" politics that try to please everyone
    - lack of champions
    - lack of money[5]

## What's in a Slogan

As was highlighted in Brooks's notes above, a lot of small cities make the mistake of focusing too much on slogans and not enough on branding. As he states, slogans are not the brands themselves, but rather phrases that support the brand established. He goes on to state that

> whatever it is that makes you different or clearly better, you must hang your hat on that. But it isn't enough for you claim that you're different or clearly better. That difference has to come by third party endorsement. Other people have to say it, too.
>
> Most communities are stuck in the "group hug mentality." They try to make everyone happy with their tourism marketing. The "membership mentality" of "we don't want to leave out any of our members" leads to generic "something for everyone" market that is ineffective.[6]

While I tend to agree with Brooks' assessment about "branding" trumping "slogans," particularly when developing a marketing strategy,

To celebrate the changes happening downtown, including that of two-way traffic, the Augusta Downtown Alliance designed limited edition t-shirts to sell to the public. The t-shirts incorporated slogans like "Don't Dis 'Gusta" and "Water Street Goes Both Ways" and proved popular among residents (author's collection).

I strongly disagree with his assertion that slogans do little to drive home a marketing message. As was seen earlier, taglines or slogans like "Built Ford Tough" or "Think Different" evoke a whole range of emotions and fit in with one of the four key sub-concepts of branding since they relate to word craft. Still, you can't have a proper slogan without first forming an identity and then working on the brand of that identity. To hammer this point home, I'm including a list of city slogans and taglines, as compiled by Brad Van Auken of the Blake Project. Van Auken evaluates the good, the bad and the downright terrible and terribly confusing slogans with which some cities have attempted to market themselves:

**Effective (they allude to a unique quality or benefit):**

- Las Vegas: "What Happens in Vegas, Stays in Vegas"
- New York, New York: "The City That Never Sleeps"
- Hershey, Pennsylvania: "The Sweetest Place on Earth"
- Austin, Texas: "Keep Austin Weird"
- Eagle Pass, Texas: "Where Yee-Hah! meets Ole!"
- Cleveland, Ohio: "Cleveland Rocks!"
- Santa Fe, New Mexico: "The City Different"
- Jim Thorpe, Pennsylvania: "The Switzerland of America"
- Coachella, California: "City of Eternal Sunshine"
- Nashville, Tennessee: "The Music City"
- Bellevue, Washington: "City in a Park"
- Rockland, Maine: "Lobster Capital of the World"

**Believable?**

- Freeland, Pennsylvania: "The Most Happening Place on Earth"
- Madisonville, Kentucky: "The Best Town on Earth"
- Glendive, Montana: "Where the Best Begins"

**What does this mean (inane or vacuous)?**

- Dunedin (NZ), "It's All Right Here"
- Rochester, New York: "I'd Rather Be in Rochester—It's Got It"
- Cambridge, Ohio: "Together for a Better Tomorrow"
- Ashburton, NZ: "Whatever it Takes"
- Rockville, Maryland: "Get into it"
- Richmond, Michigan: "With Time for You"
- Hico, Texas: "Where Everybody Is Somebody"
- Eustis, Florida: "The city of Bright Tomorrows"
- Marshall, Minnesota: "A Better Way to Live!"
- Auburn, Washington: "More Than You Imagined"

**So what?**
- Beaman, Iowa: "You're Not Dreamin', You're in Beaman"

**Boring:**
- "Visit Jakarta" (Indonesia)
- "Your Partner, Gwangju" (South Korea)
- "It's Daejeon" (South Korea)
- "Aha! Suncheon" (South Korea)

**Does this make me want to live or visit there?**
- Forestville, California: "Poison Oak Capital of the World"
- Washta, Iowa: "The Coldest Spot in Iowa"
- Allentown, Pennsylvania: "Truck Capital of the World"
- Baxter Springs, Kansas: "First Cowtown in Kansas"
- Beaver, Oklahoma: "Cow Chip Capital of the World"
- Cheshire, Connecticut: "Bedding Plant Capital of Connecticut"

**Maybe (for the right target audience):**
- Gilroy, California: "Garlic Capital of the World"
- Bertram, Texas: "Home of the Oatmeal Festival"
- Breaux Bridge, Louisiana: "Crayfish Capital of the World"
- Knik, Alaska: "Dog-Mushing Center of the World"[7]

As you can see, the most effective taglines or slogans are those that are unique and evoke a sense of "otherness" from other communities. They are effective because they embrace one or more of the five core dimensions of branding. For example, the "Keep Austin Weird" slogan of Austin, Texas, is sincere and true to the artsy-craftsy vibe they are trying to put out. Similarly, Jim Thorpe, Pennsylvania, being marketed as "The Switzerland of America" evokes the rugged nature and sophistication of the mountain city, giving it an aura of natural mystique.

It's only when, as Brooks states, cities try to be everything to everybody that slogans can fall short. Take the slogan from Rockville, Maryland: "Get Into It." What is "it" and what are you getting into? Trouble? A good time? It's impossible to know because there's no real meaning behind it. What about the slogan for Marshall, Minnesota: "A Better Way to Live." How exactly is it a better way to live? There's no way to tell.

## *Augusta: A Capital Reflection*

Greeting every visitor from every access point into Augusta is a bright blue wooden sign. This sign is your first welcome into the city and your first real chance to get to know about it as an outsider.

Bold, patriotic colors, concise messaging, and a whimsical font help define Augusta's brand as a state capital (author's collection).

Unlike traditional city signs in small towns, this particular sign does not have a "welcome to" preceding the town's name. Rather, the sign just announces the name of the city followed by a tagline.

The word "Augusta!" splatters across a red cursive font with three blue wavy lines underneath. The tagline reads "A Capital Opportunity" and is encapsulated by a white circle.

Adopted by city leaders last decade, the imagery consists of "Augusta" scrolled in whimsical font with an exclamation point at the end which denotes a sense of excitement about the place, thereby fulfilling one of the five core dimensions of proper branding. The three colors red, white and blue are familiar and seem to be used to denote the important status of the city as an American state capital, while the wavy blue lines underneath seem to salute the importance that the Kennebec River has played here. The "A Capital Opportunity" tagline is ambivalent enough to evoke a business-friendly environment, among other things, with "capital" having a triple meaning. In this regard, the meaning of capital is open to interpretation, playing upon the word in both its noun and verb forms for either something exciting "you can have a capital time," something money making "you can make capital here" or something explanatory "we're the state capital." All in all, it does a fine job in narrowing down an identity for the community.

## *Authentically Fake: How the Small Town of Sisters Marketed Itself into Relevancy*

We often think of branding as something formed in a committee or through careful reflection on an area's existing assets. Rarely, however, do we think of it as something that can be invented or faked.

"Fake it till you make it" is a common expression which suggests that by imitating confidence, competence, and an optimistic mindset a person can realize those qualities in real life.[8] Used by people seeking career advancement, it has subsequently been adapted for numerous other things including public relations campaigns and real estate developers. This was the philosophy espoused by Bill Smith of Brooks Resources when he happened upon the small city of Sisters, Oregon (pop. 2,500).

Located midway between Bend and Portland, Sisters was always the community time had passed over. Surrounded by lush green forests with rugged, snow-capped mountains towering overhead, the community had all of the charm, but none of the luck, of its larger counterparts, largely fulfilling the role of a gas stopover. When Bill Smith came there in the 1970s, it was a town of fewer than 700 with a history of livestock that was on the verge of being lost after a planned luxury resort, Black Butte Ranch, was announced 10 miles outside of town. As was recounted by developers:

> Quiet living in nature was the concept of the ranch, a very different concept from that of many destination resorts that were beginning to change rural landscapes. There would be no retail complex at Black Butte, as it was not intended to be commercial. That presented a challenge. Black Butte residents and guests would want and need a place to shop.[9]

Smith, who was the Marketing Manager for Brooks Resources, saw a solution in the town of Sisters. Unfortunately, the town was rather homely. As Smith recalls:

"It was in the middle of nowhere with not much happening. We thought about that for a minute and decided it's not our business buying towns," Smith said. "But we were looking to keep Sisters from becoming a strip mall."

In studying the city, Smith saw that the rodeo was the only event which garnered any real excitement—a weekend of raucous, brawling fun that brought income to Sisters' businesses that might otherwise not have survived the rest of the year:

Brooks Resources President Harrison thus envisioned an alternative plan. Brooks would offer a $5,000 grant to build false storefronts of Western theme to any existing business in Sisters or to new construction that honored the theme. This would give Sisters a unique image and enhance its attraction. If a business owner kept the Western theme frontage for 10 years, the loan would be forgiven.

The first restaurant to take him up on the offer was Ruth's Café, now The Gallery Restaurant and Bar. This was followed by Sisters Veterinary Clinic, Sisters Drug Store, and later Leithauser Grocery. The Leithhausers were especially enthusiastic about this offer as they were very involved with the rodeo.

When Bill Reed, Jr., built his General Land Office (which later became Reed Bros. Realty), he and his father, Bill Sr., opted to do a Western theme. Brooks Resources, which was not financially involved in that project, saw this was a good indicator that their idea was bearing fruit.

Yet another important objective of Brooks Resources was the restoration of Hotel Sisters, even though it was not part of the Brooks investment portfolio. The septic system was failing. The building was in need of a considerable amount of repair, after years of minimal maintenance. "Remodel usually involves plywood and sheet rock," Smith said, "a process that was not appealing to a remodel of a building of this stature."[10]

Again, Brooks Resources stepped in and gave financial assistance to the varied group of the building's owners to assure that the integrity of the historic pearl of Sisters was not compromised. The restored building was later purchased by Bill and Jan Reed, to reopen as a restaurant in 1985.

As more buildings became remodeled and visitors to the city increased, eyesores such as gas stations, motor lodges and other crumbling infrastructure gave way to side streets filled with shopping and dining.

In addition, the city experienced a 143 percent increase in population.

According to Patrick Davenport, the city's development director, Sisters added 100 new residential units and $75 million worth of new construction in 2017, alone. "In some ways, we've been a victim of our own success," he said.[11]

Like other tourist cities, building in the community has become pricey as demand to live there as skyrocketed. "We can't compete with Bend or Redmond; we can't be everything to everybody," Davenport said. "You build in Sisters because your heart is telling you to. And those folks become future strong community members."[12]

This sentiment was shared by Cris Converse, a longtime resident who recalls watching all the changes from the beginning on her mom's ranch: "Our western facades, they came from somewhere," she said. "It's still a local small town, a place where people volunteer at the school, a commitment and participation that keeps that character."[13]

Today, her mom's property has been divided a bit. Some of the land became a new neighborhood with views of fields and the family's 100-year-old dairy barn off in the distance. Converse said the barn could be converted into an artist space.

> There's truth to the identity the town now relies on. And it's what's separated Sisters from the stories of towns either working to keep their people or fighting to maintain independence from their neighbor's shadow.[14]

## *The Case of Biddeford + Saco: A Branding Nightmare*

While both Augusta and Sisters represent examples of how two small cities were able to get it right with regards to their branding and marketing, the same can't be said for the twin cities of Biddeford (pop. 21,000) and Saco (pop. 18,000), which undertook a disastrous attempt to rebrand their image back in 2012. Although I hesitate to highlight the same city twice, the misfire in this effort was so great that it is well worth a mention.

Situated in southeastern Maine abutting Saco Bay on the Gulf of Maine, Biddeford and Saco remain separated by the narrow Saco River. As cities with extensive industrial pasts, both have largely become bedroom communities for the ever-growing population of Portland and now serve as a gateway of sorts to the popular boardwalk resort of Old Orchard Beach. As with most twinned cities, the rivalry between these two towns was more good-natured than threatening, and the two have cooperated on festivals and other ventures in the past. So it was that the two decided to partner in a joint attempt to breathe new identity into their region.

Approaching the firm of Arnett Muldrow & Associates of South Carolina, the two cities had every reason to be optimistic over their branding. The firm, after all, was responsible for completing marketing and branding efforts for over 130 communities in 17 different states around the country and had even done work for the small cities of Skowhegan and Waterville, Maine.[15]

Launching the initiative a mere five years after their last joint rebranding effort—which produced such gems as "The urge is there, because we care," "Saco-Biddeford, catch the spirit, feel the beat," and my personal favorite, "Trash Towns USA,"[16] among others— the City of Biddeford was able to fund a new effort in part with help from a generous grant from the Orton Foundation. Visiting the city in August, two partners from the firm were given a tour of the entire area, gathering input from locals along the way about what makes their towns so special. Both cities had special public buy-ins from residents who were invited to a series of meetings in the fall and were encouraged to complete online surveys and mail-ins on their thoughts regarding the campaign.

"It was trying to see if there were commonalities to Biddeford and Saco as a region we could point out as well as ways to discover some of the distinction," said Delilah Poupore, Director of the Heart of Biddeford. "They held quite a few focus groups with citizens, businesses and different community organizations to kind of find out how they would describe Biddeford and Saco."[17]

When, on November 4, Muldrow returned to present their findings to the public, both cities were anxious. They had spent a total cost of $6,000 for this effort and wanted a good result that would be embraced by both locals and the public at large. As Ben Muldrow stated: "The most important person you're trying to reach is that person who is currently a resident," he said. "You can't get too cutesy. If the concept is not accepted by the locals, it won't work. It has to excite the people who live there and create buzz that can be built on."[18]

So, what did they end up settling on?

"Biddeford+Saco, Saco+Biddeford, one dynamic place no matter how you say it."

The slogan was a complete and utter flop.

Poupore said this phrase was initially used on promotional material and advertisements for the two cities, but that it's common for a marketing message to be used for only a few years before a new one is adopted. Craig Pendleton, executive director of the Biddeford+Saco Chamber of Commerce and Industry, said the chamber redesigned its logo to include the plus sign after the 2012 marketing campaign but neither city council formally adopted it. "We have been using it as much as possible," Pendleton said. "But without the cities embracing it, it went nowhere."[19]

The phrase was mocked widely, and the campaign lost steam.

Marketing and Communications Specialist for Saco Emily Roy said the city of Saco has undergone changes in both the administration and economic development departments since the 2012 marketing campaign. While Roy did not work for the city in 2012, she said that as far as she knows Saco did not implement the slogan.[20]

So why did it fail so badly? Lack of authenticity likely played a role.

By ignoring the five core dimensions of branding, the creators of this campaign made every conceivable mistake with regards to its messaging. Their slogan was uninspired and unoriginal, said nothing about the area's distinct qualities, was so generalized and safe as to try and appeal to everyone, and, in the end, failed to capture or inspire loyalty from the locals. The fact that public weigh-in on this also played a role in their decision went against one of the chief recommendations highlighted by Brooks earlier in this chapter.

Today, little evidence of this slogan's existence can be found online. Saco has since moved on with a much better slogan, "Friendly by Nature," a testament to its small-town charm and positioning near the ocean, while Biddeford has yet to adopt any new tagline.

Still, the cautionary tale of the "Biddeford+Saco, Saco+Biddeford, no matter how you say it" campaign is a reminder that even the best ideas can fall short if the proper branding strategies aren't adhered to.

## *Heather Pouliot and the Importance of Good Design and Branding*

As Chair of the Augusta Downtown Alliance, the owner of Core Marketing & Design, a building owner in downtown Augusta, and an At-Large City Councilor, Heather Pouliot knows a thing or two about downtown revitalization, particularly when it comes to marketing it to the public. It wasn't always that way, though.

Having grown up in Central Maine, Heather, like so many of her peers, initially moved out of the Augusta area to pursue opportunities in a larger city. "My entire life, all I wanted to do was get out of here," she recalled.

Settling in New York, she worked in real estate before moving back to Augusta in 2012 to assist with the political campaign of her future husband, Matt Pouliot, who was running for state representative. Involving herself in the Augusta Downtown Alliance in 2013, she worked in many facets of the organization before undertaking help with events, design and social media.

"I gained a lot of experience from running Matt's campaign, particularly with social media, which was really then just starting to take off in a big way," she said. "I segued that to the Alliance because of Matt's

**Heather Pouliot is the owner of Core Marketing & Design, which specializes in graphics and marketing campaigns. She emphasizes simplicity and clarity in all of her work (courtesy Dave Dostie).**

previous involvement on the Steering Committee. Having grown up here, I wanted to make Augusta a really fun place to live and felt like I could help with design work."

Having gone on to found her own marketing and design firm in 2013, Heather utilized this experience to take a crack at refining the Augusta Downtown Alliance logo.

"The first logo was designed by students at UMA and featured the iconic colors of the first three buildings to be painted in downtown Augusta. But it was too cluttered and featured graphics of a lamppost as well as silhouette figures walking down the street, with the words

'Augusta Downtown Alliance' underneath. It just looked old. I noticed other downtowns had more inviting logos so I wanted to do the same for ours."

Removing the people and lamp post from the graphic, she decided to keep the three buildings in the logo.

"Those three buildings really represented the start of revitalization in downtown Augusta and were iconic to those here at the time. Since marketing is really about consistency in colors and keeping a message on task, I felt it was important to keep them."

Heather also removed the language from the image. "The font was really bad and the language needed updating. I felt like we needed something action-oriented and something that spoke to Augusta in general." Adding the words "Meet Me Downtown Augusta" in place of the old language, she changed the font and colors to make it a bit more playful. The logo was eventually adopted by the board

"I think it's important for every community to hire a design professional, particularly if it's a small town. I also think it's important that the professional knows the city they're in, or has experience with tourism," she continued. "As for myself, I actually prefer working on projects for nonprofits, as they allow for a lot more creativity."[21]

## *Key Takeways*

When branding your community, it's important to remember these key takeaways:

1. Always adhere to the five core dimensions to base your brand upon.
2. Build your brand through one or more of those dimensions.
3. Expand upon your unique qualities in an authentic manner.
4. Never rely on public input to define you.

## *Conclusion*

> "Your brand is what people say about you when you're not in the room." —Jeff Bezos

In the world of instant gratification and connectivity, brand is everything. It's the perpetual bat signal, so to speak, that alerts the public to your identity, while giving you something to rally behind. This is something large cities have learned to do well, and that small cities aspiring for an urban experience can adapt through replication.

## 6. Marketing Your Small City ... the Right Way 111

By adhering to the five core dimensions of branding and expanding upon those same dimensions through the utilization of proper colors, language, and experience shaping, you can craft a place that is both appealing to the public as well as your residents. When done right, as in the case of Augusta, which utilized patriotic colors and carefully placed language on their welcome signs, or Sisters, which defined itself through experience-making by tacking on thematic Western elements that spoke to its rodeo festival, you can achieve a level of success. Ignore the basics and try to appeal to everyone's sensibilities, however, and you end up with an uninspired identity like Biddeford + Saco.

Branding is not rocket science, but there is indeed a level of science you need to follow in order to do it right. Just remember, in the end, the best thing you can be is authentic by showing off to the world not what you hope or aspire to be, but what you already are as a community deep down.

# 7

# Trickle Down(town) Economics

## Why Upper-Floor Development Is Key to Street-Level Retail

Anyone who follows politics is no doubt familiar with the theory of trickle-down economics. The theory, popularized during the Reagan Administration, goes something like this: if you slash taxes for the very rich, the amount of capital saved will trickle down to workers as the wealthy will invest in economic growth, thereby benefiting all. Its merits are often the subject of intense debate by Republicans, who tend to take an affirmative stance with regards to its effects, and Democrats, who remain skeptical of its impact. While those much smarter than I am could make a solid case for its effects (or lack thereof), I have only ever witnessed the theory work in one regard, that of downtown revitalization.

Now before anyone jumps the gun, understand that the notion of trickle-down economics under discussion is slightly different than the more political theory highlighted above, for unlike the political concept, this form of economics—let's call it *trickle downtown economics*—is a proven fact: develop your upper floors with residences and watch the benefits trickle down to street-level retail.

In this chapter, we'll examine how smaller cities are going about creating a more urban environment by developing their center cities around residents, not retail, and explore the right and wrong ways of doing so.

## A Brief Rundown of Upper-Floor Residences

The concept of bringing residential development to an area's urban center is nothing new. In fact, going as far back as ancient times it was par for the course. Many who operated businesses at the ground level lived above these same businesses so that they could be on hand for any developing situations. Later, as real estate became more commodified, developers would enter the game, finding a profit by leasing to business owners at the street level and tacking on additional floors to lease to residents above. This pattern continued all the way up until the mid-twentieth century, when, at least in America, these residences were abandoned by people *en masse* as tenants fled to the suburbs, leaving former apartments hollowed out.

This trend was devastating enough for larger cities, which saw huge swaths of taxpayers flee, but which nevertheless managed to hold on to some semblance of urbanity; for smaller communities, it was catastrophic. The void that would come about as a result would come to haunt these cities for years, resulting in cyclical boom-and-bust periods. Such a merry-go around of fortunes would set revitalization efforts back decades for these cities, until, in the early twenty-first century, community leaders began to give a second look into the benefits that a full-time residential population could bring to their cities.

## *Why Residents Matter: Exploring the Economic and Practical Impacts of Residential Units in a City Center*

The topic of residential expansion in downtowns is a relatively unexplored one. In fact, it's not even part of the Four Point Approach espoused by the Main Street program. Yet it's one of the most important things a community can do to sustain its revitalization efforts.

By far the biggest impact residential development has upon the downtown landscape is economic in nature. Density in and around downtown contributes to a customer base for local merchants as residents are more likely to patronize businesses that are closest to them. As has been highlighted:

> A healthy downtown residential district generates a constant flow of foot traffic to support nearby retailers, services, restaurants, and other businesses... Living downtown is particularly attractive to many who work downtown. By incorporating a higher density of residents in the downtown mix, the amount of activity increases. This in turn creates an even more vibrant desirable downtown economy.[1]

In fact, according to the International Council of Shopping Centers, residents will match $3.00 for every $1.00 spent on goods in the area

One of the conceptualized views of the Vickery Apartments in downtown Augusta, which first began leasing in the spring of 2020 (author's collection).

where they live.[2] The reasons for this are manifold, but a peek into driving trends helps explain why. According to U.S. Department of Transportation Studies, Americans are driving less than ever before. In fact:

> The average number of miles people drive has plateaued over the past three years at about 9,800 miles a year, approximately 2 percent below the amount motorists traveled in 2004, the Wall Street Journal reported. And car-based commuting trips were lower than any time since 1990, while trips for shopping and recreational activities have also fallen:
> Specifically, data show:
> - After rising for much of the 1980s and 1990s, the average number of miles traveled is falling or at least flattening out in states with large metropolitan areas with good transit like California, Illinois, Washington, Oregon, and New York.
> - Driving is also declining in rural states like West Virginia and Maine and in Sun Belt states like Arizona and Texas but rising in Southern states like Louisiana, North Carolina, and Mississippi.
> - Wyoming had the highest per capita vehicle miles traveled in the nation in 2017 at 16,901, followed by Alabama (14,498), New Mexico (14,178), Mississippi (13,673) and North Dakota (12,867), according to Census figures analyzed by the Eno Center earlier this year.
>
> The lowest amount of driving done, on average, was in New York (6,316

per capita vehicle miles traveled). Alaska (7,460), Hawaii (7,547), Rhode Island (7,573), and Pennsylvania (7,945) followed.[3]

These trends are only likely to increase as telecommuting increases in the wake of the Covid-19 pandemic.

From a strictly economic point of view, residential units downtown provide a significant boost to the health of a city as a whole because of the increase they bring in property values. In tracking from the Neighborhood Stabilization Program, which provides federal dollars for residential projects, neighborhoods that increase or upgrade their housing stock are likely to experience a 25 percent increase in property values over a five-year period.[4]

So, who are the audiences that can be served by downtown housing? Many of the most in-demand housing types are found in urban centers. Rental and senior housing are the fastest-growing sectors of the residential industry, and both exist and are increasingly being developed in and around downtown areas. Changing demographics are contributing to the increase in demand for these product types, including the following:

- Greater household formation at the youngest and oldest segments of the population, which are most likely to rent. Younger generations are making an exodus from their parents' homes as the economy improves, and seniors are living longer and requiring a broader spectrum of care.
- Limited ability for many households to obtain conventional financing for housing purchases, with as much as one-third of the population unable to qualify for a mortgage according to a National Homebuilder Survey.
- The increased desire by relocating workers to rent rather than buy for an initial period, whether because of uncertainty about the move or the inability to sell a former home in a timely fashion all drive this increased need. A study by Cort Destination Services determined that 65 percent of relocating workers planned to rent for at least the first year after a transfer, which is a reversal of trends found in the earlier part of the 2000s.[5]

Ironically, however, as overall demand for rental units has increased in the early part of the twenty-first century, statewide development of such units has actually decreased. This housing shortage has led to a sharp rise in market-rate pricing, making the development for more downtown residential development all the more imperative.

Aside from the obvious economic and practical benefits that residential units bring to city centers, residential units are shown to have positive effects in the following ways:

- Increasing stakeholder engagement and participation among the group with the greatest stake in the health of downtown. Downtown residents can be a critical first point of contact with new residents, provide eyes and ears on the street, and are easily reachable as a target sounding board for projects.
- Creating a communication network in the downtown to monitor and identify issues early. Especially critical since these individuals are present when staff go home.
- Foster highly fundable projects. Residential projects typically meet the criteria of more funding entities, especially if they can include assistance to elderly or limited income households in the area or can be focused on a limited area which meets blight or income thresholds.[6]

While many larger urban centers are aware of the practicalities and benefits that housing units can bring to a city center, including increased sustainability for local businesses in operation, increases in local property values, and the chance to create a diverse community that spans generational divides, many smaller communities are blithely unaware of how to do it. In the next section, we'll examine how some small cities have successfully tackled residential development and how these programs were incentivized and supported publicly and privately.

## *Exploring the Demographic Trends for Loft-Style Housing in Small Town, Texas*

Perhaps one of the more ironic things to come about by increasing urban housing stock in small communities is the kinds of groups it attracts, specifically Boomers and Millennials. Long at odds with each other politically, socially, and philosophically, both generational groups seemed to have found common ground in flocking to smaller urban cores for housing, albeit for different reasons.

For Boomers, who were largely raised in and stayed in the suburbs throughout their working lives, this kind of urban housing has offered the convenience of safety, while at the same time offering a reprieve from big yards and maintenance; for Millennials, who have largely trended towards more urban areas, this kind of urban housing has offered a way out of overpriced cities. The rising popularity of this lifestyle is reminiscent of how Americans often lived prior to World War II and strangely enough has helped repopulate the central cores of many of America's small towns. This doesn't mean both groups are looking for the Norman Rockwellian version of their grandfathers' America, however; rather, they are looking for a way to reshape these central areas into the urban/suburban environments they left behind.

A 2015 survey by the National Association of Realtors and Portland State University found that when deciding where to live, 79 percent of Americans in the 50 largest metropolitan areas wanted to be within an easy walk of places and things to do in their communities.[7] Such preferences are trending nationally in smaller and smaller communities and are helping to reshape the hearts of America's small towns into vibrant urban prototypes. One of the areas this has been studied in depth is in Texas where the small cities of Commerce (pop. 9,000), Denison (pop. 23,000), Denton (pop. 133,000), Paris (pop. 25,000), San Marcos (pop. 61,000), Tyler (pop. 104,000), Waco (pop. 134,000), and Sulphur Springs (pop. 16,000) were featured in a study by The Real Estate Center at Texas A&M University. Chosen for both their populations, as well as their distance from major metro areas, these cities were also chosen for their abundance of loft-style conversions in older building stock. What the study revealed was that within these eight cities, landlords reported that young professionals were the primary tenants occupying downtown loft conversions, while empty nesters came in second. It also found that majority of these residents were renters rather than owners, and that of the younger people occupying the spaces, students were not the primary demographic, but rather young professionals seeking second-move locations. Dylan Simon, an urbanist and investment sales advisor at Colliers International in Seattle, explains:

> First-move locations are where new residential renters tend to land initially. This group generally clusters around housing that is well advertised and can be found with a web browser or smartphone. Easy commutes are desirable, which correlate with the increased popularity of new high-amenity campus housing targeting today's more particular students.
> Postsecondary facilities in most cities under discussion were not within walking distance to downtown, ruling out easy commutes to campuses. San Marcos and Denton were exceptions, leading to much higher student populations frequenting those downtowns.
> Second-move locations are primarily driven by a deeper understanding of the city and its neighborhoods. When these older, more informed residents relocate, they tend to gravitate toward places where the activities, character,

lifestyle, and scale match their individual needs and wants at that point in their life. They are also looking for authenticity.[8]

Finally, the study showed that seven of the eight cities reported an increase in the percentage of renter-occupied housing units between 2000 and 2010. The exception was Denton, but Denton's reduction could be due to a significant increase in new on-campus housing constructed during that time. This would have had the effect of pulling students out of privately owned, off-campus housing and into "group quarters," a classification excluded from a city's census count.[9]

In addition, the study found that loft rental rates were generally larger than typically sized apartments that could be found in larger cities and that rents ran on average $0.75 to $1.25 per square foot, far below the market value in cities like Austin, Dallas or Houston.[10] Demand for these units was also shown to have outpaced demand for commercial retail space in the lower floors, with waiting lists being the norm.

So, what's driving these rentals? A lot of it has to do with the desire to be living somewhere distinctive. As was found in the study, many of those attracted to these types of residences are attracted to them because of the unique features that can be found in these older buildings. For while many larger urban centers tore down entire neighborhoods during the era of urban renewal, many smaller communities preserved their older building stocks. These preservation tactics have taken off with both younger and older generations who are increasingly seeking more authentic connections:

"I've found that folks don't like what I call Disney downtowns," says Beverly Abell, City of Tyler Main Street Department leader. "Cities develop over decades, and buildings with different architectural styles are acceptable to residents downtown as long as their makeovers are well done and in context with the other buildings."[11]

What was most surprising, however, is much of the influx into these places is not from lifelong residents but rather from newcomers to the area, as many of those growing up in these towns proved oblivious to the changes afoot. "You would be surprised at the number of people who live in Tyler who haven't been downtown in years," says Abell. "There is no silver bullet that's going to magically transform a downtown. It's pretty much one storefront, five jobs, and a $50,000 investment at a time."

In the end, the study conducted by Texas A&M proves that demand for upper-floor housing in smaller communities is indeed there and that revitalization done right could actually help reverse the decades of outward migration from younger residents. These trends are likely to increase over the next decade as opportunities for more remote working become available.

## Moving On Up: Garden City's Upper-Floor Initiative

Like many cities across the country, the small town of Garden City, Kansas (pop. 26,000) found itself in crisis during the height of the Great Recession (2007–2009). By the early 2010s, the city was struggling with a severe housing shortage as a lack of available lots for development, combined with a slow recovery, prevented any real growth in the city. Seeking a way to stem the bleeding, community leaders thus rallied together to develop a series of financial incentives to jumpstart the local economy. What they developed was the Downtown Second Story Residential Program.

First introduced in 2014, the Downtown Second Story Residential Program was rolled out as part of a number of incentives meant to spur growth in the downtown core. These initiatives worked by providing developers with readily available capital, made possible through expanding the downtown boundaries to fit in with Tax Increment Financing (TIF), a method that uses future gains in taxes to subsidize current improvements.

"The Second Story Residential and Neighborhood Revitalization Programs are very much available for downtown building owners who want to update or remodel their second floor spaces into viable residences," said Nicole Lucas, executive director of Garden City Downtown Vision. "Not only is there a demand for this kind of space by young professionals, but downsizing Boomers are always looking for spacious, open and light apartments and condos, especially as we continue to grow our downtown and populate Main Street with new businesses."

The incentive, which can be found on the Garden City Downtown Vision website, provides $1,000 per unit to be developed on upper floors. This incentive has the dual purpose not only of filling a much-needed residential gap in the community, but also of helping to rehab some of the city's historic buildings. The full outline of how the program works is included below:

Downtown Second Story Residential Incentive Program

The Downtown Second Story Incentive Program is intended to promote the revitalization and development of second story residential dwelling units for commercial store fronts in the Central Business District. This program is an economic development strategy that will help meet the housing needs as established in the comprehensive plan of the City of Garden City and improve the economic conditions of the Central Business district. Highlights are included below and taken directly from the program:

Program Incentives

- The City will provide free utility hook-ups for any developed or renovated residential units within the Central Business District.
- $1,000 per unit incentive for every unit developed or renovated where the private investment meets or exceeds a $10,000 per unit value. The maximum amount one (1) owner may receive in a calendar year is $10,000 (10 units).

Eligibility Requirements:

- An application for Downtown Second Story Residential Incentive Program must be filed within 60 days of issuance of a building permit.
- The improvements must conform to the City of Garden City's Building Code, Comprehensive Land Use Plan, and Zoning Regulations in effect at the time the improvements are made.
- Any property that is delinquent in any tax payment shall not be eligible for any incentive until such time that all taxes and assessments have been paid.

Incentives will be paid within 30 days of final inspection and issuance of Certificate of Occupancy

More than five years on, the Downtown Second Story Residential Program has had a major impact on spurring growth in the area. Downtown continues to be a hot spot, and the demand for second-story residential living in the central business district remains high as the open concept–loft living style remains popular across many demographics.

Even more so, the addition of new residents into the area has had a marked economic impact, as the additional residences have proved so that Main Street reported an increase of 3 percent, or $16 million in sales from 2017.[12] Downtown also saw over $162,077 in sales tax revenue for the city in 2018, with private investment running $1,329,970 and revenue in city permits rising to $24,614. By the end of 2019, the downtown saw an additional 10 businesses open, including a brewery, a boutique and a florist. These added 53 new jobs to the local economy, providing a huge boost to the city.[13] "If you have not been to downtown Garden City in a while, you don't know what you are missing," said Shelia Crane, Downtown Vision executive director. "Come on down and check out all the variety of stores and restaurants. There is a lot going on, and you will find something available for every style, age, gender and shopping occasion."

Finney County Economic Development Corp. President and CEO

Lona DuVall also voiced excitement over the downtown growth. "We have been fortunate that our downtown has stayed pretty vibrant," she said, adding that a key to recent growth has been the city's investing in the Downtown Development Fund. "The brewery was obviously a home run," DuVall said. "We are very excited."[14]

As can be witnessed, Garden City's investment in its future began with converting the upper floors of its historic building stock. By finding a way to incentivize this development, the city was not only able to solve a housing crisis but also to provide a real boost to their local economy in the form of jobs.

## Everything Old Is New Again: How Bend, Oregon, Tackled a Housing Deficit

While some communities, like Garden City, are blessed with taller-than-average skylines that allow for the development of multiple units in their upper floors, others are more typical of the more traditional nineteenth-century, 2–3 story standards that prohibit upward growth. This doesn't mean that all is lost, however; it just means that cities need to get more creative when implementing ways to add new housing stock. As we'll see from the case of Bend, Oregon (pop. 107,000), residential development does not need to be hindered simply because of a lack of readily available upper-floor space. It can instead be found by looking to previously underutilized assets.

Located in the central part of Oregon next to the Cascade Mountains, Bend has long attracted visitors to the area due to its scenic beauty and outdoor recreational opportunities. A former logging town, Bend saw its industrial might peak in the early part of the twentieth century when mills employed over 4,000 workers on both sides of the Deschutes River. So great were its fortunes that it was once considered the world's leader in manufacturing secondary wood supplies. This changed dramatically, however, in the early 1980s, when over logging led to a depletion of forest resources, devastating the timber industry in the community and causing a devastating recession that lasted throughout the decade.

By the early 1990s, things had improved somewhat for Bend. The population, which had stagnated as a result of logging, grew again as people "discovered" the area due to its scenic beauty and low cost of living. With growth rates of 6 percent or more,[15] Bend soon found itself in a predicament, however, as a severe housing shortage developed, making the city a victim of its own success. To remedy the situation, a

Central Bend Development Program was created by city leaders with aims that included:

- Create a downtown center by giving high priority to the river and downtown core projects.
- Give high priority to human scale and quality of life.
- Increase downtown's role as a center for government and business activity.
- Maintain and develop cultural, historic, and entertainment resources.[16]

Tying directly into these aims was the goal of creating housing through infill. This was encouraged primarily through the rezoning of one the inner city's most prominent mills, no longer in operation, into residential housing by changing the site from one which encouraged industrial use to one that included mixed residential and commercial space. Before they could do so, however, they needed to tackle the environmental factors that plagued the location, particularly the contamination underground. After decades of industrial use, 180 acres of former lumber mill sites had been contaminated with hazardous substances from petroleum storage tanks, wood treatment, charcoal manufacturing, and other activities.[17]

The Oregon Department of Environmental Quality began remediation, and the site developer agreed to a voluntary cleanup plan to complete it. The redeveloped site soon featured eco-friendly activities such as kayaking and fishing along and on the Deschutes River, as well as a variety of art galleries. The development preserved and repurposed portions of multiple historic buildings in the old site, including the iconic lumber mill smokestacks that enrich the neighborhood's distinctive character and celebrate its history. Not only did the redevelopment clean up environmental contamination, but also it created an economic engine for the region that employed more than 2,000 people by 2013.[18]

The entire project brought 272 new apartments to the city's core, which had a major impact on commercial and retail space. Retail vacancy rates for the Old Mill District and downtown were 6.1 percent and 2.4 percent respectively, compared to 8.1 percent overall among seven analyzed submarkets. The industrial vacancy rate in the central submarket stood at just 1.2 percent, the lowest of four analyzed submarkets.[19]

In addition, the improvements to the city center have attracted a wide range of entrepreneurs to the community, allowing Bend to become a hotspot for tech startups, even leading to Bend being named "the most entrepreneurial city in America" by *Entrepreneur* magazine in 2010.[20]

Today, the Old Mill District is one of the most celebrated and in-demand neighborhoods in the city of Bend, offering everything from high-scale shops to restaurants to grocery stores, all within footsteps of one's apartment. This convenience has made the district not only popular for residents and area newcomers moving to the city but also to tourists who have increasingly been drawn to the area through advertisements such as that included on the city's official tourism page, visitbend.com:

> From luxury townhomes to riverfront condos, *the Old Mill District* offers residents the opportunity to live in the heart of Bend's premier shopping and entertainment district that's conveniently nestled along the scenic Deschutes River.
>
> Living in the Old Mill District means you'll have unparalleled access to everything that's made Bend a world-class travel destination.
>
> Start your day with a run along the *Deschutes River Trail* or spend your lunch break *kayaking or surfing in the Bend Whitewater Park*. Play with your pooch at the RiverBend Dog Park or take the kids to *Farewell Bend Park*.
>
> Hungry? Become a regular at restaurants such as *Anthony's*, famous for their Northwest seafood and riverside dining, or *Flatbread Neapolitan Pizzeria*, which serves pizza made with the freshest organic ingredients. Grab a latte at *Strictly Organic* or wind down the evening with a glass of from *Va Piano Vineyards* or *Naked Winery*.
>
> When you live in the Old Mill District, you're part of the pulse that makes Bend such a thriving outdoor community. Enjoy a front-row seat to *Balloons Over Bend*, an annual festival where hot air balloons majestically float over the city in a breathtaking display of patterns and colors. Stroll through First Friday Art Walks, the Old Mill's monthly celebration of art and culture. And take in the wide range of concerts at the *Les Schwab Amphitheater*, Oregon's premier outdoor venue that's played host to musical legends such as Paul Simon, Bob Dylan and Peter Frampton as well as some of the most popular names in music today like Jack Johnson, Ben Harper, The Avett Brothers, and Modest Mouse.
>
> You really can have it all when you live in Bend's Old Mill District![21]

Bend's resourcefulness in creating housing where none had previously existed shows how small cities can adapt the most unremarkable places into economic engines that can fuel a city's growth.

## *Housing in Augusta: A Personal Reflection*

I will never forget the first time I drove down Water Street and had to loop around the block to find parking. It happened roughly 20 months

Downtown Augusta has become the fastest growing neighborhood in the city due to the incorporation of upper-floor apartments, such as the one featured above (author's collection).

after I had first moved here, and I had never seen anything like it. It was a feeling of excitement I will never forget after seeing the streets utterly deserted for so long.

When first moving to the city back in 2016, I was living in one of only 12 market-rate apartments downtown. Even back then, when the streets were deserted past 5 p.m., these apartments, when available, never sat vacant for more than a few days as demand for quality housing remained high. Over the subsequent years, this demand led to more development and those initial 12 apartments grew to 29 by 2018, 52 by 2020, and was forecast to be over 70 by 2021. The people living in these units, who range wildly demographically, have contributed immensely to the local economy, resulting in the opening of over 12 businesses since 2016, all of which are supported by the residents who live here.

Many, like Cushnoc Brewing, the likes of whose soft opening resulted in the parking situation described above, were motivated by the potential spending power of these full-time residents, who are all more than happy to walk downstairs for a drink and a pizza rather than drive across town.

Today, the population of full-time residents in downtown Augusta hovers close to 100 people, a feat not seen in the downtown in over half a century. Many of these people have families in these units and often go on to renovate properties in the neighboring historic district when they outgrow them. This has resulted in downtown becoming the fastest growing neighborhood in the city, and one of the most in-demand places to rent in Central Maine.

There is truly something to be said for tackling a top-down or trickle-down approach to downtown revitalization, as all the interesting retail in the world can't account for a neighborhood feel. The fact that this development was not forced but was driven by locals who care about the community has made the influx of new residents and businesses all the more meaningful. People truly feel they have a stake in the community, and that's exactly what you want to create when revitalizing: a neighborhood.

## *Andrew LeBlanc and Developing Responsibly*

Andrew LeBlanc knows all about creating great apartments in small communities. A former real estate broker, the Yarmouth native lived away before ultimately returning home. In 2019, he turned his attention to residential development in downtown Augusta. His work on the historic Vickery Complex, a block of buildings that includes the Vickery, Doughty and Laverdiere buildings, resulted in the fitting up of 23 market-rate apartment units for the city. The largest such undertaking in downtown Augusta history, the building began leasing the following year and quickly filled up with tenants.

"When I first moved back to Maine, I had already witnessed downtown development take place in Boston, with multifamily units dominating the central core. My dad happened to have a portfolio of properties available, and I got interested in developing them," he explained.

"Portland was always too frothy for me and lost its authenticity a long time ago. It

Andrew LeBlanc recently undertook one of the largest development projects in downtown Augusta history (author's collection).

hardly felt like Maine back then and even less so now. From a development standpoint, it just had a 'been there done that' kind of vibe, where developers were just about a quick buck but not really caring about the community at large. This has had a major impact on the people who rent there as developers have increasingly focused on units like condos which focus on ownership rather than rentals. It's little risk for them to build these kinds of units and as a result a seasonal population is created that doesn't even live there. People in Maine don't really trust people who rent in their cities part time and don't try to become a part of the community or culture and I didn't want to be a part of perpetuating that cycle. It's what I call irresponsible development."

He continued: "After researching Augusta, my interest piqued. It was a tertiary market as far as Maine real estate goes, with larger cities like Portland being primary, and coastal cities being secondary, but Augusta just made sense. It already had the jobs here being a state capital and a healthcare hub and all, but it lacked any large scale development to attract these people to live here."

Though he followed through with his instincts, Andrew felt a lot of resistance along the way, particularly from those in the Portland market.

"I often heard from naysayers: 'If Augusta is so great then why doesn't someone in Augusta develop it.' Well Tobias and Richard Parkhurst did just that and their vacancy rates proved that the demand was indeed there. People want to live where they work. You just have to provide them with quality. I like Augusta because it's a real community. It's about as authentic as they come. For a small city, it's pretty incredible that you have the diversity you do in the downtown, and everyone actually gets along! It's the most welcoming community I've ever been a part of and you just get a sense of excitement from being here. I think people feel that when they walk down the street," he said.

"We created these apartments for the modern Middle. When you walk into the Vickery, you feel like you're walking into a professional apartment. You can drop these apartments in any large city and not miss a beat. We crafted places that were sensitive to the original details of the building and at the same time provide all the modern amenities needed. People who rent here not only get to live in a cool building, but actually get to be a part of the history of the place."

Putting his money where his mouth is, Andrew actually moved into one of his units just a few months after leasing the rest.

"Augusta is just such a vibrant place and I wanted to be a part of it. You can't get the quality of life you can get here in many larger communities and I feel that we've developed these apartments in such a way so as not to disrupt that quality of life," he said. "Oftentimes, you have these big entities driving development who don't really care about maintaining the local culture there. You even see this in certain parts of Maine, where these massive conglomerates buy up property and impose their will on the people already there. Augusta development isn't like that. Things have happened organically here and because of that I feel like it's sustainable," he continued.

"It's been such a great thing to see this downtown develop over time and I feel it's a testament to those who came before me. When you do responsible development, you're not pushing people out, you're embracing what's already there and I feel like our development did just that."[22]

## Key Takeaways

When it comes to revitalizing a downtown area, particularly in a small city, the keys to success are proceeding from the top down. The key takeaways you should keep in mind when doing so are:

- A trickle-down approach to revitalization is the best way to ensure sustained success.
- You can achieve a trickle-down approach by concentrating on adding residential units to your upper floors.
- Residents add vibrancy to your downtown and can serve as an economic engine for retail and restaurants.
- There are a variety of ways to incentivize residential growth through public-private partnerships.
- The demand for residential units often outweighs the demand for retail space.
- Downtown residents often span the Millennial-Boomer generational divide.
- To maintain authenticity, residential growth should happen organically and not be forced.

## Conclusion

> "You can't rely on bringing people downtown, you have to put them there."—Jane Jacobs

Travel to any successful urban center in America and what will you find? People. People are what gives a downtown vitality during the day, and it's people who will give a downtown that same vitality at night.

In following a trickle-down approach to downtown revitalization, one doesn't let retail dictate the needs of residents, but rather lets residents dictate the needs for downtown. As can be seen in the cases from Bend, Texas, Garden City and Augusta, retail units can be placed in upper floors of buildings or around existing assets, and are in high demand, actually outpacing the demand for commercial and retail space. Such demand has led to a high amount of growth in each of these downtowns with new businesses opening up to take advantage of the full-time residents who have moved there. These residents moving in have offered a renewed sense of vibrancy to the area giving each place an authentic neighborhood feel.

While each community has incentivized development in their own way through various programs, the fact that each has developed residential units in an organic manner respecting both the historic architecture present as well as the community at large, has helped fuel demand for the units, particularly among Boomers and Millennials who value authenticity above all else. Such actions will no doubt continue to have a positive effect on the communities as residents rise up and stake their claim in the future of their adopted cities' growth.

# 8

# Get a Little Artsy

There's a rather famous quote from Steven Pinker's Pulitzer Prize Finalist book, *How the Mind Works*, that goes: "Modern and postmodern works are intended not to give pleasure but to confirm and confound the theories of a guild of critics and analysts, to *épater la bourgeoisie*, and to baffle the rubes in Peoria."[1] His basic meaning: people in small towns are too ignorant to understand or embrace art or culture.

While the rather dated quote speaks to the general air of smugness that many in larger urban areas have about those residing in smaller cities, it nevertheless raises a valid point in that art and culture are rarely prioritized in cities of fewer than 150,000 people. This is unfortunate as these two things are key not only to growing one's community but also in fostering a sense of creativity among the people who live there.

In this chapter, we'll explore some of the ways that art can serve as a creative *tour de force* for a smaller community, while at the same time providing another engine for economic growth. After all, "The sign of a great state or a great city is the strength of its cultural life," said J. Clayton Hering, president of Northwest Business for Culture and the Arts.[2]

By examining smaller communities not traditionally associated with big universities—which, because of a high student presence, are more likely to place emphasis on art and culture—we'll take a look at the creative route that some places have taken to foster increased appreciation for arts and culture. Before we delve in, however, let's explore the generational trends associated with such outlets and how younger professionals, particularly Millennials, interact with it.

## *Millennials and Art: An Enduring Bond*

Millennials are the first generation in nearly 100 years to embrace the full spectrum of urban living, with access to art and culture being a major driving force behind their decision to uproot. In fact, not since the Lost Generation of the early 1920s—in which authors and artists of all kinds clustered in droves in major cities like Barcelona, Paris and New York—have so many young people flocked to urban centers in search of a more culturally enriching experience.

Whether it was the result of an entitled youth, the ravages of economic turmoil, or the increasing influence of social media, the link between Millennials and their fascination with art cannot be denied. As a generation that has been defined by sharing, such an obsession with all things culture has only been exacerbated by social media.

"Some people believe that Millennials are tied to their smartphones, and therefore might be less interested in the fine arts. In fact, just the opposite appears to be true: there's a generational shift in which younger people are more attracted to art than older generations," said Albert Scaglione, founder and CEO of Park West Gallery. "During the auctions we hold around the world, we see more young people every day."[3] A study conducted through Park West Gallery supported Scaglione's theory about this generational divide, particularly with regards to Millennial preferences for places that emphasize art and culture. In the study, they found that:

> Millennials are almost twice as likely as Baby Boomers to say they both know something about art (63 percent to 34 percent), and almost universally agree that they appreciate art, the research found. In fact, four out of five Millennials said that art was important to them, the highest percentage of any age group.[4]

In addition, the study also found that social media is driving additional interest in art among all demographics, especially Millennials, allowing people to find and interact with art in new ways. Some of the other key findings include:

- 53 percent of people say they have interacted with art on social media.
- 55 percent say that social media plays an important role in discovering new art.
- 54 percent say social media enhances the way they experience art.
- 79 percent of Millennials say social media allows them to interact with art in new and interesting ways, versus 61 percent and 37 percent of Gen X and Baby Boomers, respectively.
- 65 percent of Millennials say they buy artwork with the intention of sharing it with others on social media, versus 45 percent and 25 percent of Gen X and Baby Boomers, respectively.[5]

Because of this instant connectivity, art has increasingly become more experience oriented. For unlike previous generations,

> Millennials are known for seeking out experiences more than they are known for purchasing objects. At the same time, they also prefer to showcase their personal styles and individuality in work and living spaces. As a result, Millennials seek out art that connects with them on a personal level. They also tend to seek out artists with whom they relate on a personal level.
>
> One particular experience that Millennials value is that of **discovery**. Think about music that was popularized for Baby Boomers and members of Gen X. Members of those generations mostly consumed and valued music that was carefully curated for them by recording and radio station executives. Yes, there were exceptions to this (e.g., the punk movement or the college rock scene), but the general truth remains.
>
> Millennials and members of Gen Z consume music much differently. They peruse YouTube for unknown artists, attend local shows, swap Spotify playlists, and generally reject the notion that radio executives are best suited to tell them what to listen to.
>
> Likewise, they enjoy the process of discovering visual artists as well. To do this, they use technology, connections through friends and associates, and social media to find and connect with artists, galleries, and industry experts. This puts Millennials in the unique position of often discovering fine artists early in their careers.[6]

With such an emphasis placed on experience and discovery, art is increasingly shedding the constraints of its exclusive past becoming a more objectively oriented medium that embraces the masses. This has had the result of inspiring many young adults to take risks they would not have normally taken by embracing their inner creativity and enrolling in art classes. It also speaks to the ever-growing popularity of such things as paint nights and the 30-day writing challenges espoused by many on social media.

As more young professionals position themselves around enclaves of bohemian culture, supporting the arts has never been more important. Fortunately, many small cities have done just that by investing in art galleries and museums and even by playing host to music festivals, all in an attempt to compete with their larger counterparts and make their cities more appealing. Before we explore this phenomenon further, let's take a look at what we mean by arts and culture.

## *Defining Art and Culture*

There's a fairly memorable scene in an episode of the BBC comedy series *Absolutely Fabulous* entitled "Death" in which one of the main

t↻ 🌀 will_sears

**This abstract mural designed by Portland-based artist Will Sears can be seen from both bridges spanning the river. Completed in 2018, it sits on the backside of Cushnoc Brewing Company. Note that the letters for Augusta are hidden throughout (author's collection).**

characters, Edina, invests a large chunk of her fortune in modern art in order to bequeath the collection to the nation when she dies. Her desire to do so stems from the sudden death of her father, as it forces her to come to grips with her own mortality. Upon returning with her friend Patsy after the art is delivered, Edina attempts to explain the meaning of each piece to Patsy before stumbling upon her father laid out in a coffin in the middle of the sitting room. Surprised by the addition of her father's body to the collection, Edina stumbles through an explanation before stating: "It's a dead body, Pats," with Patsy responding, "Yes, Eddie, but is it art?"

Patsy's humorous retort is something most of us have asked at some point or another, as it raises the valid question: what exactly is art, and is there a difference between art and culture? While we won't attempt to define the former too narrowly—as art is subjective by nature—we can, in fact, attempt to explain both as they relate to one another. As Sandy Fitzegerald explained in her blog CultureFighter, understanding the difference between art and culture is important "because if people do not understand the difference between the art and culture [and] what separates them then you are always beginning from the wrong place."[7]

She goes on to define art as one of the aspects of culture:

> It is a very defined creative approach to making objects or making concepts. It is defined as a physical thing that we create be it a painting or a movie or whatever. So, it is almost like creating. It is a craft or a skill by which we create an object. And that object can be conceptual as well as physical. But is very definite. It is very defined activity and it is a very defined product that you have in art. Whereas the culture is everything, what we are surrounded by.[8]

In terms of refining this even more, art is a physical manifestation of creativity that can take the form of many mediums while contributing and influencing the greater society that surrounds it. As noted, painting, sculpture, music, literature and the other arts are often considered to be the repository of a society's collective memory with art preserving what fact-based historical records cannot: how it felt to exist in a particular place at a particular time. In this sense:

> Art is communication; it allows people from different cultures and different times to communicate with each other via images, sounds and stories. Art is often a vehicle for social change. It can give voice to the politically or socially disenfranchised. A song, film or novel can rouse emotions in those who encounter it, inspiring them to rally for change.
>
> Researchers have long been interested in the relationship between art and the human brain. For example, in 2013, researchers from Newcastle University found that viewing contemporary visual art had positive effects on the personal lives of nursing home-bound elders.
>
> Art also has utilitarian influences on society. There is a demonstrable, positive correlation between schoolchildren's [sic] grades in math and literacy, and their involvement with drama or music activities.[9]

So, in understanding the key differences between art and culture, just how can small cities encourage the growth of art? It turns out there are quite a few ways. Art is hardly the narrowly defined, staid medium it was regarded to be in the past. You don't need a painting to have artwork, and you don't need a gallery to influence culture, for art can take on many forms of creative expression ranging from cinema to murals and even literacy. In the case studies presented, we'll see how certain communities utilized this loose definition of art to foster a more innovative culture.

## *Augusta: A Reflection on Art*

While not exactly a cultural desert, the arts scene in Augusta is definitely wanting. Home to historic museums, like the Maine State Museum, Museum in the Streets, the Holocaust and Human Rights Museum and Old Fort Western, it is bereft of art galleries or live performance theaters, proving a real hindrance for those seeking more cultural options. Though places like the Viles Arboretum offer opportunities to view sculptures, and the Richmond Gallery run by the University of Maine at Augusta in downtown shows off student projects, you'd be hard pressed to find anything particularly artistic. This was the dilemma I ran into when first moving to the city in 2016.

Recognizing the importance that art and artists can bring to the local economy, one of the first things we did as a Board was seek out ways to bring more color to the downtown. One of the ways we did that was by establishing a mural initiative.

Working with the art department at the University of Maine at Augusta, which was conveniently located up the street from our office, we solicited designs from students in exchange for course credit, for the placement of a mural on the corner of a building near one of the downtown gateways. Selecting a very traditional postcard style mural, the final design featured a grandfather and grandson taking in the view of Old Fort Western and the Maine Statehouse with "Augusta" emblazoned across the top. The students then worked with the head of the department to outline the mural and fill it in with color.

While the end-product was stunning, it was never exactly my favorite due to the traditional imagery produced. Nevertheless, it proved to be the perfect art project for the city at that time for three main reasons:

1. It allowed for us to involve university students in an engaging manner.

2. It piqued the interest of the public, who watched the progress of the mural as it took shape throughout the week.

3. It represented the first real step for permanent artwork. downtown

The success of the project, and the subsequent media coverage, helped fuel another mural exactly one year later, when members of the Kennebec Leadership Institute approached us about doing a community mural on an old retaining wall across the river from city hall.

Working this time with a local artist, we met as a committee and settled on a traditional, yet slightly more abstract, design featuring a flowing montage of Augusta landmarks, representing different periods in city history. The artist then laid out the design, and members of both KLI and the community were invited to fill it in with color. Turnout for the event was high, with people of all ages looking to make their mark on the final piece. A plaque was later installed in a ceremony celebrating everyone who participated.

With two murals now behind us, the Augusta Downtown Alliance decided to continue the initiative into 2018, this time with a fully abstract piece on the backside of Cushnoc Brewing Company. Working with an artist from Portland known for his use of geometric shapes, we chose a design with bold colors that could be readily seen from the other side of the river. The resulting piece set off a maelstrom of differing opinions in town as its presence on prominent building ignited debates about the merits of the design.

The flirtation we had in 2018 with abstract design led us to pursue an even more abstract piece in the summer of 2020. Working with an artist from California, whose work was prominently featured in a local restaurant, we commissioned the boldest piece of artwork yet for downtown Augusta. Unlike past works, which focused on more inanimate objects, this artist was well known for his emphasis on elongated, alien-like faces, complete with large eyes inscribed with various messages relating to the local environment. Giving the artist *carte blanche* as far as design and color scheme went—but seeking input for messaging from the business owners sponsoring the mural—what resulted was a bold hodgepodge of pinks, blues, purples, oranges and reds that completely transformed the backside of Commercial Street.

Garnering all sorts of attention due to the boldness of its design, many in the Augusta Downtown Alliance held their breath in the days after completion waiting for the inevitable backlash from the locals. To everyone's surprise, however, the overall reception proved positive, and despite a few traditionalists and naysayers, the mural proved a hit, instantly becoming one of the most Instagrammable murals in the city.

**Completed in the summer of 2020, this mural by noted muralist Kris Markovich incorporates messages of positivity, while also giving a wink and a nod to Smart Eye Care sponsor Jessilin Quint. It was the first mural to be included on Commercial Street and has since set off a flurry of revitalization in that section of downtown (author's collection).**

The mural initiative launched by the Augusta Downtown Alliance had several unintended effects on the community. For one, it moved the needle and redirected attention back to the central core of the city. Secondly, it inspired other entities to pursue their own works, with private businesses and even other nonprofits getting in on various artistic projects such as painting the treads on city stairs. Lastly, and most significantly, however, it got city leaders talking about forming an official arts commission to review future sites for work. Such a commission is currently in discussion.

While the mural initiative certainly achieved its goal of making Augusta a more culturally enriching place, its success was only due in part to the way it was approached. For, rather than launching a number of murals all at once, the initiative instead focused on an organic model that gradually eased the public into more and more abstract designs. This not only had the effect of inspiring conversations around what was appropriate for art, but also had the effect of garnering a "what's next for downtown" sense of anticipation from both the media and the public.

Art, like development, should always come from a place of authenticity that is organic, and never be force-fed to the public. Doing so ensures community buy-in and will lead to a further blossoming of culture down the road. This was one of the biggest takeaways we learned from our initiative, and it is certainly a model that can be adapted to any small city around the country.

## *A Culture of Literacy: Lake Worth Experiments with Little Free Libraries*

Isabel Allende one said: "The library is inhabited by spirits that come out of the pages at night." If that is true, then count Lake Worth, Florida (pop. 34,000), among the most haunted cities in America.

Located in southeast Florida, roughly 70 miles north of Miami, the small city of Lake Worth known locally as "The Art of Florida Living" for its dynamic arts scene, which includes numerous galleries, earned an even greater reputation in the 2010s as it became Florida's unofficial capital for little free libraries in the state. So, what exactly are little free libraries?

Defined as a book exchange mechanism, a little free library is a small wooden box that has a "take a book, return a book" policy that encourages community literacy. They come in many shapes and sizes, and anyone may take a book or bring a book to share. Little Free Library book exchanges have a unique, personal touch and have been compared to mini town squares for the exchange of information that occurs. According to littlefreelibrary.org, there are more than 32,000 registered Little Free Library book exchanges in all 50 states and more than 70 countries. The movement started in 2009 when a Wisconsin man built a model one-room schoolhouse as a tribute to his mother, a former teacher who loved reading, and filled it with books.[10]

Having first researched little free libraries in the winter of 2015, Mary Lindsey, a Lake Worth resident and free library advocate, was immediately drawn to the mission espoused by littlefreelibrary.org and sought ways to bring that mission alive to the community's residents: "I saw a picture of a Little Free Library on Facebook, Googled it and found [LittleFreeLibrary.org] ... and decided this was a project for Lake Worth. I purchased one Library and took it to the city administration to make my case. The city was heavily influenced to support the project based on the success of LittleFreeLibrary.org and the support you all offer! It was important to the City Manager that trial and error had already been done ... and we had a successful model to follow."[11]

Mary began her mission by canvassing neighborhoods that would be interested in hosting such little free libraries, holding about 30 books each, in their public spaces. Forty-eight residents including Three Lake Worth groups—Neighborhood Association Presidents Council, College Park Neighborhood Association and the Friends of Lake Worth Library—jumped at the opportunity and applied for and received money from the Palm Beach County Office of Community Revitalization to make and install the libraries.

"Initial funding came through a $15,000 neighborhood improvement grant I applied for through the Palm Beach County Office of Community Revitalization," said Mary. "In hindsight, I would have started with less than two dozen Little Libraries all at once. These little magic book boxes proliferate like bunny rabbits! Subsequent funding has come through donations from private individuals; local businesses like bars, restaurant, art galleries and Credit Unions; other nonprofits; Neighborhood Associations and civic groups like Rotary Clubs."[12]

Ten of the original libraries were placed in city parks, new greenways and in front of municipal buildings and were managed by city officials who stocked them with books along with information about community events, while the other 24 were given to little library "stewards" who agreed to maintain and stock the libraries for two years.

"We estimated that we would need 100 Libraries, and we allocated 25 for each of our city's four districts spread out in such a way to achieve our goal. People who wanted to be a steward and have one in their yard were assigned on a first come first served basis according to our distribution plan," said Mary. "Anyone who wanted one that was too close to one already planted could get one and be a part of our project for a $300 donation. It's remarkable that so many people, businesses and organizations have donated funding for Libraries and asked that we place them wherever they are needed most!"[13]

While the initial batch of little free libraries were purchased from littlefreelibrary.org for around $250 apiece and were pretty basic in design, the next batch installed featured more extravagant designs courtesy of a local craftsman. All of the libraries, however, involved local volunteers to help decorate, paint, stain and weatherproof them.

"The way our Libraries are masterfully painted has been a huge part of creating community support and community-wide pride," said Mary. "All of our artists are volunteers (we provide the paint) and many of them are so grateful to have their work on permanent public display that they go above and beyond to help us."

Many of the stewards took to the project with gusto. Karla Engel said when she and her husband lived in Milwaukee, they helped residents put up tiny libraries. When Engel moved back to Lake Worth, she posted her experiences with the libraries on Facebook, a move that got Lindsey's attention. "It's the perfect blend of artistry and literature," said Engel, adding that her library will be mostly filled with children's books—namely Dr. Seuss.[14]

Today, Lake Worth boasts around 100 little free libraries across various parks, greenways and neighborhoods around the city. That's roughly one little free library for every 300 residents—by far the largest number of little free libraries of any town in the state. While this is impressive in and of itself and speaks to the success of the program, its biggest success story is the creative innovation it fostered among the general population, who, in working together, were able to combine two art forms—painting and literacy—in a single project.

As Mary sums up: "When anyone asks me, and people ask me all the time, how we did do what we've done in such a short time, I tell them it was easy. We started with a fully engaged community from the get-go. And then I tell them, stewards! stewards! stewards! They are the critical component."[15]

## *Of Mice and Main: How Greenville's Interactive Art Display Became a Tourist Sensation*

Sometimes the best inspiration for artwork can come from out from childhood. This was certainly the case for the Mice on Main sculptures installed in Greenville, South Carolina (pop. 69,000).

Located in the piedmont region of western South Carolina, where the foothills meet the mountains, Greenville was historically known as a retail hub up until the 1970s, when many of the retail shops fled to the suburbs. An aggressive revitalization of the central core, which involved moving the Greenville County Museum of Art to a downtown location, along with the conversion of the city's Main Street to two-way traffic, with heavy emphasis on greenscaping, helped stave off further bleeding, spurring a revival of business moving back to the city center.

Today, downtown Greenville is known as mecca for the arts. There live music, art galleries and theater shows are readily promoted. The most popular artwork, however, is one that can barely be seen.

Begun in 2000, Mice on Main—a series of bronze mice scattered in different locations around Main Street—began not from the vision of an artist, but rather one of a high schooler, Jim Ryan.

Inspired from the Margaret Wise Brown book, *Goodnight Moon*, which featured nine mice, and was among his favorites as a child, Ryan first proposed the art installation as part of his senior project at Christ Church Episcopal. His idea was to install these mice from the Hyatt to the Westin Poinsett Hotel.

Making his way through the red tape involved at the city level, Ryan secured funding for different unforeseen fees by working a job. He then went about raising the money, with the assistance of donors and the mayor, to complete his project. Hooking up with a local sculptor Zan Wells on creating the nine mice from the book, each with their own look and character, Ryan placed them in various permanent locations throughout the street.

"The idea behind it was to not only add to public art in our downtown area, but also to increase foot traffic downtown," Ryan said years later in an interview with Christ Church.[16]

Upon installation, the mice proved an instant hit and were promoted citywide as part of a new scavenger hunt for locals and tourists to enjoy. One spring day in 2007, Linda Kelly and her granddaughter, Sara, were hunting for the mice. Sara asked, "Grandmother, is there a book about the mice?" When Kelly told her about *Goodnight Moon*, Sara said she meant a book about Greenville's mice. "Why don't you write one?" she said to Kelly. And she did.[17]

With Ryan's go-ahead, Kelly and Wells spent the summer of 2007 working on their children's book. They approached Alan Ethridge, executive director at the Metropolitan Arts Council, to ask for help with publicity and advice on selling the book.

"We had ordered 2,000 books, which Zan and I thought were just a huge number of books—we would never sell them," Kelly says. Wrong. On the day of the book release and signing, Kelly saw people lined up all the way down the street and around the corner of the Metropolitan Arts Council, where the launch party was being held. They quickly sold out of books. "We sent our husbands home to get more," Kelly says. "We were just floored."

Soon, downtown retailers were calling Kelly to get their own copies of the book to sell. The rest is, well, history. "It just really has taken a life of its own," Kelly says.[18]

Both the project and the subsequent book have made Mice on Main more popular than ever before, with local residents and tourists alike flocking to the downtown center to hunt them. It's proven especially popular with young couples, many of whom have reportedly had their first dates hunting mice. Couples have gotten engaged in front of a mouse, and there's even been a Mice on Main–themed wedding.

Linda Kelly has collected many of these stories over the years. She treasures them. "I think of them as real," Kelly says. "I check on them about once a month."[19]

With the growing popularity of Kelly's book, Mice on Main soon spurred a whole variation of merchandise ranging from games to

These steps along Commercial Street were completed at the same time as the mural and even included the mural's base colors. Painted by volunteers from the Augusta Downtown Alliance, the Stephen King quote was later added by Kris Markovich and reads: "Remember, hope is a good thing, maybe the best of things, and no good thing ever dies." It has since become Augusta's most Instagrammable location (author's collection).

t-shirts to mugs to pillows and stuffed animals. Each year, sales from the "Mice on Main" book and board game are generously donated to the *Metropolitan Arts Council's SmartARTS program* in *Greenville County Schools*, Ethridge says. The program has received infusions of more than $115,000 since 2009, according to Ethridge.

Kelly and Wells "have been outstanding ambassadors for the Mice on Main scavenger hunt along Main Street and for the vast Mice on Main merchandise," Ethridge says. "It is a wonderful program that provides a memorable downtown experience."

That experience is shared by all ages. Near the end of our conversation, Kelly tells the story of hearing a young couple ask a city worker if he could help them find "Teeny Tiny Millie, who is way up high."

"She's hard to find," Kelly acknowledges.

The man had replied that he couldn't help. "We don't tell where the mice are," he said. Kelly, who imagines legions of city workers being sworn to secrecy, laughs with delight. "I love that they protect the mice," she says. "'It would ruin everything if the city worker had said, 'Yeah, she's right over there.'"[20]

At the end of the day, Mice on Main's success is not based on what it has produced economically or even artistically for the city of Greenville but comes down to what it has meant for those living in the community. The mice have taken on personalities of their own and have become a point of pride for everyone in the city, all because of a senior project inspired from a childhood book.

## *Marfa, Texas: An Instagrammer's Paradise*

Times Square, The Las Vegas Strip, South Beach, Marfa's Prada: Upon first glance, one of these things is clearly not like the others, but take a closer look and you'll see how one small Texas city has captured social media by storm becoming one of the most Instagrammed locations in the U.S.

Located in the middle of the Chihuahua Desert in western Texas, the city of Marfa (pop. 2,000) was originally a railroad stopover and experienced population growth in the 1920s and 1940s with the opening of the Marfa Army Airfield. After World War II, the airfield closed, and the city's prospects began to dim. This changed in the 1970s, when New York minimalist artist Donald Judd, seeking a quiet retreat, moved there, installing two hangars of his artwork. From there, Marfa slowly acquired more fame as an artist's haven, establishing the Chianti and Judd Foundation to maintain Judd's work following his death, as well as the Lannan Foundation, which hosts a writers-in-residency program. It wasn't until the mid–2000s, however, that Marfa's artist connections really took off after installing Prada Marfa.

Designed to resemble a Prada store, the building was made of adobe bricks, plaster, paint, glass pane, aluminum frame, MDF, and carpeting. The installation's door is nonfunctional. On the front of the structure, there are two large windows displaying actual Prada wares—shoes and handbags chosen and provided by Miuccia Prada from the fall/winter 2005 collection. Prada allowed Elmgreen & Dragset to use the Prada trademark for this work.

Initially, Elmgreen & Dragset wanted to mount their fake Prada elsewhere. They particularly liked the sound of "Prada Nevada." They struggled, however, to find support in the state. The New York–based Art Production Fund stepped in, connecting the artists with contacts throughout the small Texan city, including arts institution Ballroom Marfa. "Marfa turned out to be the perfect location for the work, with the nearby Judd Foundation and the legacy of Minimalism," the pair tells Artsy. They believe that Judd's simple sculptures, which were often made of wood or metal and could resemble furniture, impacted the future aesthetics of retail interiors. The duo views its own work as a time capsule, an investigation into how humans mark the natural world.[21]

Originally meant to be a reflection on contemporary consumerism, particularly with regards to luxury branding and gentrification, Prada Marfa has since been seen as a statement for how the fashion world penetrates even the most rural of places. While the installation was initially temporary, the onset of social media, beginning with Facebook, attracted droves of people driving into the middle of the desert to catch a shot in front of the iconic structure, and has since become a permanent display. Its popularity peaked when it was featured on *Gossip Girl*, a popular TV series, which ran on the CW network from 2007 to 2012.

As premised on "the scandalous lives of Manhattan's elite," there's a lot of art, fictional and otherwise, but the Prada Marfa sign, as displayed near the entrance of the Van der Woodsen family penthouse, is the show's Eckleburg eyes. Since its first appearance early in season two—which also debuted a Richard Phillips painting—the sign appears at some point in nearly every episode, a peculiar object in the backdrop of a mind-numbing, deeply chaotic-neutral soap opera.

The sign's appearance on the show propelled it into a very specific sort of ubiquity: Pinterest virality, countless YouTube tutorials, dorm room décor prints, and Etsy and Redbubble copycats. The signage's reputation has, too, seeped into the legacy of Prada Marfa itself: a hundred-plus episodes of *Gossip Girl* and a photo op from noted Texan Beyoncé later, *Vogue* referred to the sculpture as "the fashion girl's Statue of Liberty." What was once commentary on the absurdity of luxury was then placed back into the context of (albeit fictional) absurd luxury, becoming a new, absurd symbol of luxury turned back on itself.[22] Today, Prada Marfa is easily one of the most famous and Instagrammed locations in Texas, with social media influencers driving well out of their way to capture a shot in front of it.

Capitalizing off the popularity of this installation, several new pieces have since been installed in and around Marfa that are specifically tailored to the Instagram crowd. These include works like the neon pink "Was It Real?" sign—which pays homage to the mysterious Marfa lights, a phenomenon of blinking lights that have been appearing above the skies since the 1880s—and the famous El Cosmico Hotel, an artistically-inspired glamping site that utilizes colorfully decorated trailers and has amassed a following from celebrities, including Beyonce.

## *Cynthia Roodman and Art in Augusta*

Cynthia Roodman is the owner of The List Salon & Gallery in downtown Augusta. A hairstylist for the past 20 years, she is an art enthusiast and has been involved in all kinds of art promotions for the City of Augusta. As a member of the Design Committee for the Augusta Downtown Alliance, she played a leading role in helping to establish the city's first downtown art walk and has been a strong advocate for encouraging art both within and outside her salon.

"I grew up in Morrill, Maine, on a dairy farm," she

**Cynthia Roodman is a big advocate for increased arts in the community and often hosts works from local artists in her salon, The List (courtesy Scott Monroe).**

explains. "My parents never left the dairy farm and when I was a little kid, I knew it was my goal to leave every six months and travel the world to see different things. The first time I went to Europe and I saw art, I was in awe and wanted to commit my life to that. I cried when I saw my first Monet. I saw every brush stroke and I remember sitting there and just crying. Right then I knew art was a passion."

An avid traveler, Cynthia relocated several places in her youth before eventually settling back in Maine.

"I came to Augusta via Montana and South Dakota where I had met my husband who was an immigrant farm worker. I wanted to be near my parents and the ocean, and South Dakota really didn't offer the kind of diversity I wanted," she says. "Upon returning, I enrolled in Capillo and started working as a manager at Visage [a hair salon]. I promptly turned it into an art gallery and salon because there was no art in downtown Augusta at that time. I had grown up in the Midcoast which featured lots of art and I wanted to bring a bit of that here."

While declining to label herself an artist, Cynthia does dabble in photography and has submitted photographs to various art shows, including the art walk in downtown Augusta.

"I am not good with words so my artwork deals with photographs. I feel like artwork is an expression of yourself without using words. People can judge it, but it's your opinion and your opinion can't be wrong," she continued. "My artwork tells a story because it shows people and gives a mood of a particular place. I like artwork because it allows people to express themselves."

In discussing her favorite piece of art, she says: "It's hard for me to pinpoint my favorite art work. Growing up in Maine I grew up with Andrew Wyeth's work. *Christina's World* spoke to me as a child and I think I felt that connection even more because he was from Maine," she said. "As an adult, I was initially drawn to classic impressionists and photography, but honestly, I embrace all art. Every piece has a story to tell me. I love Ainslee Adams. Even our local photographer Dave Dostie is amazing. We are so lucky to have him because his photos make me feel the mood of the community."

Hosting regular exhibits in her salon, Cynthia is proudest of giving local artists a means of showing off their work.

"I committed to featuring artists who are in my chair or through their relatives. That's how I create a community by having that link. When I host a show it's all about networking and community buy-in and it's been wildly successful. Every artist I've had has sold work. I have 75 hours worth of clients in my chair a week. With the other two stylists in my salon, that's over 120 hours of clients looking at artwork."

She continues: "I cannot stand bougie artists. Art is not supposed to be bougie. I've committed myself to giving shy artists a chance to display their work who might otherwise be too nervous to show off their art in a gallery. I want my place to give you confidence. That's why I do it."

Regarding her favorite work of public art in Augusta, Cynthia says she likes the mural done over Cushnoc the best.

"I love the piece done by Will Sears," she says. "It has the letters of Augusta hidden in it and the colors used are so vibrant! Every time you enter downtown from the other side of the river, it greets you. It makes feel like I'm part of the difference. It welcomes me. What I appreciate about Augusta is that they're open to all the new ideas we present to them. I love that they're allowing us young people to have a voice because in so many other towns we're not allowed to have a voice. It feels really good."

## *Key Takeaways*

When it comes to establishing art in your small city, there are several key takeaways you should keep in mind:

- Art and culture have two different meanings, with the former going to support the latter.
- Art is broad and not easily defined as it encompasses a vast array of mediums.
- Art should never be forced upon a community in order to build a culture. It should be gradually introduced and expanded.
- Art requires authenticity to thrive and should be kept within the context of the community in which it is placed.
- The best kinds of artworks are those that are interactive, fun and draw in outsiders.

## *Conclusion*

> "Art is an evolutionary act. The shape of art and its role in society is constantly changing. At no point is art static. There are no rules."—Raymond Salvatore Harmon.

No offense to Steve Pinker, but small cities can appreciate art just as much as their urban counterparts. In fact, if it is coming from a place of authenticity, as many of the communities highlighted above have shown, art can foster an even more meaningful impact. This is because unlike larger cities, which have readily available capital from developers and artists at their disposal, most art in smaller cities is developed, paid for, and installed by members of the communities themselves. Because of this buy-in, it becomes possible for even the most culturally deprived places to establish a flourishing arts scene, as it encourages participation across all levels, making small town art something truly special indeed.

9

# Leveraging the Unexpected

*A Proactive Approach to Disaster Mitigation*

There's no doubt that small cities have a disadvantage when it comes to dealing with emergencies. With smaller populations, smaller economies, and a smaller media presence, most small cities are often left to their own devices in times of distress. This doesn't mean that emergency situations can't be mitigated effectively, however. In fact, with the right approach, a disaster not only can be mitigated but also can be utilized to your advantage. As will be demonstrated below, it's all in how you leverage the unexpected. Before we delve further into the subject, let's first examine a little bit more about disaster situations and their effects on smaller communities.

## Disasters in Smaller Communities

Michelle Dean once defined crises as the great unifier, stating: "Crisis forces commonality of purpose on one another."[1] This is definitely true in small cities, whose citizens often band together in times of distress.

As noted, emergency preparedness professionals in smaller cities are often forced to tackle a disaster differently than their larger counterparts would. This is due to a whole host of factors highlighted by Rural Emergency Preparedness and Response (2019): These include:

- Limited funding for rural response agencies, such as EMS, fire departments, or local public health departments, that could affect the availability of staffing, equipment, training, public

outreach and education, and other emergency preparedness and response activities
- Greater geographical coverage areas, which could result in longer response times during an emergency
- Demographic challenges, such as rural areas with concentrations of elderly, disabled, and poor residents
- Infrastructure for communication and warning systems may be substandard or nonexistent
- Coordination and cooperation among a complex network of local, state, and federal agencies during an incident[2]

Federal help in emergency situations often lags behind for smaller communities struck by disaster, as evidenced in Marshalltown, Iowa (pop. 27,000), which experienced little in the way of relief following a devastating tornado:

> In Marshalltown, state and local officials weren't familiar with the complex process needed to receive individual assistance, leaving them scrambling when an EF3 tornado barreled into town July 19, 2018.
> Residents and officials still are rebuilding Marshalltown after being denied individual assistance. The EF scale ranks tornadoes by their damage and wind speed, with EF5 as the most destructive.
> When the twister struck at about 4:30 p.m., Michelle Spohnheimer, the city's housing and community development director, and employees were crammed into a single-stall restroom in the basement of her office.
> The tornado—one of three that hit Iowa that day—damaged more than 1,800 homes and 200 other structures.
> "The severity of it is not something that we really are accustomed to experiencing, and so when a tornado like that hits a community, it can be extremely devastating," Spohnheimer said. "We were very fortunate to have no fatalities."
> The tornado struck two factories before hitting a poorer part of town, said Kim Elder, the coordinator and homeland security representative of Marshall County.
> "Just before it lifted, it went from an EF1, EF2 and worked its way into the EF3," Elder said. "The EF3 is where it destroyed the majority of those low-income, smaller homes, older homes and the factory. That's the majority of the damage as it worked its way across Marshalltown."
> Many of the residents were uninsured or underinsured, Elder said.
> Fugate said FEMA's individual assistance program is designed to mitigate this type of destruction. But in Marshalltown, the complex application formula left hundreds without assistance from FEMA.[3]

Often in larger cities, residents will wait for direction from state or federal authorities before taking any action of their own. Given that this is not a viable option for most rural communities, as evidenced by the example above, smaller cities often must band together in times of distress, forming relationships between civic leaders, volunteers, and non-profit groups for cleanup. Because of this, it becomes necessary for smaller cities to practice emergency preparedness in addition to emergency response. So, what's the difference between the two?

Emergency preparedness refers to actions performed before an emergency. Examples can include planning and coordination meetings; writing communication or standard operating procedures; training staff, volunteers, and community members; conducting emergency drills and exercises; and ensuring that emergency equipment is available, in good repair, and ready to use.

> Emergency response refers to actions taken after an emergency or natural disaster to help minimize the negative effects. Examples can include emergency communications; coordinating first responders and volunteers; providing emergency medical care to injured; coordinating temporary shelter for evacuated or displaced survivors; and organizing supplies and equipment for those assisting in and affected by the emergency or disaster.[4]

As we'll see from the examples below, the small cities that are most successful in dealing with disaster mitigation are often the ones that prepare for them and take action. It is such means which give them the advantages of their larger counterparts.

## *Seven Steps of Crisis Management*

While Augusta's approach to leveraging the Covid-19 pandemic into something manageable was something many communities struggled with, its response in the face of such adversity proved unique among others. This was due in no small part to the way it approached the situation. For, as recounted above, in any crisis situation, particularly in smaller communities, it is often necessary for multiple entities to pool the resources at hand and work together. Utilizing such a collaborative approach ensures that relief is received more quickly and that damage is kept to a minimum.

According to BBN International, there are seven steps an entity should take when it comes to crisis management:

1. Anticipate
   The first step is to prepare. Be proactive and arrange an intensive brainstorming session to go through all the potential crises that could occur at your organization. The simple rule of thumb is to accept Murphy's Law, "What can go wrong, will go wrong."

2. Create a plan and test it
The crisis response plan should be tailored for your organization, and it should include both operational and communications components—in a crisis, what will you do and what will you say? In order to ensure the messages contained in the crisis response plan are delivered effectively and with credibility, it needs to be tested.

3. Identify your crisis communication team
A small team of senior executives should be identified to serve as your organization's crisis communications team. Ideally, the CEO will lead the team, with the firm's top public relations executive and legal counsel as his or her chief advisers, after that the size of the team depends on the needs of your business. This team should set the communications process for your business.

4. Establish notification and monitoring systems
Knowing what's being said about you in traditional and social media, by your employees, customers, and other stakeholders often allows you to catch a negative "trend" that, if unchecked, could turn into a crisis.

5. Communicate, communicate, communicate
The first rule of crisis management is to communicate. Early hours are critical and they set the tone for the duration of the crisis. Be as open as possible; tell what you know and when you became aware of it; explain who is involved and what is being done to fix the situation. Be sure to correct misinformation promptly when it emerges.

6. The death of the super injunction
While crisis experts assert that the legal route is still a valid approach to take, from a reputational point of view, it can sometimes do more harm. ... Also, be aware that the legal route takes time. Time is not on your side in a crisis. [Author's note: While the context provided doesn't necessarily apply to general communities in disaster, it could be interpreted and adapted to mean self-reliance without government aid.]

7. Post-crisis analysis
After a crisis, formal analysis of what was done well, what could be done better next time and how to improve various elements of your crisis response plan. ... As the crisis comes under control, a company should examine how effective their plan was during the crisis and the impact the incident has had on its employees, brand(s) and reputation. If any of those three have taken a hit, a company may need take steps to address them.[5]

While these seven steps are intended for business organizations, they can just as well be applied for community organizations. For, as 2020 proved, every organization is vulnerable to crises, and the days of playing ostrich by burying your head in the sand and hoping the problem goes away are long gone. Thus, having a concerted response is not only necessary but vital to the health of your community. Below, we'll examine several small communities that managed to practice these tenets rather effectively.

## *Planning for a Twister: How Tuscaloosa Weathered the Storm*

To anticipate an outcome and plan for a crisis, you don't need to be a psychic, you just need to be prepared, and to be prepared you need to create a plan and test it. No community handled these tenets quite as beautifully as Tuscaloosa, Alabama (pop. 101,000).

Long prone to severe weather, given their Deep South location, the small city of Tuscaloosa was dealt a severe blow when, in 2011, a devastating tornado ripped through the heart of their city, destroying over 12 percent of the built infrastructure. While this would have decimated larger communities, which would have waited for federal aid, Mayor Walter Maddox chose not to panic, but rather to act. As recounted:

> When asked if he was ready for a disaster like the city saw in 2011, Maddox said yes, thanks to extensive FEMA training just two years before.
> 
> Maddox was a rock in his community, comforting constituents who had lost loved ones and homes and encouraging first responders and city employees.
> 
> "He was calm, yet in charge, and he was optimistic and it mattered a lot," Tuscaloosa Fire and Rescue Chief Alan Martin said.
> 
> Maddox said his heart might have been back in the command center, always concerned about the small details, but he was out doing what he needed to do.
> 
> "I've gotten way too much credit when it comes to this response," Maddox said. "We didn't do anything magical here at city hall. It belongs to our citizens who stepped to the plate, in a way that none of us will ever forget, and our employees, who by training and sheer guts would not let us fade into the night."[6]

By anticipating that such a disaster could happen and conducting the proper training with FEMA to counteract it, Maddox not only helped stave off what could have been a lengthy recovery process, but also inspired confidence in his citizens.

## *Augusta Keeps Its Head Above Water*

Augusta sits in a pretty precarious position. Located at the literal Head of Tide on the Kennebec River, it is subject to constant threats of flooding due to tidal shifts. Such flooding risks are exacerbated during full moons but are particularly threatening from January till April when ice jams can form in the narrower southern portion of the river, causing water to back up over the banks. When, on January 15, 2018, one such ice jam occurred, Augusta sprang into action, avoiding catastrophe.

Monitoring the situation, which indicated a flood risk, Augusta Public Works, in tandem with the Augusta Police Department, released text alerts to all residents and business owners downtown to remove their cars from Front Street and move them to higher ground. They also messaged businesses to secure their lower floors and move any products to higher ground. Afterwards, they forwarded the message on to the Augusta Downtown Alliance, who shared it to their followers on social media. By late afternoon, all cars were removed from the lower lots and parking was closed off. While the river rose steadily throughout the evening, it wasn't until midnight when river levels breached 20 feet over the banks, well past the 12-foot flood stage. As Chris Legro, a meteorologist with the National Weather Service, recalled, "The river levels spiked pretty quickly," Legro said. "The river remained far above flood stage for about an hour before it receded to 16.1 feet by 11 a.m. Sunday."[7]

Though the flood devastated the nearby community of Hallowell, which saw 20 vehicles submerged and 24 businesses suffering product losses from flooded basements, the Augusta business and residential community emerged relatively unscathed in the disaster, losing only two vehicles and seeing only minor damages.[8] Such successes can no doubt be attributed to the forward thinking organizations who worked together to identify a crisis communication team, establish a notification system and communicate a message of impending danger to the public.

## *Greensburg Takes Matters into Its Own Hands*

When it comes to disaster situations, time and again too many small cities and downtown organizations sit back and wait for disaster relief to come from the federal government. Rather than leading the way, they pass the buck off to an external force. Successful cities and organizations, however, do not wait. This was demonstrated best by the small town of Greensburg, Kansas (pop. 777), after 95 percent of the city was destroyed by a violent F-5 tornado.

"We lost half the population [to relocation] right away," recalls Greensburg Mayor Bob Dixson, who was the postmaster at the time. "They had no place to live. A lot of older residents moved to neighboring communities. But we were very blessed—2.8 million of our friends and neighbors came to help us," he says, referring to the population of Kansas. "The Kansas Department of Transportation, the Kansas National Guard, many cities, counties and towns sent trucks and ambulances and equipment and volunteers."[9]

Rather than wait for state and sederal monies to come through and dictate rebuilding efforts, the city of Greensburg put up their own money, establishing a property tax incentive program for businesses to reestablish themselves.

As the Alliance did with their partner Gardiner Main Street (159-160), Greensburg borrowed from its own budget, at the risk of incurring a deficit. This allowed them to control how funds would be dispersed and in doing so allowed them to establish new green building standards for those in receipt. As city administrator Steve Hewitt recalled, "To ever expect that you can rebuild a community with no debt or price tag to a community, it's just not realistic."[10]

The town's unique story, one of devastation and forward-thinking reconstruction, attracted media attention, becoming the subject of two TV series and several books. In 2007, Discovery Channel reached out to Greensburg to film a TV series that would document the green reconstruction of the town. A deal was inked for *Greensburg*, and environmental activist/actor Leonardo DiCaprio signed on to the project. The series ran for three seasons and documented the day-to-day struggle facing residents. A second mini-series, the four-episode *Build It Bigger: Rebuilding Greensburg*, premiered in November 2008 on the Science Channel.[11]

Greensburg's recovery six years after the disaster, and the subsequent fame of its green rebuilding efforts, show just how impactful it can be when a community joins together and sets their own rules, rather than suing for money and waiting for someone else to come to the rescue.

## *Sebring Looks to Others for Post-analysis Advice*

While natural disaster, though tragic, can often be prepared for in advance, human tragedies cannot. This is especially true when it comes to senseless actions.

When, in 2019, the small city of Sebring, Florida (pop. 10,000), suffered the deaths of five of its citizens in a bank standoff gone awry, they found themselves in an unprecedented situation. Sebring looked to other cities, like Parkland, Florida, which had overcome similar circumstances to help them cope with the tragedy.

As funerals were being planned Friday for the shooting victims, community leaders, clergy and others were realizing just how tough it was going to be to move forward and heal—and maybe look to forgive the accused shooter.

"There is a high level of people being on guard right now," said the Rev. George Miller of Emanuel United Church of Christ in Sebring. "And I don't think many people are used to that feeling of what it's like to be on guard and anxious."

And forgiveness? "Forgiveness takes a long time if we are to honestly forgive someone," Miller said.[12]

Seeking out answers, community members looked to cities that had suffered similar crises, including Orlando, which experienced a mass shooting at Pulse Nightclub, and Parkland, which had suffered a mass shooting at Stoneman Douglas High School in 2018.

As Parkland mayor Christine Hunschofsky said, "In a small, tight-knit community like Sebring, which is like ours in Parkland, it's not just a part of the city that's impacted. It's all-encompassing. When a tragedy hits a community it's so natural and easy to focus on everything that's wrong that it's very important to also look at what's right."

While nothing will make up for the loss of human life, Sebring's post-crisis analysis strategy of working with cities who had suffered similar circumstances no doubt helped them to cope with the shock and to examine ways of moving forward.

## *Reflecting on Augusta: A Virus Like No Other*

In late winter of 2020, the Covid-19 virus crossed the Pacific, hitting the nation like a scatter bomb. Beginning with just a few isolated cases in Washington State, the virus spread rapidly across the Rockies until, by the end of March, every state had succumbed to its clutches. A wave of panic, followed by mandatory shutdowns of non-essential businesses, effectively ended the late boom period of the 2010s. Unemployment, previously at historic lows, rose rapidly, increasing from 3.5 percent to 14.7 percent by May. Nowhere were these effects felt more than in small cities like Augusta.

## *Anticipating the "New Normal"*

The phrase "new normal" is perhaps the ugliest combination of words in the English language. A complete contradiction in

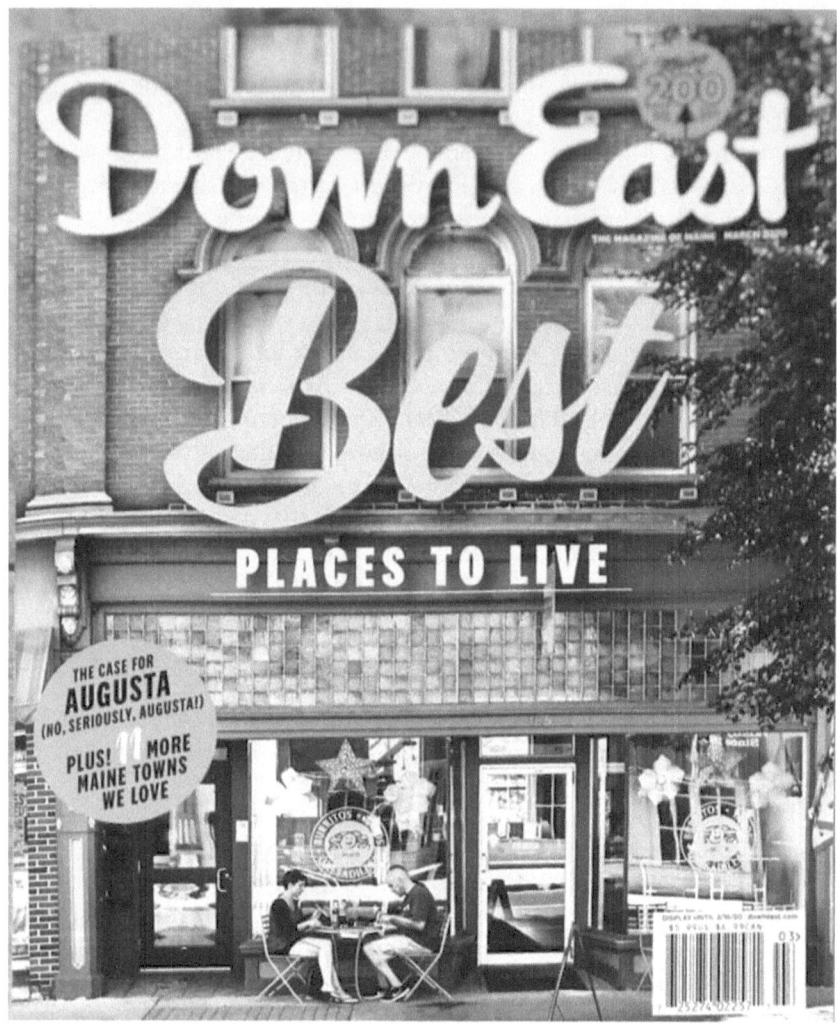

In March 2020, Augusta was featured on the cover of *Down East* magazine and recognized as one of the "Best Places to Live" in Maine due to its thriving downtown district. Less than two weeks after its publication, however, the Covid-19 pandemic shuttered the city (author's collection).

terms—for how can something that's normal be new?—the phrase is often thrown around loosely whenever something comes on without warning. For, Augusta, this new normal was unlike anything the city had been seen.

Just four days prior to March 18, the date when Maine's Governor Mills ordered the closure of dine-in for restaurants and bars, downtown

## 9. Leveraging the Unexpected    157

A sign outside a retail business in downtown Augusta reads "Apart But Still Together" during the 6.5 week statewide lockdown that barred indoor shopping (courtesy Dave Dostie).

Augusta was packed with revelers celebrating the upcoming St. Patrick's Day holiday. By March 16, however, rumors of an impending lockdown over a rise in coronavirus cases had gotten out and the damage was swift. Downtown had become a ghost town. Fortunately, however, civic and downtown leaders were two steps ahead.

Two days before the governor issued her own declaration of emergency, representatives from the City of Augusta and the Augusta Downtown Alliance (Alliance) converged in a downtown coffee shop to discuss the future. Knowing that a mandated declaration was only days away and not content to sit on the sidelines and wait, it was determined that a prudent course of action would be followed by having the city preempt the order and issue their own declaration. What followed was an order largely based on CDC guidelines that included the following addendums:

- Limits to 50 people or less for gatherings
- Restrictions to in-house dining, with takeout and delivery encouraged
- Allowance for pre-packaged beer/wine/liquor sales and delivery

Following the meeting, the message was spread quickly to each business owner, with the explanation that the city's decisive action would give them more leverage in discussions with the governor prior to her own order. While politically dicey, the move worked.

When, in fact, the governor's declaration went into effect two days later, no business owner could say they were shocked. The order delivered was a mirror image of the one issued by Augusta and even included pre-packaged beer/wine/liquor deliveries (later to be expanded to cocktails) for good measure. All of this was no doubt a direct nod to the city's initial implementation. More importantly, it bought business owners valuable time to adapt and transition. This, however, was just the first step.

## Creating a Plan and Testing It

No city—or country for that matter—had a plan for Covid-19. It came on so fast that there really was no way to plan for it. Nevertheless, the Augusta Downtown Alliance had funds in reserve for emergency situations. As a result, it was able to continue functioning. These reserved

Downtown Augusta was a virtual ghost town during the first week of the Covid-19 pandemic. As time went on, however, businesses shifted strategies and began to lure visitors back (courtesy Keith Luke).

funds were something that was implemented by the Board of Directors just in case things went south during a particular year and proved incredibly helpful throughout the crisis. In addition, the Board had voted on a conservative budget with specific items that were line-itemed and others that were a bit softer. This allowed for some fluidity in how non-allocated funds were spent.

## Communicating the Message

Immediately following the state's declaration, downtown business owners found themselves in a two-fold scenario: adapt or die.

Deprived of in-house diners, downtown restaurants made the tough decision to reduce staff, limit liquor orders and rebrand their menus. Rising to the occasion, many adjusted swiftly, but the customers did not. That's when the Alliance stepped in.

Forming a direct line of communication between the city, the state, and the Alliance, we made ourselves accessible through social media, via phone, and through in-person visits to businesses so that we could pass along any of the latest updates and answer any questions regarding quarantine restriction phases, upcoming funding opportunities and ways to support one another. This also extended to the Board level, through emails.

In terms of tasks, one of the first major things the Alliance did was to gather information from each of the restaurants and create a marketing campaign. This campaign featured a simple graphic showcasing all restaurants participating in delivery/takeout in the downtown area followed by their contact information. Within hours of posting, the resulting graphic had a reach of over 6,500 people with 55 shares from the Alliance home page alone. Orders to restaurants went up and overnight delivery and takeout orders became more profitable. This was just the tip of the iceberg, however, as we went all out on communication.

## Taking Charge of the Situation

As we saw from some of the samples included above, the federal government is often slow to respond to disasters, particularly in the more rural communities. This is why the Alliance took an aggressive stance on getting money out to the people in as fast as a manner as possible. This was done in the first week of the CARES Act (the bill passed by Congress to ease the burden of financially strained merchants) by helping business owners navigate the complications of Payment Protection and EIDL, by inviting them into the office to fill it out for them and walk them through any of the other options that were made available.

Applying on behalf of more than a half a dozen businesses, the Alliance managed to secure roughly $60,000 in forgivable loans for Water Street merchants. Nevertheless, it soon became apparent that these federal funds would be slow in coming and that if anything were going to be done in the immediate future, help would have to come from the Alliance itself.

Not content to sit on the sidelines, the Augusta Downtown Alliance swept into action to establish their own form of relief with the Kennebec Valley Downtown Relief Fund. Partnering with Gardiner Main Street, their counterpart located just seven miles downriver, both organizations designed a grant, borrowing $4,500 from non-allocated items within their respective budgets. From that initial $9,000 seed, both partners worked together to aggressively campaign for matching donations from both their communities, as well as from private entities. Within ten days, they had raised over $50,000.

Establishing an application process, a committee was assembled, needs assessed, and checks distributed. Twenty businesses in all received aid by the time all was said and done, with checks ranging up to $3000, covering everything from payroll to rent.

By taking action and not waiting for federal action, the Alliance was able to keep businesses afloat and fulfill the sixth principle of BBN International's seven steps of crisis management: not relying on outside intervention to solve our issues.

## *Analyzing What's Working*

Perhaps one of the main things the Augusta Downtown Alliance did in the wake of the shutdowns was analyze what other communities were doing to stave off closures and help restaurants address the new restrictions, which included:

- Mandatory masks for all servers
- Plastic guards for all bar areas
- Contact tracing for customers (requiring name and phone numbers)
- Reduced dine-in capacity
- Six-foot distancing between tables

Fortunately there were templates from other cities on how to move forward. Borrowing an idea from restaurants that had recently reopened in Europe, city officials from Augusta presented the idea of parklets, or outdoor dining spaces, to members of the Augusta Downtown Alliance for review. These parklets would allow for restaurants to expand their seating onto sidewalks, parking spaces and roadways to help with social distancing while increasing seating capacity.

After gauging support from the business community, the Alliance worked with members of city council to add this measure to the agenda, getting participating restaurants the prerequisite forms so that they could expand their seating outdoors. Two restaurants actually chose parklets in parking spaces, while two others were fast-tracked permission to utilize road and sidewalk space.

While supporting small businesses through the restrictions process was part of the Alliance's post-crisis analysis, it was by no means the only way it sought to gain leverage over Covid-19. From the outset, members of the Alliance forged positive feelings by becoming more community focused. Turning their thoughts outside their geographic limitations, members of the organization began to advertise window space by celebrating graduates of the Class of 2020. This campaign launched with great fanfare, and within a week, dozens of posters were dropped off and distributed across the downtown, eliciting increased traffic from curious parents and students alike.

In addition, the Alliance sought to increase comfort and positivity in the community by sending out press releases regarding new residential construction, as well as new building sales and business interests. They even recorded a PSA for the local radio station that ran throughout the eight weeks of lockdown announcing that downtown was open for business.

Lastly, the Augusta Downtown Alliance focused on a business-as-usual approach, mimicked in other communities, emphasizing decorative elements such as American flags and flower arrangements, and even going so far as to release drone footage of a vital downtown. All of this had the effect of convincing the public that despite everything negative, the center of the city was still very much alive.

## *Shawn McLaughlin and Dealing with Crises*

Shawn McLaughlin knows a thing or two about the restaurant and bar industry. He also knows a thing or two about dealing with a crisis.

Having grown up in Medford, Massachusetts, Shawn moved to

Maine in 2013 and within a couple of years had networked himself into Cellardoor Winery, where he oversaw a build-out of their second location in Portland. He then managed the place for six months before becoming the Vice President of Sales and Operations at neighboring Stroudwater Distillery.

Moving to downtown Augusta in 2017 with his fiancée and future wife, Soo Parkhurst, Shawn was at first not keen on the move. "I didn't really see it for what it was at the time," he recalls. "But then, after living here for a bit, I began to become involved with the downtown more and I saw how the city was on the rise and trying to reinvent itself. I began to see its potential."

Working with the partners from Cushnoc Brewing Co., Shawn opened his own downtown gastropub called State Lunch in 2020.

"I wanted to take my bartending experience and open a place that the community could benefit from," he said. "I wanted to fill the gap and provide the kind of experience I was used to in Boston and Portland."

Shawn McLaughlin opened his restaurant, State Lunch, just 19 days before a statewide lockdown barred indoor dining (courtesy Dave Dostie).

Defining a gastropub as a place that focuses equal parts on cocktails, food and atmosphere, Shawn's gamble paid off and the place proved an instant hit with the public, with wait times out the door. Then, 19 days after opening, Covid-19 hit, and the state was locked down.

"I can't tell you what the feeling was like," Shawn said. "It was devastating. For the first five minutes, I can't even tell you the thoughts that went through my mind. But then, I pulled myself together and decided to rise above it."

Shifting his model from upscale pub fare to to-go orders, deliveries, cocktail mixes and family-style platters, Shawn retrained his wait staff and went to work. "Augusta was so great to us when we opened, and I wanted to be there for them and provide a sense of normalcy during their tough times. Once again, Augusta didn't disappoint. They supported us in so many ways. They ordered food, they stopped by to chat, and they bought gift cards. The amount of community support I received was overwhelming. It solidified my thinking in that I made the right choice to invest here."

Reflecting on the community impact, he said: "I've lived in big cities and compared to what I've got here, it's just not the same. Here, I feel like the whole city is rooting for you to win. There's no competition, just support."

He continued: "My advice to anyone in an emergency situation is to be open-minded enough to adapt and pivot. My philosophy is 'evolve or die.' You are responsible for yourself in this life and you can't blame outside things for your failures or shortcomings.

"I think small cities can definitely replicate the urban experience. I do it every day in my own little way. Augusta is exciting because we're doing something really special here. We have the opportunity to make it into something incredible and the people in Augusta have balls. Heather, Andrew, Tobias—they all have made an impact and from day one I've been impressed on what they done for this place to make it better. This place works because it's a slow organic build rather than a pre-designed one. The people adding to this community live and work here and care about it as opposed to the money. It's a pretty great thing."[13]

## Key Takeaways

The following are some of key takeaways from this chapter:

- Small communities are at a disadvantage when it comes to disaster situations.
- Small communities have resources available in dealing with disasters but need to utilize them effectively.
- The key to utilizing the resources at hand are emergency preparedness and emergency action.
- The seven crisis management steps are crucial in an emergency situation.
- Cities that mitigate disaster effectively follow the seven crisis management steps which include: anticipating an outcome; setting up a communications team; establishing a communications network; communicating a message; self-reliance; and establishing a post-crisis analysis to examine what's worked in other communities who have dealt with similar situations in order to adapt them to your situation.

## *Conclusion*

"I always tried to turn every disaster into an opportunity."—Nelson Rockefeller

Unexpected situations are a part of life, and any leader of a community organization needs to be prepared on how to deal with them. This is particularly true in small communities where outside aid is neither swift nor forthcoming.

By properly leveraging the unexpected, an organization can not only mitigate the lasting ramifications of a disaster but also help can retain trust in their leadership. Remember, small cities work differently than their larger counterparts, which are often among the first to receive aid packages, and while not all of them have gigantic resources readily available, they are anything but helpless. Volunteers, community members, church groups, civic leaders and more are all at your disposal and will pitch in, in the event of any emergency. The trick is to anticipate, take action, and communicate effectively throughout. In every emergency situation, there lies an opportunity for learning and growth, and if handled properly, an effective response to a disaster can ensure that your community reemerges stronger than it was before.

# 10

# Avoid the Three Deadly Fallacies of Urban Planning

There is a fairly common argument made relating to downtown revitalization that goes something along the lines of this: "I support the efforts you're doing, but before we spend any money improving the area, we have to give people a reason to come down. There needs to be a draw." I myself have heard this multiple times in Augusta City Council meetings and every time I have, I shake my head in amusement.

On the surface, an argument like this seems sensible, even logical. It's a "build it and they will come" approach. When you dig a little deeper, however, you begin to pick apart the logical flaws. For how can you create a draw without first investing in the area to make it attractive enough to support that draw? This is an example of fallacy.

So how do we define fallacies?

In the strictest and classical form, a fallacy represents an error in logic. All of the arguments that are guilty of that error may be said to be *instances* of that fallacy, so fallacies are generally considered to be *types* of arguments.

> However, there is a growing movement among modern students of fallacy to consider fallacies, not as errors in a single argument, but as illegitimate moves in the broader context of a dialectical discussion. Aristotle himself seems to support this view, referring to his examples of bad reasoning as "elenchoi" or *refutations* rather than as arguments.[1]

When it comes to revitalizing communities, arguments regarding correct approaches often evoke fallacies of many kinds. While there are many that can be presented, we'll focus on three of the most common ones below.

## Building for Drivers: The Fallacy of Not Enough Parking Downtown

How many times have you ever heard someone say one of the following? "I was going to go to Target, but there's just not enough parking." Or "I have tickets to go see the Patriots, but I think I'll stay home because of parking." Or even "I really want to go to the movies, but the parking is terrible." Chances are you haven't heard any of these statements.

Now, how many times have you heard the following statements? "There's just no parking downtown." Or "Downtown needs to add more parking." Or even "Nothing could ever be done downtown until we get the parking in order." Chances are you hear it all the time. Why? Because our suburban culture tells us this is so.

As a society we have become so accustomed to large-scale parking lots with 300 spaces or more that we often don't blink an eye walking the equivalent of a block or two to get to our destination. Try this in a downtown area, however, and we complain loudly on Facebook about how terrible it is to park.

In these times, there is a cognitive disconnect between the suburban shopping experience and the downtown experience. Most sane people would never expect to find a space right next to a Walmart or grocery store during peak hours but somehow expect to park in front of their downtown destination every time regardless of the hour. All too often city leaders fall for the trope of "not enough parking" and seek to overcompensate by adding suburban style parking plans to their revitalization efforts. Their logic seemingly goes: if we build more parking, more people will come.

At first glance, it seems logical enough. Why not make downtown more accessible to those with cars? But ask yourself this: have you ever gone out of your way to go somewhere because the parking was good? We do not say, for example, "I really want to go this restaurant because they have a huge parking lot." The fact is that parking is an excuse, not a source of the problems, particularly for downtowns. Small cities are by no means immune to it, either. The Laberge Group actually breaks these parking misconceptions down into five common myths and realities, which I'll paraphrase below:

> **MYTH**: People hate walking.
> **REALITY**: People will park where parking is provided, particularly if there is adequate signage and lighting.
> **MYTH**: Parking should be free.

## 10. Avoid the Three Deadly Fallacies of Urban Planning    167

**REALITY:** Everyone already pays for parking, they just don't know it. The costs for parking are factored into everything from rents, lease fees, sale prices and taxes. These expenses are passed on from developers to merchants and finally to the consumer. Because of this, there is nothing wrong with charging for parking through metered system.
**MYTH:** It's hard to find parking downtown.
**REALITY:** Almost all parking problems are perception-based and can be resolved through good direction and signage.
**MYTH:** Parking should be equally available to everyone.
**REALITY:** Segmented parking is a must for a successful downtown. Customers and shoppers should have the highest priority, while visitors, residents, office workers and business owners—especially business owners—should park the farthest away.
**MYTH:** A parking problem is a bad thing.
**REALITY:** Parking problems in your downtown are actually indicative of a healthy business environment. It shows that your area is in demand and popular with consumers.

The truth of the matter is that downtown parking, more than anything else, is a perception problem rather than an actual problem. Adding more parking by erecting huge parking spaces doesn't make your downtown more accessible to motorists, but it does makes it less attractive. As with everything else, there needs to be a balance applied when dealing with parking.

## Nevada City: A Case for Meters and Meter Hikes

One of the biggest myths around parking (and one that is addressed above) is how parking should be free and open to anyone, and that by charging for parking, you are deterring traffic away from your downtown. This is a fallacy.

In his book *The High Cost of Free Parking*, economist Donald Shoup argues that free parking is not only a bad idea as it encourages cars to cruise for limited spaces, but also costs cities money. He estimates that parking spaces cost an average of $1,750 to build and $400 to maintain. Annual free parking subsidies can cost up to $127 billion nationally.[2] In addition, he found that free parking stimulates car-based development that economically injures the poor, as it's the poor who are least likely to have access to a vehicle, yet will remain on the hook for budget shortfalls related to parking that cause hikes in property taxes, sales taxes, etc. His research also showed that free parking actually has a zero net effect on the business environment. His suggestion: install meters and charge fairly and accordingly for what the spaces are worth, then deploy those funds raised for the public benefit.

This is something the small community of Nevada City, California (pop. 3,000) took to heart. Located in northern California, roughly 60 miles northeast of Sacramento and 84 miles southwest of Reno, the city is a playground for tourists, who use it as a base for recreation in the nearby Tahoe National Forest, South Yuba River and the Sierra Mountains. Because of this, their main commercial district is often prone to parking demand. Yet, even with metered parking, the city found issues, primarily with the revenue (or lack thereof) being generated from 25-cent meters—which was why the city council took decisive action in 2019 to increase parking fees.

> "It was the first cost increase in decades, if ever," said Erin Minett, a recently elected city council member who pushed for the increase. People used to come to the city and laugh—"Oh, it's only 25 cents, how cute!" she said. (Even the city's website advertises the remarkably cheap meters: "What a bargain! Bring change with you when you visit us!")[3]

Raising the price of the city's 237 parking meters from 25 cents to a dollar was more than just economical, it was downright crucial for survival. The $10,000 a month being generated by the meters proved too little to cover the salaries of the public employees managing them, and the city was in constant shortfall for funding. Furthermore, because the pricing was so cheap, office workers and employees of businesses were known to abuse the system and take up all the critical spaces in front of their shops during shift hours—to the detriment of the city's tourists. Many in the downtown area recalled how they would simply continue to feed the meter.

Dan Strawser, a city councilor who had long advocated for free parking, was initially opposed to the price raise because the larger neighboring community of Grass Valley had free parking and seemed to be operating fine without any fees. This changed, however, when Grass Valley began installing meters:

> "At that point, I lost my next-door neighbor example," he said. So when Nevada City's city council voted to raise rates, Strawser had a considerable change of heart. He was the one who actually pushed for the dollar amount—double the 50 cents that the city's department of public works initially asked for, and still more than the 75 cents that Minett had thought wise.
>
> Other leaders were pleased. "I've always thought we do not charge enough," another council member, Valerie Moberg, told a local newspaper. And Minett sees the meter hikes as a win-win for the city and citizens, in that they'll help save lives in case of fire and free up space downtown. "I want Nevada City to stay sweet, but also keep up with the times," she said. "I thought this was a two-fer."[4]

To really drive the message home that the fees were more than just another cash grab by the city, city leaders attached a proviso to the rate hike designating that a percentage of funding go towards efforts to fight wildfires. Being one of 188 communities in California listed for extreme wildfire danger, such an effort hit home for many of the residents, particularly since Paradise, another mountain community, had suffered terribly during a previous wildfire outbreak.

> Of the estimated $550,000 a year that the new parking rates will generate, 20 percent will pay to clear flammable undergrowth, Minett said, and for an emergency siren at city hall to help people evacuate. Minett hopes that attaching a concrete social objective to the rate hikes is enough to stave off too much controversy. Nevada City has been applying for state grants to suppress wildfire risk, but it's too small to qualify for many of them.[5]

As of 2020, the hikes have been fully implemented, and while temporarily suspended in June due to Covid-19, they went back into effect in July. The city expects an 800 percent increase in funding over 2019.

## Building for Urbanism: The Case Against Planned Development

In the spring of 1979, a low-budget film called *Over the Edge* was released and later pulled from a handful of theaters because of the fear of mass rioting. Focusing on youth run amok, the film centers on a group of teenagers who turn to drugs, theft and petty acts of vandalism to escape the doldrums of small-city life. The film climaxes in a crescendo of violence once one of their own is unwittingly killed by a police officer, ultimately putting the neglectful adults in the community at risk.

What makes *Over the Edge* such a great movie is not the plot so much (although the plot is interesting in and of itself) but rather the setting that drives it. For the small city in which it takes place is not just any ordinary city, but rather a master-planned community—a town built to mimic the conveniences of city, with mixed use principles of houses, apartments and condos. This mixed use is completely development-driven and fairly isolated, leading to many of the issues witnessed later in the film. It also happens to be a perfect allegory for some of the flaws that would later define new urbanism.

### *The Issue with New Urbanism*

In the late 1970s and early 1980s, the middle class in the United States was still firmly entrenched in suburbs. With cities in decay and crime rates peaking nationwide, the suburbs offered salvation for urban dwellers seeking safe and family-oriented neighborhoods.

The rise of manicured office parks and elaborate shopping centers helped spur this drive, as commuters no longer had to leave their neighborhoods to trek into downtowns for shopping, working, or daily convenience needs. As a result, cities continued their decline due to lost tax revenues while suburbs continued to grow. It was during this period that a hybrid model combining the best of suburban and urban elements began to grow in popularity among urban planners. This model would eventually give birth to the New Urbanist movement of the 1990s.

Founded in 1993, the Congress of New Urbanism defined their intentions by stating:

> We advocate the restructuring of public policy and development practices to support the following principles: neighborhoods should be diverse in use and population; communities should be designed for the pedestrian and transit as well as the car; cities and towns should be shaped by physically defined and universally accessible public spaces and community institutions; urban places should be framed by architecture and landscape design that celebrate local history, climate, ecology, and building practice.[6]

Spreading these principles across the country, new urbanist communities soon began popping up in Colorado, Florida, and Maryland among other places, and while many of these communities outwardly showcased the elements of a city, few if any actually realized them, often falling far short of occupancy hopes. As Arian Horbovetz ponders:

> So why are these new developments so often unoccupied? Typically the apartment spaces go quickly, but the retail spaces on the ground floor often struggle mightily to find tenants... [There are] a number of key reasons for these vacancies, including issues of scale, motives, and the desire to lure chains instead of unique local businesses and establishments.[7]

Horbovetz goes on to state that another reason for New Urbanist communities often appearing inhospitable is because it tries too hard at being urban. Urbanity is not something that exists in an island form. It needs connectivity to other areas of density and walkability to make it thrive. Manufacturing that construct goes against the principles of what urbanism is. As he goes on to write.

> Urbanism, at its core, is connective and fluid, creating places where people want to be, not simply via neighborhood revitalization, but by blending that localized revitalization seamlessly into the surrounding area. There must be a sort of "transition" from one area to the next that guides the resident or visitor gently, instead of assuming that a large-scale new-urbanist creation can suddenly spur arteries of growth in inhospitable urban deserts.[8]

Historic Tax Credit projects such as the one taking place at 341 Water Street represent a more sustainable way to develop responsibly (author's collection).

Horbovetz's critiques of new urbanism are hardly unique. In fact, new urbanist city centers have been compared to "ghost towns" or even "shopping malls masquerading as cities." As Michael Sorkin wrote in the September 1998 issue of *Metropolis* magazine, "New Urbanism reproduces many of the worst aspects of the Modernism it seeks to replace ... [It] promotes another style of universality that is similarly overreliant on visual cues to produce social effects."[9]

## New London's Not-So-New Urbanist Scheme

While New Urbanist principles have more often straddled the line between suburbia and urbanity, there are some cases where they have influenced the development of small cities. One such example can be found in the port city of New London, Connecticut (pop. 27,000), which suffered disastrous consequences in attempting to build a mixed-use development.

The whole situation started when the New London Development Corporation (NLDC) was revived and successfully lobbied Pfizer to expand a $300 million research facility on the site of an old factory. This proved a major victory for the city, with Gov. Rowland himself announcing at the groundbreaking ceremony, "Years from now, this will be a case study in how to revive a community."[10]

The project was built, but the NLDC didn't stop there, for adjacent to the new facility was a neighborhood known to locals as "The Fort," a hodgepodge of nineteenth century Victorian homes that was aged, but hardly derelict. Claire Gaudini, who was running the NLDC at the time, decided to double down on the investment and redevelop all 90 acres adjoining Pfizer. The redevelopment would feature condos, apartments, a conference center and retail. There was just one catch: "The Fort" had to go.

To gain access to the homes, the city authorized the NLDC to use eminent domain to condemn and acquire the properties from those who refused to sell. Most of the 90 or so property owners—of about 115 homes and two dozen small businesses—did sell, but seven owners, who controlled 15 properties, held out. They were subject to unconscionable harassment by real estate people, but they hung on.[11]

Acquiring a lawyer, the holdouts took the NLDC to the Superior Court, then the state Supreme Court and ultimately the U.S. Supreme Court. The court rendered a 5–4 decision in favor of the NLDC, however, and the neighborhood was demolished.

While that might have been the end of the story, it was just the beginning of the tragedy, as years of court wranglings and negative press had basically rendered the NLDC as toxic. Funders for the project were scared off, and Pfizer, which was supposed to be the heart of this new development community, soon suffered a merger. The Great

## 10. Avoid the Three Deadly Fallacies of Urban Planning 173

Recession came in the following year, and Pfizer abandoned its facility. The site continues to sit empty, although there have been murmurings of renewed push for development. What was lost, though, is far greater than what will ever be gained.

"There were 90 acres. People lived on 10 acres. It would have been easy to develop around them. That's all we ever wanted," said Prof. Fred Paxton, a Connecticut College history professor who was a member of the Coalition to Save Fort Trumbull, one of two groups that tried to save the neighborhood. Indeed, well-regarded Waterford architect John Steffian drew up plans that would have redeveloped the area without sacrificing the neighborhood.[12]

Although New London's case is extreme and toes the line between urban renewal and New Urbanism, the mixed-use principles proposed borrowed heavily from New Urbanism and represent an example of development gone amuck. New Urbanism, in theory, is not bad, and there are certainly cases where these principles have actually added to a city's character. Overall, however, the danger of New Urbanism is that, as in New London, New Urbanism cares more about creating something new than enhancing something old, thereby violating the sacred notion of what makes development work: authenticity.

### *Building for Walkers: The Fallacy of Pedestrian Malls*

What's the cheapest and most convenient form of transportation a small community can adopt? Why, walking, of course! And while we can all agree that walking to the nearest daily conveniences is the ultimate urban experience, there is a right way and a wrong way to go about replicating such an experience for your community. One such wrong way is through the introduction of pedestrian malls.

So, what are they exactly? Pedestrian malls are essentially streets in retail districts that are closed off to traffic. Ironically enough, it was Victor Gruen, who was famous for popularizing the suburban shopping center, who championed the cause of the pedestrian mall in the mid–1950s. His first experiment came to light in 1959 in Kalamazoo, Michigan, at the height of the suburban craze. The concept proved immediately popular as "cities saw Gruen's concept as a cheap and quick fix that would lure suburbanites and their dollars back downtown."[13]

The pedestrian mall movement gained traction throughout the 1960s and 1970s, becoming a staple for urban planners. Unfortunately, it did not have the desired result. While those pedestrian malls opening around the country garnered plenty of media attention, they did little to inspire suburban shoppers, who failed to return to the cities. Even with stereotypical shopping mall improvements, such as fountains, benches and new lighting, shoppers simply ignored the hassle. As vacancy rates soared and once thriving businesses moved out, pedestrian malls soon became gathering places for vagrants, forcing many of the malls to revert to traffic.

While there is an ample amount of literature devoted to the failure of pedestrian malls, there have indeed been places where they have succeeded. In a report published by the Downtown Fresno Partnership, which worked diligently to reopen the city's Fulton Mall back to traffic, they found that:

- Pedestrian malls in the United States have an 89 percent rate of failure. Most have been removed or repurposed. Only 11 percent have been successful.
- Of the 11 percent successful pedestrian malls, 80 percent are in areas with populations under 100,000.
- Certain indicators need to be present for a pedestrian mall to be successful in the United States:
    ◊ Attached to a major anchor such as a university (e.g., Boulder)
    ◊ Situated in close proximity to a beach (e.g., Miami, Santa Monica)
    ◊ Designed to be a short length in terms of blocks (1–4 blocks long)
    ◊ Located in a community with a population under 100,000 (e.g., New Bedford, Massachusetts)
    ◊ Located in a major tourist destination (e.g., Las Vegas, New Orleans)
- Cities that have transformed their abandoned pedestrian malls into "complete" main streets have experienced turnarounds in their downtowns, with more investment, higher occupancy rates and more pedestrian traffic. Ninety percent of these cities see significant improvements in occupancy rates, retail sales, property values, and private sector investment in the downtown area when streets are restored.

At its height, there were over 200 pedestrian malls in the United States, but today, fewer than two dozen remain. Those that have managed to survive have fulfilled many of the necessary criteria outlined above. Even so, the criteria do not ensure a slam dunk, as evidenced by the fate of Main Mall in Poughkeepsie, which, despite being near Vassar College, was converted back to traffic in 2001.

All knowledge to the contrary, many cities continue to flirt with pedestrian malls. In fact, during the Covid-19 pandemic, there has been an uptick in street conversions from centers of vehicular traffic to ones for pedestrian use only. While not called pedestrian malls, but rather "open streets," they are essentially the same concept repackaged, and just like the previous generations of pedestrian malls before them, they are not off to a great start. In New York City, for example, Mayor Bill de Blasio promised 100 miles of "open streets" to provide social distancing easements, but what resulted was a logistical nightmare leading to traffic congestion and inequitable divisions among neighborhoods. A report from Transportation Alternative found that:

> At present, the program remains a disconnected network of public space islands with management challenges. While pocket parks and outdoor restaurants are helpful, they will not solve our transportation crisis or revive our economy. These should be finishing touches on top of a connected system to keep New York moving—not New York City's small answer to a giant problem.[14]

In addition, the report also found that Open Streets had short-changed cyclists, with just 7.88 miles, or 44 percent, of the proposed 18.07 miles of "pop-up" bike lanes being implemented. Manhattan received a disproportionate 54 percent of "pop-up" bike lane mileage despite already being the borough with the most bike lanes.[15]

With such a history of failure, it thus becomes baffling why any city leader would choose to follow this path. But alas, humans are creatures of habit, and as we will see from the sample below, panic often trumps rationality and logic.

## *Rockland Experiments Through Panic*

Albert Einstein is often misquoted as having said, "Insanity is doing the same thing over and over again and expecting different results." While he might not have said it—the saying actually comes from a 1983 mystery novel called *Sudden Death*—the message rings true: when you expect different outcomes from things that are obvious failures, you have already defeated the point of trying. So, it rings true for the small city of Rockland, Maine (pop. 7,000), which, in 2020, attempted to mimic the tried-and-often-failed concept of a pedestrian mall.

Located along Maine's rocky Midcoast, Rockland is a pretty idyllic city. A traditional community of lobstermen, with a high percentage of artists, Rockland has increasingly relied on tourists each summer to drive its economy. With the onset of the Covid-19 pandemic, however, and the restrictions imposed by the State on gatherings in indoor dining and retail spaces, Rockland was forced to rethink its traditional strategy and come up with out-of-the-box solutions to draw more people into its city center. Unfortunately, the solution the city council proposed was a pedestrian mall.

> The proposal has been compared to a traffic closure on Church Street in Burlington, Vermont, now a popular pedestrian mall, as well as pedestrian spaces in bigger cities. Rockland officials and Gov. Janet Mills last week said it could be a model for other towns and cities in the state, as a way to encourage shopping while allowing social distancing and health protocols.[16]

As their Rockland City Manager, Tom Luttrel, stated:

> We're trying to really work together [with downtown stakeholders.] It's basically been many meetings over Zoom trying to figure out what will work and what won't work. We just want to make sure that our downtown businesses, or any businesses in Rockland, stay afloat. We don't want to see all of our restaurants boarded up because their staff doesn't feel safe serving inside, or they can only do every other table.[17]

Buoyed by a sense of hope, Rockland proceeded with the plans, with the encouragement of others, including the state and various nonprofits. Two councilors were so sure of its success that they predicted lasting impacts:

> "This is a once-in-a-generation opportunity, not just for Main Street in Rockland, to try to re-envision aspects of how society is constructed," said Councilor Nate Davis. "It's not an exotic idea at all. Maybe it's an exotic idea for Maine, but it's happening all over the world."
>
> Councilor Valli Geiger, too, said the decision could be something for "the long haul" that would change Rockland "in a good way," including reworking how downtown businesses take deliveries and more, and shifting the focus from car traffic to people.[18]

While the proposal initially called for the closing of Main Street for the entire summer, cooler heads prevailed, and it was agreed that it would try the experiment for two weekends in June and take it from there. So how did it work out, you ask? In a word: *catastrophe*.

The first weekend of the closure saw near-perfect weather. The city encouraged entertainment and children's activities, and notices were put out showing proper places to park. The anticipated crowds, however, never materialized, minus a group of protestors who quickly took over the street. As the *Bangor Daily News* reported:

> More than 100 protesters, most dressed in black and wearing facemasks, filled the roadway in observance of Juneteenth, the anniversary of the last slaves learning of their emancipation after the Civil War. The gathering,

## 10. Avoid the Three Deadly Fallacies of Urban Planning

organized by Angela McIntyre, alternated between silent vigil and impassioned protest.[19]

The resulting spectacle of protests, alongside a mostly empty street, left Rockland wondering if the city would see a repeat the second weekend. Unfortunately, it did. While there were no protests the second time around, there were even fewer people than before and even fewer restaurants participating in the concept. As reported:

> Rockland was one of the first cities in Maine to announce a bold plan that would close its Main Street to traffic for the entire summer.
>
> However, that idea fell flat on two trial weekends in June, with only a few restaurants setting up outdoor dining areas on the sidewalks and beyond while the street was shut down. Additionally, the idea to close the street for the entire summer worried business owners who rely on getting deliveries on busy Route 1.[20]

So other than the obvious, why was Rockland's experiment such a failure?

Rockland's trial failed for five key reasons:

1. **The plan was hastily rushed through with poor comparative examples.**
   With councilors citing Burlington, Vermont, and Charlottesville, Virginia, among others, as comparative examples of small cities with successful pedestrian malls, they completely glossed over the fact that these were college cities and had readily available populations of students to draw upon.

2. **City officials failed to appeal to locals.**
   City officials hoped that, by shutting things down, they could effectively draw upon and reinvigorate a tourist population. Unfortunately, with no tourists present, all they had to rely upon were locals, who, more often than not, could not afford the inflated prices of food and retail in the city center

3. **City officials failed to convince downtown merchants of their plan.**
   In their haste to look action-oriented, city officials glossed over what downtown merchants wanted, not considering their needs, and ignoring their concerns. As a result, their plan was less than convincing, and retailers never got fully behind it.

4. **City officials failed to consult any urban planners.**
   Any serious undertaking in a community requires proper consideration. Such consideration is found through research and

expert opinions, especially when dealing with the livelihoods of a business community. A quick run-through with an urban planner or two would've shown them the folly of this scheme.

**5. Overconfidence.**
It's one thing to be confident that your plan will work. It's quite another to say it's a "once-in-a-generation opportunity,"[21] especially when none of the above issues were addressed from the outset. As we've said before, there is no silver bullet to small city revitalization, so confidence in your methods should be maintained, but also tempered.

## *Nancy Smith on Finding Balance Through Smart Growth*

Nancy Smith knows a lot about improving an urban landscape with the use of balance. As Executive Director of GrowSmart Maine, she sees the application of smart growth principles as essential to the health of a community.

Joining GrowSmart ten years ago, she has connected her decades of experience as a farmer and a forester to include eight years in the Maine legislature. Her role at GrowSmart includes advocacy and public events to help Maine communities build lasting prosperity while keeping what they love about their hometowns and neighborhoods.

"I have worked in forestry and farming most of my professional life, in northern and Central Maine," Smith says. "With that background, I served eight years in the Maine Legislature, representing rural businesses in both the business and agriculture committees. I did not come to GrowSmart Maine from the planning sector, instead I brought an appreciation for the value of accommodating growth and change while keeping what we all love about Maine, intact."

Nancy continues, "GrowSmart Maine and our allied organizations fill a void between what the private sector and government sector can do. We provide fundamental support that is often a few degrees of separation from tangible outcomes, but these educational resources, advocacy, and mission-driven events connect Mainers to people and ideas that inspire and support their community work."

An independent 501c3, GrowSmart Maine encourages cities to preserve and adapt what's in place in order to grow. As it states on their website, smart growth provides choices in how communities respond to growth and change by:

## 10. Avoid the Three Deadly Fallacies of Urban Planning   179

Nancy Smith is the Executive Director for GrowSmart Maine and advocates for intelligent, sustainable development in Maine's cities (courtesy Dave Dostie).

- Working to revitalize historic neighborhoods and vibrant communities suited for residents of all ages, to foster entrepreneurs and creative thinkers, and to provide a safe and inclusive place to raise children.
- Advocating for policies and projects that advance Maine's business and economic growth and development in balance

with the conservation and enrichment of our greatest assets: the beautiful and productive built and natural environments that are the bedrock of our cultural and economic heritage.
- Supporting the continuation of traditional livelihoods like fishing, farming and forestry; keeping Maine families working their heritage and making it possible for their children to do the same.
- Providing leadership by convening a broad range of voices in meaningful conversations on how to arrive at common-sense solutions as united Mainers.

One of the successes GrowSmart Maine is most proud of is its successes with encouraging the use Historic Rehabilitation Tax Credits in small communities.

"What the Federal and Maine State Historic Rehabilitation Tax Credit (HRTC) programs do is encourage reinvestment in our communities by incentivizing the rehabilitation and re-use of historic buildings for commercial purposes. These credits are intended to spur investment in communities throughout our state by creating jobs and helping cover qualifying costs related to bringing new life to these buildings," she said.

Nancy states that the advantages and benefits of the HRTC are many, citing:

- It is a critical tool for downtown revitalization as many of these historic buildings are situated in our downtowns;
- The preservation and adaptive use of historic buildings is vitally important to preserving Maine's unique quality of place, in turn attracting residents and tourists to Maine and strengthening our economy;
- Continued access to the HRTC affirms predictable business regulation;
- Continued use of the HRTC has positive climate impacts through the reuse of building materials. Offsetting the need to manufacture new building materials makes use of these buildings' embodied energy, representing a significant measure of efficiency and carbon sequestration.

She also cites the program's economic successes, referencing data compiled by the Maine Historic Preservation Commission that states that since the inception of the State's HRTC in 2008, more than 100 projects have been completed totaling construction costs of almost $556 million, with an increased municipal assessment value of more than $160 million.

"Smart growth is really about providing the choices in how

communities respond to growth and change. We do our work with the goal of ensuring future generations can also prosper while calling Maine home. Specific strategies incorporate land use and social issues such as housing, transportation, open space, predictable and effective regulations that foster a sense of community," she said. "We all see growth patterns that diminish rather than enhance quality of life. When people have to 'drive to qualify' to find housing near their work, or when a community has lost equitable access to recreational and productive open space, then bad policy decisions have accommodated sprawling development. This is why growing our communities the right way is so important."[22]

## Key Takeaways

Some of the key takeaways regarding common fallacies to avoid include:

- Fallacies often dominate the discussion when it comes to downtown revitalization.
- Fallacies are essentially talking points disguised as truth meant to simplify or shut down a broader discussion.
- Building for drivers via parking, urbanity via New Urbanism or walkers via pedestrian malls are three of the most common fallacies practiced in downtown revitalization.
- A "build it and they'll come" approach will almost always fail.
- Authenticity and organic growth are the only true guarantors of success.

## Conclusion

> "We cannot solve our problems with the same level of thinking that created them."—Albert Einstein

When you repeat something often enough, you're not likely to find the truth but rather an alternative reality. This is what many who undertake downtown revitalization efforts will find during the process of growth, particularly with regards from those with little education on the subject.

All too often fallacies regarding things like making downtown more accessible to drivers or to walkers or even to developers are wheeled to the forefront as panaceas or silver bullets for solving the issues of decades of neglect. They utilize a "build it first, and then they will come approach." In reality, however, there is no silver bullet when it comes revitalizing a community. These efforts take time and require careful, well-thought-out plans with action. Larger cities have learned from many mistakes generated during the era of urban renewal, but many smaller communities are still repeating them. To achieve a truly urban experience for your small city, it thus becomes necessary to do your research and avoid the three deadly fallacies that can take you down the wrong path.

# 11

# Mixing It Up

## Celebrating Diversity in America's Small Cities

Picture a typical small city in the American heartland. What do you see? Quaint shops and small businesses, trees and historic homes, farmlands and rolling hills—no doubt all come to mind. Now think about the people living there. What do you see? Chances are, you picture older people playing bingo; farmers in pickup trucks; young children riding bikes. You're also likely to think of all of them as White, conservative, overly religious and stuck in their ways. No one would blame you for thinking of any of this. It is, after all, the image that has been presented to us in media and film for decades, but it is hardly the whole story. Small cities, like the rest of the nation, are not immune from change and, as such, have seen influxes of different cultures, races and beliefs move into their communities. While there are still stark differences from the diversity displayed in larger cities like New York and smaller cities like Berlin, New Hampshire, make no mistake that smaller cities are, in fact, changing. We'll examine how some of these smaller cities are embracing such changes in the case studies presented below. Before we delve in, however, we'll examine a bit about different kinds of diversity and how exactly such diversity is impacting our smaller cities on the whole.

## Analyzing Diversity

It's hard to measure a year by an exact measure of time, but if you were to peg 2020, you'd be safe to bet that 8 minutes, 46 seconds would come pretty close. This was how long it took for George Floyd to fully suffocate under the knee of Minneapolis police officer Derek Chauvin. Floyd's death was a pivotal turning point for race relations in American history.

While the first half of 2020 was undoubtedly defined by the Covid-19 pandemic, the latter half of 2020 was surely defined by the subject of race. In the wake of Floyd's killing, Americans have increasingly turned a mirror on themselves and have been hosting frank talks on race and racial politics. Many of these talks have taken place in larger cities but have increasingly trickled down into America's small towns. As outrage from the video of Floyd's death grew, so too did protests in larger city centers. Small cities were hardly immune from the ramifications of the phenomenon, however, as they witnessed demonstrations of their own.

So, what's driving these frank talks now, as opposed to the discussions of 1992, which saw wide-scale protesting and rioting in the wake of the Rodney King beating? In a word: demographics.

By 2044, it is projected that the United State will reach a milestone in its history by becoming a majority-minority nation. This means that for the first time, Whites will make up just 49.7 percent of the population, while Hispanics, Blacks, Asians, Pacific Islanders and multiracial groups will make up 51.3 percent. This is due to a plethora of factors, which include falling birth rates for White Americans as well as higher patterns of immigration from minority communities, among others. These demographic changes are already apparent to Millennials and to Gen Z, who, combined, stand out among the most diverse generations in American history. These groups are predicted to make up 75 percent of the American workforce by 2024. These trends have long been emerging in larger American cities; now they are trickling down into our suburbs and smaller communities, where it's been reported that White majorities are down from a peak of 93 percent in 1980 to 83 percent in 2010.

Once exemplars of de Tocquevillian American exceptionalism, now they're subject to such gibes as a Silicon Valley executive's infamous assertion last year that "no educated person wants to live in a s***hole with stupid people." And to be sure, "the little town blues," as Brookings has characterized it, are real: Many of these smaller communities are in demographic decline as the ambitious young go elsewhere, leaving them ever Whiter and older, and the departures of large company headquarters, such as ADM and Caterpillar, have been a blow.

Yet America's smaller communities are far more diverse—and have far greater potential—than is commonly believed. The resurgence of manufacturing and energy development, sectors which tend to be more critical to smaller economies, has helped many smaller towns. Recent demographic data show a movement away from expensive coastal cities, including Millennials, who tend to look for affordable single-family homes. The number of rural home mortgages has increased for five straight years, though the increase trails the rate in urban areas, and nearly twice as many Millennials, according to the National Association of Realtors, bought homes in small cities or rural areas last year as in denser urban areas.

As Millennials increasingly flood into these areas, diversity is following. These changes are having a lasting impact on such places, leading many within these communities to ponder their new situations. As studies have shown, however, such changes are not something to be feared, but to be embraced:

> One common justification for diversity—which has a very long history in the U.S.—revolves around the cultural contributions that people from a variety of backgrounds bring. These can be simple things like food, clothing styles, music or holidays—taco trucks on every corner, Korean barbecue on every block. St. Patrick's Day, Hanukkah, Cinco de Mayo and Chinese New Year.[1]

So what exactly is diversity, then, and how is it being defined?

For the longest time, the American mindset defined diversity solely along the basis of race. This was not surprising as race was the main focal point defining the Civil Rights Act and Voting Rights Act, and, in fact, has dominated every conversation from school bussing to affirmative action in the decades since. It even played a major role in the 2020 presidential election.

While race continues to maintain such a defining role, the concept of diversity is now, to put a play on words, more diverse than ever. For what used to be a mainly Black and White issue has become a larger and growing conversation about immigration rights, LGBTQ+ inclusion, religious tolerance, and political and intellectual variation, among others.

In general, diversity can be broken down into three broad categories: External, Internal and Sociopolitical:

- External Diversity is composed of outward physical characteristics, which can include their race, sex, skin color, ethnicity etc.
- Internal Diversity is composed of traits that are not as outwardly defined as their external appearances and can include attributes such as education, sexual orientation, interests, family status, cultural heritage, economic standing, etc.
- Sociopolitical Diversity is composed of influences that have come to shape a person's worldview based on their life experiences. These include their political and religious beliefs.

These forms of diversity are ever-present in major urban centers, which have traditionally been gathering places for those of varied backgrounds. It's only in recent times that these sorts of conversations are trickling down into smaller cities, and as we'll see from some of the examples below and having a cultural impact.

## *Holt Churches Initiate Conversations About Diversity*

While cities like Morrisville and St. Joseph have embraced diversity by circumstance, some communities have taken a more proactive approach by actively driving diversity initiatives through the encouragement of visitations. This is certainly the case for Holt, Michigan (pop. 24,000).

Located south of Lansing, Michigan's state capital, the city of Holt is part of Delhi Township and has one of the most homogenized populations in the state. According to statistics gathered from the 2010 *U.S. Census Bureau*, Holt is 86.3 percent White, 5.6 percent African American and 5.4 percent Hispanic, which was Whiter overall compared to the rest of Michigan.

"Holt is not diverse, but I feel like they are still accepting of other people," said Avni Tokhie, an Indian American transplant to the community. "Since it's a small town, people probably think the residents here are close[d]-minded, but I have not run into any of those people so far."[2]

Town Supervisor C. J. Davis cites the general agrarian nature of the community as the reason for its lack of diversity, stating, "People here were raised by a bunch of farmers and a lot of the African Americans went into the city to live because it was closer to jobs and closer to the plants."[3] He does note, however, that overall things are changing. One of the reasons is the local churches.

Home to 16 Catholic churches, Holt is hardly a hotbed for religious eclecticism, but it is these very churches that are driving the change for a more a diverse city. One of the ways it is doing so is by literally bringing in minorities from surrounding areas to attend services:

> Audrey Taylor, a constant fixture at her church near Holt, said the majority of registered members at her church are white, but that a large number of minority children are bussed in from surrounding poor neighborhoods for services each Sunday morning.
> "My church is more accepting of minorities because we're trying to help them," said Taylor.[4]

While this is not so much a community-led initiative as it is a church-led one, Michigan State University Professor of Social Work Dr. Ronald Hall believes that initiatives like this are a good way to promote diversity, as they create alliances.

"I think churches in Holt could start the process by interacting with black churches," said Hall. "There are quite a number of African American churches in the Lansing area and if those churches could interact together, I think that's a way you can begin to form a community alliance."[5]

While not a first among church groups, as churches have traditionally opened the doors to diverse groups in the past, including Vietnamese Boat people, Cuban refugees and Iraqi asylum seekers, the active exchange of parishioners between churches in Lansing and Holt does represent a major step forward in race relations as it displays an active willingness among a certain sector in the community to develop a more welcoming community.

Because concerns over diversity have never been at the forefront of Holt development, no funds are currently being allocated toward enlightening the public about people of different races or ethnicities.

According to Davis, townships operate differently than cities, leaving little money to be spent on initiatives that might improve diversity. "When we spend money on issues like this, unlike city budgets, we have people within the township asking why we are spending their taxes doing this and that," said Davis. "But, as a township, we try to make it welcoming for everybody."[6]

Contrary to what Davis said, Tufts University Professor of Sociology Susan Ostrander believes there are many things communities can do to educate people about diversity, many of which don't involve spending a lot of money. "Public schools can also make sure that curricula is inclusive and that children and teachers are culturally competent," said Ostrander. "Community organizations, including churches, can sponsor discussions about why diversity matters."[7] Ostrander also suggests that local businesses should consider selling ethnic foods and other products, as well as hiring people from diverse groups.[8]

## Huntington: A City Open to All

You might not think of small-town West Virginia as a bastion of progressive tolerance, but that's exactly what you get when you enter the city of Huntington (pop. 45,000).

Located in far southwestern West Virginia on the border of Ohio, Huntington began as a sleepy agricultural city until becoming a railroad hub in the 1870s serving as a vital link between Richmond, Virginia, and cities in the Midwest. Growth was stymied, however, after a disastrous flood in the 1930s left tens of thousands homeless—a condition worsened with the decline of the steel industry following World War II. Both events led to a population loss of over 45,000 residents between 1950 and 2000.

Today, Huntington is on the rebound. Home to Marshall University, one of the top research institutes in the state, the city plays host to a substantial student population, contributing to the culture of the area.

While Huntington continues to grow its population and culture in the twenty-first century, their policy towards diversity has attracted increasing amounts of attention, primarily due to their "Open to All" campaign.

Originally modeled from the LGBT Advisory Committee in 2015 formed by Mayor Steve Williams to help advance the discussion about equality and justice for the LGBT community, the initial campaign launched in the aftermath of the West Virginia Senate's voting down of a controversial Religious Freedom Protection Act in 2016. The Open to All campaign was launched with the goal of promoting diversity and inclusion by broadening views beyond race, gender and sexual orientation. It encourages maintaining a safe and welcoming environment for all employees, customers, visitors and vendors, regardless of race, religion, ancestry, sex, age, disability, sexual orientation, gender identity, gender expression, or income status.[9] Featuring a pledge to be inclusive, despite one's differences, the campaign has since attracted many merchants. "We have a hundred businesses on board now, so it's kind of celebrating the success of the campaign," Murdock said.[10]

In addition to the pledge, window stickers are used as designation markers for participating Open to All businesses and organizations. "We wanted businesses to have a visual way to show we don't want to discriminate. We want to make it well known, in fact, that we are open to all," Murdock said. "Actually putting the sticker on the door is a great way for folks to really know where your business stands and you know when you go in that business you're not going to be treated any differently regardless of race, religion, sexual orientation, etc."[11]

The campaign re-launched two years later and expanded upon its initial range of promises. It now includes the Huntington Regional Chamber of Commerce, among others. Carmen "Mitzi" Sinnott, a member of the Mayor's Diversity Advisory Committee, said the re-launch comes after the Diversity Advisory Committee joined with the LGBTQ Advisory committee. "We really collectively decided we wanted to expand the campaign to all communities that have been formerly marginalized and historically oppressed," she said. "It really just made sense for Huntington to live up to its full potential. We want to be a city where everyone can thrive and everyone is welcome."[12]

The city's campaign attracted the attention of numerous Human Rights organizations who heralded its welcoming nature in a state not traditionally known for its inclusivity. So successful was it that Huntington received a score of 95 on a 100-point scale and was also one of 41 cities to earn an "All Star" designation for advancing LGBTQ equality without relying on state law as part of the Human Rights Campaign's 2017 Municipal Equality Index.[13]

Even churches within the community have taken enthusiastically to the initiative.

The Rev. Jacque Parlato, of Central Christian Church in Huntington, spoke about the importance of religious organizations joining the campaign, like her congregation did years ago. The campaign hopes to branch its cash mob promoting into a worship mob event on Sundays where crowds will join in on worship services to show appreciation.

Williams also said that, as part of the campaign, he has been working to include diversity in higher ranking positions. Huntington Fire Chief Jan Rader, the first female fire chief in West Virginia, also said it is

Augusta hosts several minority-owned businesses throughout its downtown. The burgeoning Iraqi community has contributed greatly to the vibrancy of the area, opening *halal* shops like this one (author's collection).

important for government entities to take the pledge. Both the city's IT director and municipal judge are minorities, she said.[14]

Huntington's aggressive stance against discrimination is an important step, not only to making visitors feel comfortable but also to extending inclusion to those who live in the community as well. As Kim Baker, owner of River & Rail Bakery, said: "To build a strong community we must recognize all its aspects and respect the individual differences," she said. "Hate weakens our society and it degrades joy and prosperity. The richest lives are those full of compassion, cooperation, tolerance and gratitude."[15]

## *A Celebration of Food and Culture: The Case of Morrisville and St. Josephs*

Celebrating diversity with food is an American tradition that dates back centuries. From our earliest days, when Native Americans broke bread with the Pilgrims, to every subsequent group that has added to the varied diet we have since grown accustomed to, sharing our plates has been a defining part of our culture. Such exchanges between groups are not unique, for multicultural societies such as ours, however, and are rooted deep within history:

> Dating back to the Greek Empire, it can be seen that food and dining as a group was as much about enjoying company and conviviality as it was about the cuisine.
> 
> This continued throughout the Roman Era, during which the convivium (Roman dinner party) became a mainstay in society. We may have come a long way since then, but the intrinsic role food plays within societies and families as a bonding agent has remained.[16]

Professors Kaitlin Woolley and Ayelet Fishbach coauthored a study published in 2016 in the *Journal of Consumer Psychology* that showed colleagues who ate similar foods together experienced higher rates of trust and closeness than those who ate alone. "People tend to think that they use logic to make decisions, and they are largely unaware that food preferences can influence their thinking," Fishbach wrote. "On a very basic level, food can be used strategically to help people work together and build trust." She goes on to state that eating is actually a social phenomenon that involves conversation with loved ones about one's daily activities or current happenings in the world, allowing real bonds to be forged.

So it is that two cities, Morrisville, North Carolina (pop. 29,000), and St. Josephs, Minnesota (pop. 7,000), came to find common ground with new residents.

## Morrisville: Where East Meets West

Morrisville, North Carolina, is a small city located in the heart of the Research Triangle—a major research center anchored by the cities of Raleigh, Durham and Chapel Hill. Containing three of the largest research institutions in the state—University of North Carolina–Chapel Hill, Duke University and North Carolina State University—the region has long been an economic driver, particularly in the burgeoning tech industry.

A former railroad hub that saw skirmishes between Confederate and Union troops towards the end of the Civil War, the city remained a primarily agricultural region, until witnessing exponential growth, as a result of the booming technology sector. Today, Morrisville is among the fastest growing towns in North Carolina. In fact, the population has grown by more than 200 percent in the last 12 years and is forecast to grow at a similar pace for the foreseeable future.

The town is also younger than many neighboring communities, with 27 percent of the population under the age of 18 and only 4 percent over the age of 65. What makes Morrisville different from other cities, however, is not its younger residents or its explosive growth, but rather the diversity that has flocked to it and shaped it. For, in 2020:

> Morrisville has the largest concentration of Asian Indian residents in the region. A 2015 special census of the town of Morrisville showed the population to be 50 percent white, 27 percent Indian American, 13 percent African American, and six percent Hispanic. Four percent identified themselves as having a mixed ancestry of two or more races. More than 30 percent of the town's residents were born outside the United States.[17]

While such a conglomeration of diverse backgrounds could intimidate residents of many small communities, this has not been the case with Morrisville, which has embraced the changes head on. In fact, the Morrisville Town Council includes two of the first Indian Americans elected to office in the state. Politics, however, is not the only unifier for the community, however, as the city has embraced its new residents by throwing the annual East Meets West festival.

Beginning as the "Taste of Morrisville" in 2011, the festival blossomed into its current iteration under the guidance of the Chamber of Commerce, which sought to find a way to merge the traditionally Southern roots of the native residents with those of the newcomers. To do this, they included a list of food vendors selling small plates of Italian, Mediterranean, Indian, Peruvian, Irish, Chinese, Mexican and American Southeast cuisine. Community leaders taste and judge foods from around the world, and the public votes and selects their favorites. There are also numerous activities for children, including cultural dancing, face painting, and arts and crafts, as well as on-stage entertainment that includes performances by Chinese students, Indian and Irish dancers, and Middle Eastern belly dancers, as well as a private school band, a youth theater group, and a hip-hop dance group. Past festivals have included blues, reggae, and bluegrass groups as well.[18] "One of the most distinct features about Morrisville is its variety of cultures," said Mayor Mark Stohlman. "The East Meets West festival is incredibly important to the town council as a means of connecting with the public and celebrating the cultures that make our town unique."[19]

While the festival is about highlighting the diversity of the community, it's also about drawing these crowds into the local culture, as well. The city council views the East Meets West festival as an opportunity for residents of foreign cultures to experience North Carolina traditions, such as pulled pork and bluegrass music, for the first time.

Such inclusivity drew the attention of the National League of Cities (NLC), and in March 2017, they presented the East Meets West festival with the City Cultural Diversity Award for cities with less than 50,000 residents.

The blending of cultures in the East Meets West Festival certainly provides the perfect recipe from which to celebrate both old and new in a relaxed environment. The free event is open to the public and takes place each year in early autumn. As Morrisville Chamber of Commerce President Sarah Gakill states, "Families and businesses appreciate the opportunity to celebrate Morrisville's diversity at the East Meets West festival each year."[20]

## *Spreading Cultural Diversity Through Culinary Diversity in St. Joseph*

While not as elaborate as the festival put on in Morrisville, the small city of St. Joseph, Minnesota, has been dabbling with cultural diversity by celebrating new restaurateurs in their downtown.

Located in central Minnesota, St. Joseph is a relatively quiet community. Home to the all-female College of Saint Benedict, a Roman Catholic liberal arts school, it has long been an overwhelmingly White community, with a strong Scandinavian heritage. Recently, however, the city has been attracting newcomers of more diverse backgrounds seeking an escape from the city. One such newcomer is Mateo Mackbee, who opened Krewe in late spring of 2020. A tribute to his Louisianan mother, Mary Mackbee, a former principal, Krewe specializes in New Orleans cuisine like gumbo and jambalaya.

Mackbee, 47, and Erin Lucas, 27, his girlfriend and business partner, moved from Minneapolis two years ago. They were driven by a shared desire to bring awareness of racial inequities to rural communities and to find an alternative to the limited career options available to them in the metro area. "I had grown kind of weary of the restaurant scene in the Twin Cities, where it was hard for someone like myself," Mackbee said. "I'm a little bit older and a little bit darker than most of the people on the line."[21]

Staking out a claim in rural Minnesota, Mackbee had initially seen success with a pop-up restaurant in a nearby community. Lured by the landlord who owns the properties where the restaurant sits now, they have since opened a bakery alongside Krewe. "A lot of people who grew up here, they've never known a person of color," said Steve Peterson, a retired General Mills executive who attends Kopka's church. "There's something about these guys being here that helps." In addition to his restaurant and bakery, Mackbee has also sought to bring in more diversity through Model Citizen, a nonprofit program he created with the Rev. Mark Kopka, a Lutheran pastor, who seeks to introduce students of color to farming.

With an acre of land in nearby Paynesville, donated by Nordland Lutheran Church, Mackbee hopes to inspire more youth to stake out rural areas and to educate them on virtues of agriculture.

"One of the things we noticed is that all of these kids are literally surrounded by farmland," Mackbee said, "but they don't have the opportunity to step onto it."

"We see this farm as a model for the area," Peterson said, "to encourage other young people to be entrepreneurs and to do what's right for the land."

By year's end, Mackbee and Lucas plan to have a chicken coop, sheep, and a wood-fired oven to cook for outdoor parties. The ingredients will show up on their menus. And, ideally, the farm will enrich the community in other ways.

Standing outdoors on a windy afternoon, Mackbee looked toward a patch of forest at the edge of the still-unplowed farmland. "I need to get the kids out here to see it and to smell it," he said.[22]

## A Mixed Welcome in Lewiston

While the cases above represent examples of proactive ways various cities and organizations have been seeking out diversity for the betterment of their communities, the case of Lewiston, Maine, provides an example of a more mixed welcome.

Located in southern Maine, midway between Portland and Augusta, Lewiston (pop. 36,000) is a traditional mill town that specialized in the processing and manufacturing of various textiles. As its industrial heritage continued to dominate much of its growth in the nineteenth and twentieth century, the city attracted a significant number of Irish and Quebecois millworkers to the area, helping to make the city the second most populous in the state.

Lewiston's flirtation with immigration at the turn of the century was like that of many others in New England at the time: immigrants were often excluded from the more nativist elements of the city. Though these early immigrants were eventually able to overcome discrimination, the lesson of their exclusion did not apparently transfer over to the new round of immigrants that began flooding in at the start of the twenty-first century, most notably Somali Bantus.

Beginning in 2000, Somali Bantus, who had been given priority status for resettlement by the U.S. government, had begun a secondary internal migration from Clarkston, Georgia, where they had originally been placed into public housing, to Maine. Desperate to get away from the crime they experienced, several members of this group began settling in and around Lewiston. Word soon spread from these early arrivals that Lewiston was affordable with a low crime rate and good schools. Soon, more Somalis followed, and within two years, Lewiston had a sizable community on their hands, with 1,000 arrivals in total, accounting for nearly 3 percent of the total population.

Unlike previous groups who had immigrated into Lewiston, the Somalis who settled there were ethnically Black and Muslim. They were also driven by factors other than work, with safety and housing being among their chief motivators for resettlement. Because of this, the new arrivals were quick to draw the suspicions of the native population with rumors beginning to spread regarding their motivations. As the *New York Times* reports:

> People whispered that Somalis were getting free cars, courtesy of the government, $10,000 grants, even free air-conditioners and groceries. Word had it that they got to jump to the head of the line for government-subsidized apartments. None of this was true, but the intensity of the false rumors reflects the distinct unease surrounding the sudden arrival of so many Somalis to this fraying mill town....[23]

Predicting that the new community would place a strain on the city's social services, including its English as a Second language program, Mayor Laurier T. Raymond drafted an open letter to the Somali community asking that they restrict further migration into the city. The mayor's letter, written in English to a community with many non–English speakers, said: "Please pass the word: We have been overwhelmed and have responded valiantly. Now we need breathing room. Our city is maxed-out financially, physically and emotionally."[24]

The mayor's letter, though intended to be well-meaning, set off an explosion of ill will among the Somali community, ultimately gaining statewide and national exposure. Somali elders responded with their own letter, accusing the mayor of being an "ill-informed leader who is bent towards bigotry."

They wrote that many Somalis or their children were American citizens and were helping Lewiston's economy by moving into vacant apartments and opening new stores.

"We think your letter is an attempt to agitate and incite the local people and license to violence against our people physically, verbally and emotionally," they wrote.[25]

Though the mayor stopped short of a full apology, he did, in fact, acknowledge his shortcomings in not meeting with the community leaders directly before penning the letter, saying: "We understand the social and economic pressure that new entrants bring to the community. We hope that others appreciate the potential richness and opportunity newcomers bring to the city." Still, the damage was done.

Less than a year after the letter was written, a small White supremacist group demonstrated in Lewiston in support of the mayor, prompting a simultaneous counter-demonstration of about 4,000 people at Bates College and the organization of the "Many and One Coalition." Only 32 attended the rally by the White supremacist group. The mayor was out of state on the day of the rallies, while governor John Baldacci and other officials attended.

Later in 2006, a severed frozen pig's head was thrown into a Lewiston mosque while about 40 men were praying. This was considered very offensive by the Muslim community, as swine is proscribed in Islam. A man admitted to the act and claimed it to be a joke.

While tensions have since cooled, with many Somalis becoming part of the business community downtown, and younger Somalis playing a direct role in helping Lewiston High School's soccer team win a series of championships, the lack of open and honest communication between the city government, and later their lack of support during rallies, is a wound that has continued to fester.

## Soo Parkhurst on Growing Up in Maine

Soo Parkhurst is one of the most accomplished women in Central Maine. Co-owner of O&P Glass with her brother, Tobias, she owns three buildings in downtown Augusta and serves on multiple nonprofit boards, including the Colonial Theater. She also happens to be an Asian American woman in the oldest and Whitest state in the country. Reflecting on her background, she has this to say:

> I was adopted when I was 5 months old from Seoul, South Korea. I was born in Kyonggi do, South Korea, and came to America on July 26, 1986, and for the last 34 years we have been celebrating this day like it's a second birthday. I grew up in Fairfield, Maine, until I was about 9 years old and moved to Readfield, Maine. If I hadn't moved I would have went to Lawrence High school instead of Maranacook High School—which when thinking back on it I am super grateful for the transition because I may have had a different experience at Lawrence. I went to a super accepting and open-minded school.
>
> I was always that resistant adopted child who didn't care about my roots or where I came from. My parents were always trying to introduce me to these Korean cultural fairs and the opportunity to learn about my motherland but for some reason I didn't care. And in all reality, I wasn't ready to care. I felt like a permanent exchange student if that makes any sense. Being adopted never felt like that big of a deal because I hadn't started researching yet. For me, growing up, being adopted meant collecting coins in a 5 gallon blue jug and rolling the money with my dad on the weekends. Ever since I can remember, my parents, brothers, visitors, threw their extra change in this jug that was given the name "KOREA FUND." It was always for our big trip to South Korea when I was ready. That was always stressed: "ONLY WHEN I WAS READY."
>
> I define myself as an Asian-American Woman. But, I do think I am still trying to figure out who

Soo Parkhurst grew up in the Augusta area and now co-owns O&P Glass with her brother Tobias. She has been a major player in the development of downtown's north end (courtesy Dave Dostie).

## 11. Mixing It Up

I am—I think we all are. I think growing up as a kid in Maine, I always saw myself as white. When you grow up around all white people, you actually believe you are white. But, more so as an adult, I define myself as a professional, a sister, daughter, aunt, a person who cares deeply about family and someone who is always evolving ... it's less about race. No matter what method of self-definition I choose, they are all subject to misinterpretation. Everyone has biases, and those biases will reflect the way a person interprets my self-description.

I can't really say I've experienced much racism here, but there has definitely been an ignorance factor, perhaps not coming out of hate, but more from curiosity. People ask A LOT of questions and genuinely care about my life and how I ended up here. When I was in the 1st or 2nd grade I did have a teacher call home saying she thought I may have adoption issues. When asked why she thought that, my teacher told my mother it's because I went off on a kid who called me Chinese. Kids don't know any better and I don't even think they even realized I was different. Of course some kids would make the "slanty eye motion" with their fingers pressed against their eyes, but for some reason it just didn't bother me.

My take on ignorance is that I'm not going to change someone's ignorant views by reacting with a comment back. That's something that is deeper than I can fix with a reaction. I just kind of make it known I heard them and shake my head. I can only respond to ignorance with a fact—like a lot of people assume you are this or that without knowing anything. I actually had a table of Chinese women arguing if I was Chinese or Japanese and some said I must be Chinese because of the size of the bridge of my nose. This is even after I told them I was Korean. So, my point is that this has happened to me in many different settings and I think it's not so much racism but more coming from a place of curiosity. What I can say is I have never experienced racism where I feared for my life.

Comments like "the little Asian girl" probably will never stop. Some people will indeed take comments like that as racist, derogatory, and sexist, but to me, I use it as a way of being positive. Yes, to many in Maine I'll always be the "little Asian girl," but I'm also smart, outgoing and funny. It's the same thing when I speak and people say "wow, your English is very good." They aren't trying to be mean, they are genuinely shocked. They just didn't know English is the only language I know and they don't know my story.

Mine is definitely not the story of all minorities living in this state that's for sure. My journey has one of the better outcomes for someone being adopted and also a minority. I often wonder what my experience would have been like if I hadn't been adopted by a family that was completely white and my Korean family moved to Readfield instead. I'm sure my two experiences would not compare. My best friend is Indian, however, and she grew up exactly the same way I did and her family moved from India to Canada to Maine. I've asked her about her experiences as well and she hasn't experienced any racism where we grew up. I think Maine is just overly accepting and more curious than anything else. When my parents were adopting me, they were told they could not adopt a black child because Maine was too white.

In general, Maine people are friendly and everyone knows everyone. Maine is an aging state that is predominantly white and I compare my experiences here to winning the lottery. You would think growing up in the least diverse state in America I would of had a much more terrible experience, but I just happened to grow up in environments and schools that accepted me.[26]

## *Key Takeaways*

When considering diversity, it's important to remember these key takeaways:

- Diversity is important in providing an authentic urban experience.
- Diversity can be broken down into the following categories: Internal, External and Sociopolitical.
- Diversity is important for creating a welcome environment for all.
- Diversity doesn't have to be a challenge, it can be achieved through simple acts such as invitations, food exchanges and pledges to be more inclusive.
- Diversity should always involve open and honest communication.

## *Conclusion*

> "Cities have the capability of providing something for everybody, only because, and only when they are created by everybody."—Jane Jacobs

You can't have a proper salad without a mix of ingredients, and the same thing goes for our cities. Diversity of people, ideas and cultures is part of the fabric of living in an urban environment, and while our smaller cities are no doubt more homogenous than our larger counterparts, this doesn't mean we can't embrace the changes that occur within them.

As the case studies above show, diversity doesn't necessarily need to be artificially construed, but it should be celebrated. By providing a non-exclusive, welcoming environment, we not only go a long way

## 11. Avoid the Three Deadly Fallacies of Urban Planning 199

towards learning from those who are different than us, but also, we go a long way towards inviting them in to experience our own cultures as well.

Diversity is not an easy task for most places, but if done right, with honest, open communication it can be accomplished in a way that is beneficial for all.

# Conclusion:
# Not a Moment to Lose

Is it possible to replicate an urban experience in a small city? Yes. Is it possible to achieve this without surrendering your small-town charm? You bet it is!

As the case studies outlined across the American cities highlighted have shown, the trick to replicating an urban experience doesn't necessarily stem from development. You don't need a major office complex to move in to provide you with new blood, a massive apartment complex to give you an edge on housing, or a den of artists to give your city a makeover: everything you need is already in place.

As was alluded to in the introduction, small cities, like large cities, were not established with the intention of limiting their development. They spent most of their history competing for the very same resources including people, jobs, and cultural attractions as their much larger counterparts. It was only in the twentieth century that many small cities began to give up competing and adopt feelings of inferiority as vehicular travel, de-industrialization and the rise of expansive office parks emptied out their towns in favor of larger metro areas. Now, no longer confined by these things, small cities are rediscovering their downtowns and redefining what it means to be a small community once again.

In the previous chapters we have touched upon the various ways small cities not only can compete but also how they can grasp the moment at hand by urbanizing the centers of their communities. This includes forging an identity, organizing a movement, improving aesthetics, redefining traffic flow, marketing to outsiders, encouraging good instincts and responsible residential development, leveraging the unexpected, and supporting art and diversity. In addition, we also touched upon some of the more common mistakes to avoid when undergoing a revitalization effort, namely so-called "silver bullet methods" like increasing parking, building for urbanism, or building for walkability, none of which utilize a mixed approach that is necessary to increase a sense of density.

As we have seen with the case studies, all communities represented display a diversity of population, culture, and regional identities, and all have fairly successful stories that can be shared and incorporated into any other community. While some share some advantages over others, and not all are easily boxed into neat packages, they nevertheless represent some of the best examples nationwide of what small communities have done to define and revitalize themselves. By focusing on their successes—as well as failures, in certain cases—it is hoped that other small communities in the midst of change can adapt and adopt a proper strategy for moving forward.

If you take away anything from this book, it is hoped that you remember authenticity is key to any successful revitalization, for when it comes to urbanity, you can't force or fake your way through the process. You need to be true to who and what you are. This doesn't mean you can't experiment or bring in new ideas, but it does mean you should take stock of the resources you have and go from there.

If it's been said once, it can be said again: the process of revitalization is a long road. It's a marathon, after all, not a sprint. Mistakes can be made along the way, but if you stay true to the fundamentals that make up the foundation of urbanism, then you can achieve the goals of a denser, thriving city center that will ultimately emanate outward.

Small cities need not remain on the sidelines and wish for better days, for those days are here. No other period in modern history is as favorable to the growth of small cities as the 2020s. For a variety of reasons, Americans are once again giving these places another look. How leaders within these communities choose to capitalize off this moment is entirely up to them. The time for change is now, and there's not a moment to lose.

# Chapter Notes

## Introduction

1. Shen, Maxine. (August 18, 2020). "Cuomo Blames POLICE for Crime Wave: New York governor says cops must address 'lack of trust' in communities as Big Apple shootings surge 82% and threatens to pull funding for NYPD if reforms are not in place next year." *Daily Mail*. Retrieved August 26, 2020. https://www.dailymail.co.uk/news/article-8637797/New-York-Gov-Cuomo-blasts-lawlessness-state-NYC-lack-trust-fuels-urgent-crisis.html.

2. Madori-Davis, Dominic. (May 19, 2020). "Wealthy New Yorkers fled the city when the coronavirus outbreak started. New data shows where they went—and which neighborhoods emptied out the most." *New York Times*. Retrieved August 26, 2020. https://www.businessinsider.com/where-wealthy-nyc-residents-went-during-coronavirus-outbreak-nyt-report-2020-5

3. McFall, Caitlin. (August 5, 2020). "Cuomo Begs Wealthy New Yorkers to Come Back to Save the City: 'I'll buy you a drink.'" Fox News. Retrieved August 26, 2020. https://www.foxnews.com/us/cuo mo-begs-wealthy-new-yorkers-to-come-back-to-save-the-city-ill-buy-you-a-drink

4. Hendricks, Michael. (March 31, 2020). "The End of Cities?" E21. Retrieved August 28, 2020. https://economics21.org/have-we-reached-the-end-of-cities

5. Hough, Sue. (August 5, 2020). "Small Town Markets Have Huge Investment Potential in 2020-Here's Why (And How to Capitalize on It)." Bigger Pockets. Retrieved August 28, 2020. https://www.biggerpockets.com/blog/small-town-markets-have-huge-investment-potential-in-2020

6. *Ibid.*

7. Frey, William H. (April 6, 2020). "Even Before Coronavirus, Census Shows U.S. Cities' Growth Was Stagnating." Brookings.edu. Retrieved August 31, 2020. https://www.brookings.edu/research/even-before-coronavirus-census-shows-u-s-cities-growth-was-stagnating/

8. *Ibid.*

9. Greene, Andy. (December 23, 2013). "John Mellencamp: My Life in 15 Songs." *Rolling Stone*. Retrieved August 31, 2020. https://www.rollingstone.com/music/music-lists/john-mellencamp-my-life-in-15-songs-11308/

10. *Ibid.*

11. Pant, Paula. (June 15, 2020). "Benefits of Living and Working in a Small Town." *The Balance*. Retrieved September 1, 2020. https://www.thebalance.com/benefits-of-living-and-working-in-a-small-town-453928

12. Cartier, Brad. (May 14, 2020). "The Rising Interest in Rural and Small Town Real Estate." Fool.com. Retrieved September 1, 2020. https://www.fool.com/millionacres/real-estate-market/articles/the-rising-interest-in-rural-and-small-town-real-estate/

13. *Ibid.*

14. *Ibid.*

15. "Advantages of Small Town Living." (2020). City of Toccoa. Retrieved September 2, 2020. https://www.cityoftoccoa.com/advantages-of-small-town-living.cfm

16. *Ibid.*

17. *Ibid.*
18. "Section 7: The Urban Experience." (2014). *The People Place and Space Reader.* Retrieved September 2, 2020. https://peopleplacespace.org/toc/section-7/
19. *Ibid.*
20. Ocejo, R.E., Kosta, Ervin B., Mann, A. (March 13, 2020). "Centering Small Cities for Urban Sociology in the 21st Century." *City & Community.* Retrieved September 2, 2020. https://onlinelibrary.wiley.com/doi/full/10.1111/cico.12484

## Chapter 1

1. McMahon, Edward T. (October 2018). "The Secrets of Successful Communities." New Hampshire Municipal Association. Retrieved July 22, 2020. https://www.nhmunicipal.org/town-city-article/secrets-successful-small-communities
2. *Ibid.*
3. *Ibid.*
4. "The Main Street Movement." (2020). Main Street America. Retrieved July 10, 2020. https://www.mainstreet.org/mainstreetamerica/themovement
5. "Who We Are." (2020). Main Street America. Retrieved July 10, 2020. https://www.mainstreet.org/about-us
6. *Ibid.*
7. "The Main Street Movement." (2020). Main Street America. Retrieved July 10, 2020. https://www.mainstreet.org/mainstreetamerica/themovement
8. "Who We Are." (2020). Main Street America. Retrieved July 10, 2020. https://www.mainstreet.org/about-us
9. "Wheeling Heritage." (2020). Main Street America. Retrieved July 11, 2020. https://www.mainstreet.org/mainstreetamerica/mainstreetawards/gamsa/new-item/wheeling
10. *Ibid.*
11. *Ibid.*
12. "Wheeling Heritage Wins Prestigious 2019 Great American Main Street Award." (2019). West Virginia Department of Commerce. Retrieved July 12, 2020. https://commerce.wv.gov/wheeling-heritage-wins-prestigious-2019-great-american-main-street-award/
13. "How Community Heart and Soul Works." (2020). Community Heart & Soul. Retrieved July 12, 2020. https://www.communityheartandsoul.org/what-we-do/
14. *Ibid.*
15. *Ibid.*
16. *Ibid.*
17. *Ibid.*
18. "Introduction. "(2020). One Holyoke CDC. Retrieved July 13, 2020. https://www.oneholyoke.org/about-us/introduction/
19. "Americorps Vista." (2020). Retrieved July 13, 2020. https://www.nationalservice.gov/programs/americorps/americorps-programs/americorps-vista
20. *Ibid.*
21. "Downtown Nampa Main Street Coordinator." (2013). Americorps Vista. Retrieved July 15, 2020. https://my.americorps.gov/mp/listing/viewListing.do;jsessionid=jGnyQ5yP3xz5YRn81Y2LqxkJB8bhx1fBypb2B3hl1Yzxd1JWQWF5!491985738?id=48339&fromSearch=true
22. Interview with the author, June 30, 2020.

## Chapter 2

1. Hayden, Dolores. (1995). *The Power of Place: Urban Landscapes as Public History*, 36.
2. Relph, Edward. (2008). *Place and Placelessness.* London: Sage Publishing, 141.
3. Good, Karen. (2002). "Preservation of Small Town Character in the Town Center of Rutland, Massachusetts." https://scholarworks.umass.edu/cgi/viewcontent.cgi?article=1035&context=larp_ms_projects
4. *Ibid.*
5. Hall, Michael. (2010). "Owen County Quilt Trail. Historic Kentucky."
6. *Ibid.*
7. *Ibid.*
8. *Ibid.*
9. *Ibid.*
10. *Ibid.*
11. www.conchrepublic.com/our-founding-in-1982/.
12. Interview with the author, July 2020.

## Chapter 3

1. Quinn et al., 2008. "Preference for Attractive Faces in Human Infants Extends Beyond Conspecifics." HHS Public Access. https://www.ncbi.nlm.nih.gov/pmc/articles/PMC2566458/
2. Bhadauria, A. (August 2016). "Investigating the Role of Aesthetics in Consumer Moral Judgment and Creativity." University of Wisconsin Milwaukee. Retrieved July 20,2020, https://dc.uwm.edu/cgi/viewcontent.cgi?article=2343&context=etd
3. Ibid. https://dc.uwm.edu/cgi/viewcontent.cgi?article=2343&context=etd
4. Peltonen, Mari. (February 3, 2020). "A Specialist in Urban Study Aesthetics Wants To Turn the City Into a Living Room For All." https://www.helsinki.fi/en/news/sustainability-news/a-specialist-in-urban-aesthetics-wants-to-turn-the-city-into-a-living-room-for-all
5. Auer, Michael J. (October 1991). "The Preservation of Historic Signs." Preservation Briefs. Retrieved July 16, 2020. https://www.nps.gov/tps/how-to-preserve/briefs/25-signs.htm
6. Ibid.
7. "Article 3: Planning Area and Regulating Plan Design." Retrieved July 20,2020. https://user-3vpeqil.cld.bz/Design-Manual/20/#zoom=z
8. Suttie, J. (April26, 2019). "Why Trees Can Make You Happier: Research suggest that being around trees is good for our mental and social well being." Greater Good Magazine. Retrieved July 20, 2020. https://greatergood.berkeley.edu/article/item/why_trees_can_make_you_happier
9. Ibid.
10. "Trees to Return Downtown." (May 16, 2007). Duluth News Tribune. Retrieved July 21, 2020. https://www.duluthnewstribune.com/news/2248734-trees-return-downtown
11. Ibid.
12. Ibid.
13. "City of Edmonds Flower Basket Program." (2020). City of Edmonds. Retrieved July 21, 2020. http://www.edmondswa.gov/edmonds-newsletter-home/2910-city-of-edmonds-flower-backet-program.html
14. "Creating Mini Parks for Increased Physical Activity." (2011). National Recreation and Park Association. Retrieved July 21, 2020. https://www.nrpa.org/contentassets/f768428a39aa4035ae55b2aaff372617/pocket-parks.pdf
15. "New Pocket Park Opens Downtown." (July 14, 2020). The Cheyenne Post. Retrieved July 22, 2020. https://www.thecheyennepost.com/news/new-pocket-park-opens-downtown/article_ec9e3974-c5f6-11ea-90be-4b0082100303.html
16. Cotton, Max. (July 10, 2020). "Cheyenne's First Pocket Park Opens." Wyoming News Now. Retrieved July 22, 2020. https://www.wyomingnewsnow.tv/2020/07/10/cheyennes-first-pocket-park-opens/
17. Barnhart, Kirsten. (May 13, 2020). "Speaker System Fills Downtown Van Wert With Music." Times Bulletin. Retrieved July 22, 2020. https://timesbulletin.com/Content/News/News/Article/Speaker-system-fills-downtown-Van-Wert-with-music/2/4/224310
18. Ibid.
19. Ibid.
20. Interview with the author, July 12, 2020.

## Chapter 4

1. Dishman, Lydia. (July 31, 2015). "Scientific Proof That Your Gut is Best At Making Decisions." Fast Company. Retrieved July 24, 2020. https://www.fastcompany.com/3049248/scientific-proof-that-your-gut-is-best-at-making-decisions
2. Ubid.
3. Sturt, D., Nordstrom, T. (July 3, 2019). "6 Dangers of Having Great Leadership Intuition." Forbes. Retrieved July 24, 2020. https://www.forbes.com/sites/davidsturt/2019/07/03/6-dangers-of-having-great-leadership-intuition/#7648be362ed2
4. Karas, David. (January 6, 2019). "One Man's Mission to Revitalize Small Town America." The Christian Science Monitor. Retrieved July 25, 2020. https://www.csmonitor.com/World/Making-a-difference/2019/0106/One-man-s-mission-to-revitalize-small-town-America
5. McCrea, Nick. (April 9, 2013). "With Closure of Biddeford incinerator

What Will Main Do With Its Trash?" *Bangor Daily News*. Retrieved July 25, 2020. https://bangordailynews.com/2013/04/09/news/bangor/shuttered-incinerator-raises-concerns-about-how-maine-will-handle-trash-in-the-future/

6. Karas, David. (January 6, 2019). "One Man's Mission to Revitalize Small Town America." *The Christian Science Monitor*. Retrieved July 25, 2020. https://www.csmonitor.com/World/Making-a-difference/2019/0106/One-man-s-mission-to-revitalize-small-town-America

7. Catoe, Mandy. (March 19, 2017). "Helping Towns Rediscover Their Spark: Sims Foundation brings in partner with track record of helping communities." *The Lancaster News*. Retrieved July 25, 2020. https://www.thelancasternews.com/content/helping-towns-rediscover-their-spark

8. *Ibid*. https://www.thelancasternews.com/content/helping-towns-rediscover-their-spark

9. Pinkerton, J. (April 25, 2019). "The Kansas City Metro Posts Solid Growth." KC Economy.com. Retrieved July 26, 2020. https://kceconomy.org/2019/04/25/the-kansas-city-metro-posts-solid-population-growth/#:~:text=The%20Kansas%20City%20metro%20area,The%20Dallas%2DFt.

10. O'Brien, Shannon. (November 5, 2019). "Proposed Downtown Olathe Apartments Stir Controversy, Questions About Old Settlers' Future." Fox4kc.com. Retrieved July 26, 2020. https://fox4kc.com/news/proposed-downtown-olathe-apartments-stir-controversy-questions-about-old-settlers-future/

11. *Ibid*.

12. *Ibid*.

13. Ritter, Sarah. (November 11, 2019). "This Joco Downtown Could Get' First Big' Redevelopment. Will It Force Businesses Out?" *The Kansas City Star*. Retrieved July 27, 2020. https://www.kansascity.com/news/local/article237114019.html

14. Interview with the author, July 20, 2020.

15. Maxwell, J. (May 5, 2003). "Good Leaders Learn How To Trust Intuition Not Just Logic." *Maximum Leadership*. July 27, 2020. https://www.bizjournals.com/pittsburgh/stories/2003/05/05/smallb2.html

16. *Ibid*.

## Chapter 5

1. Henerby, Ann. (2015). "The Rules of the Road: Then Versus Now." https://www.enotrans.org/article/the-rules-of-the-road-then-versus-now/

2. Eno Center for Transportation. "The Life of Eno." (2019). https://www.enotrans.org/the-life-of-eno/

3. Henerby, Ann. (2015). "The Rules of the Road: Then Versus Now." https://www.enotrans.org/article/the-rules-of-the-road-then-versus-now/

4. Edwards, Keith. (2019). "Work to Convert Downtown Augusta to Two Way Traffic Set to Begin Monday." https://www.centralmaine.com/2019/07/26/work-to-convert-downtown-augusta-to-two-way-traffic-set-to-begin-monday/

5. Walker, W. et al. (2015). "Downtown Streets: Are We Strangling Ourselves on One Way Networks." https://nacto.org/wp-content/uploads/2015/04/Are-We-Strangling-ourselves-on-one-way-networks_Walker.pdf

6. Wayland, S. (2012). "A Business Case for Conversion from One-Way to Two-Way Streets" https://raisethehammer.org/article/1605/a_business_case_for_conversion_from_one-way_to_two-way_streets

7. *Ibid*.

8. Riggs, W. Appleyard, B. (2016). "The Economic Impact of One to Two-way Street Conversions: Advancing a Context 5 Sensitive Framework." https://spa.sdsu.edu/documents/Economic_Impact.pdf

9. Gilderbloom, John. (June 11, 2014). "Two-way Streets Can Fix Declining Downtown Neighborhoods." *Planetizen*. Retrieved June 19, 2020. https://www.planetizen.com/node/69354.

10. *Ibid*.

11. Glasser, C. (2020). "New Albany Did What Louisville Has Not: Pushed Through Downtown Street Redesign." https://www.leoweekly.com/2020/02/new-albany-louisville-not-pushed-downtown-street-redesign/

12. *Ibid*.

13. *Ibid*.

14. Steuteville, R. (2019). "Cities benefit from restoring two-way traffic: Two-way streets prove safer, more walkable, and more supportive of business than one-way streets for Midwestern cities." https://www.cnu.org/publicsquare/2019/07/09/cities-benefit-one-way-two-way-conversions
15. Ibid.
16. Ibid.
17. Wellner, B. (2015). "Harrison Street Closes: Brady Now Two way." https://qctimes.com/news/local/harrison-street-closes-brady-now-two-way/article_35da94e4-17da-5de7-8ceb-8d17b81d11c2.html.
18. Noe, M. (2015). "Brady Street Business Owners Say Two Way Traffic Is Providing a Boost." https://www.wqad.com/article/news/local/drone/8-in-the-air/brady-street-business-owners-say-two-way-traffic-is-providing-a-boost/526-128ba320-9a08-4d05-b274-e0106fc599b1
19. Ibid.
20. Maine Traffic Resources. (2015). "Downtown Augusta Two Way Traffic Feasibility Study."
21. Edwards, K. (2019). "No Accidents But Parking A Concern Since Augusta Downtown Traffic Went Two Way." https://www.centralmaine.com/2019/12/20/no-accidents-but-parking-a-iconcern-since-augusta-downtown-traffic-went-two-way/
22. Ibid.
23. Interview with the author, July 15, 2020.

## Chapter 6

1. "Psychology Behind Developing Brand Loyalty." (2020). USC Dornsife. Retrieved July 28, 2020. https://appliedpsychologydegree.usc.edu/blog/psychology-behind-developing-brand-loyalty/
2. Ibid.
3. Ibid.
4. McCray, Becky. (April 2, 2013). "How to Market a Small Town." Small Biz Survival." Retrieved July 28, 2020. https://smallbizsurvival.com/2013/03/how-to-market-a-community.html
5. Ibid.
6. Ibid.

7. VanAuken, B. (September 12, 2014). "Evaluating City Mottos, Taglines, and Slogans." *Branding Strategy Insider*. Retrieved July 29, 2020. https://www.brandingstrategyinsider.com/evaluating-city-mottos-taglines-and-slogans/#.XxIf7RdKjIU
8. Powell-Brown, Ann (2003). "Can You Be a Teacher of Literacy If You Don't Love to Read?". *Journal of Adolescent & Adult Literacy*. Vol. 47 No. 4: 284–288.
9. Malone, Bonnie. (April 28, 2015). "How Sisters Became Sisters." *The Nugget Newspaper*. Retrieved July 29, 2020. https://nuggetnews.com/Content/Current-News/Current-News/Article/How-Sisters-became-Sisters/5/5/23509
10. Ibid.
11. Houghton, K. (February 4, 2018). "Through Boom or Bust, Oregon Small Town Rides Theme to Maintain Identity." *Bozeman Daily Chronicle*. Retrieved July 31, 2020. https://www.bozemandailychronicle.com/news/through-boom-or-bust-oregon-small-town-rides-theme-to-maintain-identity/article_2c793ae8-cfc5-5de0-b4ce-695933e8e403.html
12. Ibid.
13. Ibid.
14. Ibid.
15. Pendleton, Craig. (September 2012). "Craig's Column." *Biddeford-Saco Chamber News*. Retrieved July 31, 2020. https://myemail.constantcontact.com/September-News-.html?soid=1109032175955&aid=Va-r2Ag6RLc
16. "Co-Branding: Residents Picks for Biddeford-Saco's New Slogan." (March 19, 2007). *MaineBiz*. Retrieved July 31, 2020. https://www.mainebiz.biz/article/co-branding-residents-picks-for-biddeford-sacos-new-slogan
17. McPherson, Grant. (February 1, 2018). "Saco Hires PR Firm. Former Logo Up in the Air." *Biddeford-Saco-OOB Courier*. Retrieved August 1, 2020. https://chambermaster.blob.core.windows.net/userfiles/UserFiles/chambers/3069/File/SacohiresPRfirm.pdf
18. "Portland Crafts Slogan to Put City on the Map." (April 4, 2013). *Portland Press Herald*. Retrieved August 1, 2020. https://www.pressherald.com/2013/04/30/portland-crafts-slogan-to-put-city-on-the-map_2013-05-01/#

19. McPherson, Grant. (February 1, 2018). "Saco Hires PR Firm. Former Logo Up in the Air." *Biddeford-Saco-OOB Courier*. Retrieved August 1, 2020. https://chambermaster.blob.core.windows.net/userfiles/UserFiles/chambers/3069/File/SacohiresPRfirm.pdf
20. *Ibid.*
21. Heather Pouliot reference goes here.

## Chapter 7

1. "Evaluating Housing Opportunities." (June 24, 2011). University of Wisconsin. Retrieved August 2, 2020. https://fyi.extension.wisc.edu/downtown-market-analysis/analysis-of-opportunities-by-sector/housing/
2. "The Art of Revitalizing Downtown Residential." (October 9, 2012). Vierbicher. Retrieved August 3, 2020. https://www.vierbicher.com/market-expansion-the-art-of-revitalizing-downtown-residential/#
3. Short, Aaron. (January2, 2020). "Americans Are Poised to Drive Less in 2020: This could be the year when Americans start making fewer car trips." StreetsBlog USA. Retrieved August 4, 2020. https://usa.streetsblog.org/2020/01/02/are-americans-poised-to-drive-less-in-2020/
4. "The Art of Revitalizing Downtown Residential." (October 9, 2012). Vierbicher. Retrieved August 3, 2020. https://www.vierbicher.com/market-expansion-the-art-of-revitalizing-downtown-residential/#
5. *Ibid.*
6. *Ibid.*
7. Hunt, D. Harold. (August 17, 2017). "This Old Loft Downtown Living in Small Town Texas." Texas A&M Real Estate Center. Retrieved August 1, 2020. https://www.recenter.tamu.edu/articles/tierra-grande/This-Old-Loft
8. *Ibid.*
9. *Ibid.*
10. *Ibid.*
11. *Ibid.*
12. Mescberger, Alessa. (April 1, 2019). "Progress 2019: Downtown Garden City Sees Variety of New Business Openings." *The Garden City Telegram*. Retrieved August 1, 2020. https://www.gctelegram.com/news/20190401/progress-2019-dowtown-garden-city-sees-variety-of-new-business-openings
13. *Ibid.*
14. *Ibid.*
15. Bend Oregon U.S. Census. (2020) http://www.bend.or.us/index.aspx?page=634
16. "How Small Towns and Cities Can Use Local Assets to Rebuild Their Economies: Lessons From Successful Places." (May 2015). United States Environmental Protection Agency. Retrieved August 2, 2020. https://www.epa.gov/sites/production/files/2015-05/documents/competitive_advantage_051215_508_final.pdf
17. *Ibid.*
18. *Ibid.*
19. *Ibid.*
20. *Ibid.*
21. "The Old Mill District." (2020). Visit Bend. Retrieved August 2, 2020. https://www.visitbend.com/about-bend-oregon/moving-bend-oregon/neighborhoods/the-old-mill-district
22. Interview with the author, June 30, 2020.

## Chapter 8

1. Park West Gallery. (September 25, 2018). "Are Millennials Interested in Art? Yes, New Park West Gallery Study Finds." Ciston PR Newswire. Retrieved August 2, 2020. https://www.prnewswire.com/news-releases/are-millennials-interested-in-art-yes-new-park-west-gallery-study-finds-300718490.html
2. "How Millennials Influence the Art Market." (December 18, 2019). *Widewalls*. Retrieved August 3, 2020. https://www.widewalls.ch/magazine/millennials-art-market
3. *Ibid.*
4. Park West Gallery. (September 25, 2018). "Are Millennials Interested in Art? Yes, New Park West Gallery Study Finds." Ciston PR Newswire. Retrieved August 2, 2020. https://www.prnewswire.com/news-releases/are-millennials-interested-in-art-yes-new-park-west-gallery-study-finds-300718490.html
5. *Ibid.*

6. Ibid.
7. Fitzgerald, Sandy (2012). "What is the Difference Between Arts & Culture?" Culturefighter. Retrieved August 4, 2020. https://www.culturefighter.eu/concept-of-creative-industries/critique/what-is-the-difference-between-arts-and-culture
8. Ibid.
9. "How Does Art Affect Culture and Society?" (2020). Reference.com. Retrieved August 3, 2020. https://www.masterpiecemixers.com/art-affect-culture-society/
10. "Little Free Library." (2020). Retrieved August 4, 2020. https://littlefreelibrary.org/
11. "One Small Town Over 100 Free Libraries." (2020). Little Free Library. Retrieved August 4, 2020. https://littlefreelibrary.org/one-small-town-over-100-little-libraries/
12. Ibid.
13. Ibid.
14. Thompson, Kevin D. (August 28, 2016). "Little Free Libraries Will Soon Be Popping Up in Lake Worth." *Palm Beach Post*. Retrieved August 5, 2020. https://www.palmbeachpost.com/article/20151016/NEWS/812020894
15. "One Small Town Over 100 Free Libraries." (2020). Little Free Library. Retrieved August 4, 2020. https://littlefreelibrary.org/one-small-town-over-100-little-libraries/
16. Lee, Anna. (July 16, 2020). "After 20 Years Mice on Main Continue to Delight and Enthrall." *Greenville Journal*. Retrieved August 5, 2020. https://greenvillejournal.com/arts-culture/after-20-years-mice-on-main-greenville-continue-to-delight-and-entrall/
17. Ryan, Jim. (2015). "How the Mice on Main Came to Main Street." Mice on Main. Retrieved August 5, 2020. http://www.miceonmain.com/historyofmiceonmain.html
18. Lee, Anna. (July 16, 2020). "After 20 Years Mice on Main Continue to Delight and Enthrall." *Greenville Journal*. Retrieved August 5, 2020. https://greenvillejournal.com/arts-culture/after-20-years-mice-on-main-greenville-continue-to-delight-and-entrall/
19. Ibid.
20. Ibid.
21. Cohen, Alina (May 25, 2018). "The Fake Prada Store in the Texas Desert That Became an Art Mecca." Artsy.net. Retrieved August 6, 2020. https://www.artsy.net/article/artsy-editorial-fake-prada-store-texas-desert-art-mecca
22. Carter, Eileen. (April 12, 2020). "In Defense of the Prada Marfa Sign in 'Gossip Girl.'" Garage.com. Retrieved August 6, 2020. https://garage.vice.com/en_us/article/n7jp98/in-defense-of-the-prada-marfa-sign-in-gossip-girl

## Chapter 9

1. James, Geoffrey. (2020). "33 Encouraging Quotes For Times of Crisis." Crisis.com. Retrieved August 7, 2020. https://www.inc.com/geoffrey-james/33-encouraging-quotes-for-times-of-crisis.html
2. "Rural Emergency Preparedness and Response." (January 25, 2019). Rural Health Info Hub. Retrieved August 5, 2020. https://www.ruralhealthinfo.org/topics/emergency-preparedness-and-response
3. Justine Coleman and Isaac Windes. (August 23, 2019). "Small Communities Struggle to Cope with Large Disasters." Non Doc. Retrieved August 7, 2020. https://nondoc.com/2019/08/13/small-communities-struggle-to-cope-with-large-disasters/
4. "Rural Emergency Preparedness and Response." (January 25, 2019). Rural Health Info Hub. Retrieved August 5, 2020. https://www.ruralhealthinfo.org/topics/emergency-preparedness-and-response
5. Bradshaw, Andrew. (July 3, 2017). "7 Steps to Crisis Management." BBN International. Retrieved August 8, 2020. https://bbn-international.com/2017/07/03/7-steps-to-crisis-management/
6. Brown, Melissa. (March 22, 2015). "Mayor Walt Maddox: Tuscaloosa's Tornado Tested Leader." *Tuscaloosa Real Time News*. Retrieved August 9, 2020. https://www.al.com/news/tuscaloosa/2015/03/mayor_walt_maddox_tuscaloosas.html
7. Pafundi, Jason, and Dennis Hoey. (January 25, 2018). "Flooding Puts Areas of Augusta, Hallowell Under Icy Water." *Kennebec Journal*. Retrieved

August 6, 2020. https://www.sunjournal.com/2018/01/15/flooding-puts-areas-of-augusta-hallowell-under-icy-water/
   8. *Ibid.*
   9. Quinn, Patrick. (April 13, 2013). "After Devastating Tornado, Town Reborn Green." *USA Today*. Retrieved August 8, 2020. https://www.usatoday.com/story/news/greenhouse/2013/04/13/greensburg-kansas/2078901/
   10. *Ibid.*
   11. *Ibid.*
   12. Price, Wayne T. (January 25, 2019). "Day After Sebring Shooting, City Cope with Tragedy, Struggles to Make Sense of 5 Deaths." *Florida Today*. Retrieved August 9, 2020. https://www.floridatoday.com/story/news/2019/01/25/sebring-shooting-suntrust-bank/2677401002/
   13. Interview with the author, August 2020.

## Chapter 10

   1. "What is a Fallacy?" (2020). Palomar. Retrieved August 11, 2020. https://www2.palomar.edu/users/bthompson/What%20is%20a%20Fallacy.html
   2. Stromberg, Joseph. (June 27, 2014). "Why Free Parking is Bad for Everyone." Vox.com. Retrieved August 15, 2020. https://www.vox.com/2014/6/27/5849280/why-free-parking-is-bad-for-everyone
   3. Bliss Laura. (July 12, 2019). "A Small Town Decides Parking Can't Be a Bargain Anymore." City Lab. Retrieved August 17, 2020. https://www.bloomberg.com/news/articles/2019-07-12/why-a-small-town-wants-to-charge-more-for-parking
   4. *Ibid.*
   5. *Ibid.*
   6. "The Charter of the New Urbanism." (2020). Congress for the New Urbanism. Retrieved August 15, 2020. https://www.cnu.org/who-we-are/charter-new-urbanism
   7. Horbovetz, Arian. (October 9, 2018). "The Failure of 'Just Add Water' Urbanism." *Strong Towns*. Retrieved August 15, 2020. https://www.strongtowns.org/journal/2018/10/9/the-failure-of-just-add-water-urbanism
   8. *Ibid.*
   9. DeWolf, Chris. (February 18, 2002).

"Why New Urbanism Fails." *Planetizen*. Retrieved August 15, 2020. https://www.planetizen.com/node/42
   10. Condon, Tom. (April 2, 2018). "New Movie Will Revive Painful Lesson in How Not to Redevelop a City." *The CT Mirror*. Retrieved August 17, 2020. https://ctmirror.org/2018/04/02/new-movie-will-revive-painful-lesson-not-redevelop-city/
   11. *Ibid.*
   12. *Ibid.*
   13. Lange, Alexandra. (September 30, 2019). "Who's Afraid of the Pedestrian Mall?" Curbed.com. Retrieved August 17, 2020. https://www.curbed.com/2019/9/30/20885226/best-pedestrian-mall-design#:~:text=Fulton%20Mall's%20success%20offers%20clues,shoppers%20who%20are%20already%20there.
   14. Yakas, Ben. (July 22, 2020). "Report: DiBlasio's Open Streets Plan Falls Short of What NYC Needs." Gothamist.com. Retrieved August 18, 2020. https://gothamist.com/news/report-de-blasios-open-streets-plan-falls-short-what-nyc-needs
   15. *Ibid.*
   16. Milliken, Maureen. (May 12, 2020). "Rockland to Close Main Street to Traffic to Spur Shopping." *MaineBiz*. Retrieved August 18, 2020. https://www.mainebiz.biz/article/rockland-to-close-main-street-to-traffic-to-spur-shopping
   17. *Ibid.*
   18. *Ibid.*
   19. Andrews, Ethan. (June 23, 2020). "A Defiant Juneteenth in Rockland." *The Free Press*. Retrieved August 20, 2020. https://freepressonline.com/Content/Download-the-current-issue-as-a-pdf/Features/Article/A-Defiant-Juneteenth-in-Rockland/93/78/69634
   20. Abate, Lauren. (July 18, 2020). "Rockland's Main Street Won't Be A Pedestrian Plaza This Summer. But Here's the New Plan." *Bangor Daily News*. Retrieved August 20, 2020. https://bangordailynews.com/2020/07/18/news/midcoast/rocklands-main-street-wont-be-a-pedestrian-plaza-this-summer-but-heres-the-new-plan/
   21. *Ibid.*
   22. Email to the author, August 1, 2020.

## Chapter 11

1. Smith, Noah. (September 13, 2018). "Diversity Is An American Strength, Not Weakness." *Bloomberg*. Retrieved August 22, 2020. https://www.bloombergquint.com/view/diversity-is-an-american-strength-not-weakness

2. Kendler, Courtney. (October 22, 2015). "Diversity: Can It Be Saved in Small-Town America?" Michigan State University School of Journalism. Retrieved August 22, 2020. https://news.jrn.msu.edu/2015/10/diversity-can-it-be-saved-in-small-town-america/

3. Ibid.
4. Ibid.
5. Ibid.
6. Ibid.
7. Ibid.
8. Ibid.

9. Johnson, Shauna (January 10, 2019). "Huntington's Open to All Campaign Marks Milestone." *Metro News*. Retrieved August 22, 2020. https://wvmetronews.com/2019/01/10/huntingtons-open-to-all-campaign-marks-milestone/

10. Ibid.
11. Ibid.
12. Ibid.
13. Ibid.

14. Hessler, Courtney. (January 9, 2018). "Huntington Expands Its Open to All Campaign." https://www.herald-dispatch.com/news/huntington-expands-its-open-to-all-campaign/article_2558db9e-60b2-5113-aed3-f160a06327c8.html

15. Davis, Clark. (March 3, 2016). "Huntington Announces LGBT Inclusive Open to All Campaign." West Virginia Public Broadcasting. Retrieved August 22, 2020. https://www.wvpublic.org/post/huntington-announces-lgbt-inclusive-open-all-campaign#stream/0

16. "Why Does Food Bring People Together?" (2016). Labelle Assiette Blog. Retrieved August 22, 2020. https://labelleassiette.co.uk/blog/food-bring-people-together/

17. Williamson-Baker, Sarah. Gaskill, Sarah. (June 15, 2017). "How One Small Town in North Carolina Celebrates Cultural Diversity." National League of Cities. Retrieved August 22, 2020. https://www.nlc.org/article/how-one-small-town-ini-north-carolina-celebrates-cultural-diversity

18. Ibid.
19. Ibid.
20. Ibid.

21. Anderson, Brett. (July 22, 2020). "Small Town Minnesota Eatery Serves A Lesson in Diversity." *Star Tribune*. Retrieved August 22, 2020. https://m.startribune.com/small-town-minnesota-eatery-serves-a-lesson-in-diversity/571862571/

22. Ibid.

23. Belluck, Pam. (October 15, 2002). "Mixed Welcome as Somalis Settle in Maine City." *New York Times*. Retrieved August 22, 2020. https://www.nytimes.com/2002/10/15/us/mixed-welcome-as-somalis-settle-in-a-maine-city.html

24. Ibid.
25. Ibid.

26. Interview with the author, August 5, 2020.

# Bibliography

Abate, Lauren. (July 18, 2020). "Rockland's Main Street Won't Be a Pedestrian Plaza This Summer. But Here's the New Plan." *Bangor Daily News*. Retrieved August 20, 2020. https://bangordailynews.com/2020/07/18/news/midcoast/rocklands-main-street-wont-be-a-pedestrian-plaza-this-summer-but-heres-the-new-plan/

"Advantages of Small Town Living." (2020). City of Toccoa. Retrieved September 2, 2020. https://www.cityoftoccoa.com/advantages-of-small-town-living.cfm

"Americorps Vista." (2020). Retrieved July 13, 2020. https://www.nationalservice.gov/programs/americorps/americorps-programs/americorps-vista

Anderson, Brett. (July 22, 2020). "Small Town Minnesota Eatery Serves a Lesson in Diversity." *Star Tribune*. Retrieved August 22, 2020. https://m.startribune.com/small-town-minnesota-eatery-serves-a-lesson-in-diversity/571862571/

Andrews, Ethan. (June 23, 2020). "A Defiant Juneteenth in Rockland." *The Free Press*. Retrieved August 20, 2020. https://freepressonline.com/Content/Download-the-current-issue-As-a-pdf/Features/Article/A-Defiant-Juneteenth-in-Rockland/93/78/69634

"Are Millennials Interested in Art? Yes, New Park West Gallery Study Finds." Park West Gallery. (September 25, 2018). Ciston PR Newswire. Retrieved August 2, 2020. https://www.prnewswire.com/news-releases/are-millennials-interested-in-art-yes-new-park-west-gallery-study-finds-300718490.html

"The Art of Revitalizing Downtown Residential." (October 9, 2012). Vierbicher. Retrieved August 3, 2020. https://www.vierbicher.com/market-expansion-the-art-of-revitalizing-downtown-residential/#

"Article 3: Planning Area and Regulating Plan Design." Retrieved July 20, 2020. https://user-3vpeqil.cld.bz/Design-Manual/20/#zoom=z

Auer, Michael J. (October 1991). "The Preservation of Historic Signs." Preservation Briefs. Retrieved July 16, 2020. https://www.nps.gov/tps/how-to-preserve/briefs/25-signs.htm

Barnhart, Kirsten. (May 13, 2020). "Speaker System Fills Downtown Van Wert with Music." *Times Bulletin*. Retrieved July 22, 2020. https://timesbulletin.com/Content/News/News/Article/Speaker-system-fills-downtown-Van-Wert-with-music/2/4/224310

Belluck, Pam. (October 15, 2002). "Mixed Welcome as Somalis Settle in Maine City." *New York Times*. Retrieved August 22, 2020. https://www.nytimes.com/2002/10/15/us/mixed-welcome-as-somalis-settle-in-a-maine-city.html

Bend, Oregon, US Census. (2020). http://www.bend.or.us/index.aspx?page=634

Bhadauria, A. (August 2016). "Investigating the Role of Aesthetics in Consumer Moral Judgment and Creativity." University of Wisconsin Milwaukee. Retrieved July 20,2020, https://dc.uwm.edu/cgi/viewcontent.cgi?article=2343&context=etd

Bliss, Laura. (July 12, 2019). "A Small Town Decides Parking Can't Be a Bargain Anymore." *City Lab*. Retrieved August

17, 2020. https://www.bloomberg. com/news/articles/2019-07-12/why-a-small-town-wants-to-charge-more-for-parking

Bradshaw, Andrew. (July 3, 2017). *7 Steps to Crisis Management*. BBN International. Retrieved August 8, 2020. https://bbn-international.com/2017/07/03/7-steps-to-crisis-management/

Brown, Melissa. (March 22, 2015). "Mayor Walt Maddox: Tuscaloosa's Tornado Tested Leader." *Tuscaloosa Real Time News*. Retrieved August 9, 2020. https://www.al.com/news/tuscaloosa/2015/03/mayor_walt_maddox_tuscaloosas.html

Carter, Eileen. (April 12, 2020). "In Defense of the Prada Marfa Sign in 'Gossip Girl.'" Garage.com. Retrieved August 6, 2020. https://garage.vice.com/en_us/article/n7jp98/in-defense-of-the-prada-marfa-sign-in-gossip-girl

Cartier, Brad. (May 14, 2020. "The Rising Interest in Rural and Small Town Real Estate." Fool.com. Retrieved September 1, 2020. https://www.fool.com/millionacres/real-estate-market/articles/the-rising-interest-in-rural-and-small-town-real-estate/

Catoe, Mandy. (March 19, 2017). "Helping towns rediscover their spark: Sims Foundation brings in partner with track record of helping communities." *The Lancaster News*. Retrieved July 25, 2020. https://www.thelancasternews.com/content/helping-towns-rediscover-their-spark

"The Charter of the New Urbanism." (2020). Congress for the New Urbanism. Retrieved August 15, 2020. https://www.cnu.org/who-we-are/charter-new-urbanism

"City of Edmonds Flower Basket Program." (2020). City of Edmonds. Retrieved July 21, 2020. http://www.edmondswa.gov/edmonds-newsletter-home/2910-city-of-edmonds-flower-backet-program.html

"Co-branding: Residents' Picks for Biddeford-Saco's New Slogan." (March 19, 2007). *MaineBiz*. Retrieved July 31, 2020. https://www.mainebiz.biz/article/co-branding-residents-picks-for-biddeford-sacos-new-slogan

Cohen, Alina (May 25, 2018). "The Fake Prada Store in the Texas Desert That Became an Art Mecca." Artsy.net. Retrieved August 6, 2020. https://www.artsy.net/article/artsy-editorial-fake-prada-store-texas-desert-art-mecca

Coleman, Justine and Isaac Windes. (August 23, 2019). "Small Communities Struggle to Cope with Large Disasters." Nondoc.com. Retrieved August 7, 2020. https://nondoc.com/2019/08/13/small-communities-strugg le-to-cope-with-large-disasters/

Condon, Tom. (April 2, 2018). New Movie Will Revive Painful Lesson in How Not to Redevelop a City." *The CT Mirror*. Retrieved August 17, 2020. https://ctmirror.org/2018/04/02/new-movie-will-revive-painful-lesson-not-redevelop-city/

Cotton, Max. (July 10, 2020). "Cheyenne's First Pocket Park Opens." *Wyoming News Now*. Retrieved July 22, 2020. https://www.wyomingnewsnow.tv/2020/07/10/cheyennes-first-pocket-park-opens/

"Creating Mini Parks for Increased Physical Activity." (2011). National Recreation and Park Association. Retrieved July 21, 2020. https://www.nrpa.org/contentassets/f768428a39aa4035ae55 b2aaff372617/pocket-parks.pdf

Davis, Clark. (March 3, 2016). "Huntington Announces LGBT Inclusive Open to All Campaign." West Virginia Public Broadcasting. Retrieved August 22, 2020. https://www.wvpublic.org/post/huntington-announces-lgbt-inclusive-open-all-campaign#stream/0

DeWolf, Chris. (February 18, 2002). "Why New Urbanism Fails." *Planetizen*. Retrieved August 15, 2020. https://www.planetizen.com/node/42

Dishman, Lydia. (July 31, 2015). "Scientific Proof That Your Gut Is Best At Making Decisions." *Fast Company*. Retrieved July 24, 2020. https://www.fastcompany.com/3049248/scientific-proof-that-your-gut-is-best-at-making-decisions

"Downtown Augusta Two Way Traffic Feasibility Study." Maine Traffic Resources. (2015).

"Downtown Nampa Main Street Coordinator." (2013). Americorps Vista. Retrieved July 15, 2020. https://my.americorps.gov/mp/listing/view

Listing.do;jsessionid=jGnyQ5yP3xz5YRn8lY2LqxkJB8bhx1fBypb2B3l1Yzxd1JWQWF5!491985738?id=48339&fromSearch=true

"Downtown Parking Myths, Realities and Solutions." PDF Slide. Retrieved August 11, 2020. https://pdfslide.net/reader/f/downtown-parking-myths-realities-and-solutions-parking-myths-realities-and-solutions

Edwards, K. (2019). "No Accidents but Parking a Concern Since Augusta Downtown Traffic Went Two Way." https://www.centralmaine.com/2019/12/20/no-accidents-but-parking-a-concern-since-augusta-downtown-traffic-went-two-way/

Edwards, Keith. (2019). "Work to Convert Downtown Augusta to Two Way Traffic Set to Begin Monday." https://www.centralmaine.com/2019/07/26/work-to-convert-downtown-augusta-to-two-way-traffic-set-to-begin-monday/

"Evaluating Housing Opportunities." (June 24, 2011). University of Wisconsin. Retrieved August 2, 2020. https://fyi.extension.wisc.edu/downtown-market-analysis/analysis-of-opportunities-by-sector/housing/

Fitzgerald, Sandy (2012). "What is the Difference Between Arts & Culture?" *Culturefighter*. Retrieved August 4, 2020. https://www.culturefighter.eu/concept-of-creative-industries/critique/what-is-the-difference-between-arts-and-culture

Gilderbloom, John. (June 11, 2014). "Two-way Streets Can Fix Declining Downtown Neighborhoods." *Planetizen*. Retrieved June 19, 2020. https://www.planetizen.com/node/69354.

Glasser, C. (2020). "New Albany Did What Louisville Has Not: Pushed Through Downtown Street Redesign." https://www.leoweekly.com/2020/02/new-albany-louisville-not-pushed-downtown-street-redesign/

Good, Karen. (2002). "Preservation of Small Town Character in the Town Center of Rutland, Massachusetts." https://scholarworks.umass.edu/cgi/viewcontent.cgi?article=1035&context=larp_ms_projects

Greene, Andy. (December 23, 2013). "John Mellencamp: My Life in 15 Songs." *Rolling Stone*. Retrieved August 31, 2020. https://www.rollingstone.com/music/music-lists/john-mellencamp-my-life-in-15-songs-11308/

"Growth Was Stagnating." Brookings.edu. Retrieved August 31, 2020. https://www.brookings.edu/research/even-before-coronavirus-census-shows-u-s-cities-growth-was-stagnating/

Hall, Michael. (2010). *Owen County Quilt Trail*. Owenton, KY: Owen County Extension Homemakers.

Hayden, Dolores. (1995). *The Power of Place: Urban Landscapes as Public History*. Cambridge: MIT Press.

Hendricks, Michael. (March 31, 2020). "The End of Cities?" E21.org. Retrieved August 28, 2020. https://economics21.org/have-we-reached-the-end-of-cities

Henerby, Ann. (2015). "The Rules of the Road: Then Versus Now." https://www.enotrans.org/article/the-rules-of-the-road-then-versus-now/.

Hessler, Courtney. (January 9, 2018). "Huntington Expands Its Open to All Campaign." https://www.herald-dispatch.com/news/huntington-expands-its-open-to-all-campaign/article_2558db9e-60b2-5113-aed3-f160a06327c8.html

Horbovetz, Arian. (October 9, 2018). "The Failure of 'Just Add Water' Urbanism." *Strong Towns*. Retrieved August 15, 2020. https://www.strongtowns.org/journal/2018/10/9/the-failure-of-just-add-water-urbanism

Hough, Sue. (August 5, 2020). "Small Town Markets Have Huge Investment Potential in 2020—Here's Why (& How to Capitalize on It)." *Bigger Pockets*. Retrieved August 28, 2020. https://www.biggerpockets.com/blog/small-town-markets-have-huge-investment-potential-in-2020

Houghton, K. (February 4, 2018). "Through Boom or Bust, Oregon Small Town Rides Theme to Maintain Identity." *Bozeman Daily Chronicle*. Retrieved July 31, 2020. https://www.bozemandailychronicle.com/news/through-boom-or-bust-oregon-small-town-rides-theme-to-maintain-identity/article_2c793ae8-cfc5-5de0-b4ce-695933e8e403.html

"How Community Heart and Soul Works." (2020). Community Heart & Soul. Retrieved July 12, 2020. https://

www.communityheartandsoul.org/what-we-do/

"How Does Art Affect Culture and Society?" (2020). Reference.com. Retrieved August 3, 2020. https://www.masterpiecemixers.com/art-affect-culture-society/

"How Millennials Influence the Art Market." Widewalls Editorial. (December 18, 2019). *Widewalls*. Retrieved August 3, 2020. https://www.widewalls.ch/magazine/millennials-art-market

"How Small Towns and Cities Can Use Local Assets to Rebuild Their Economies: Lessons from Successful Places." (May 2015). United States Environmental Protection Agency. Retrieved August 2, 2020. https://www.epa.gov/sites/production/files/2015-05/documents/competitive_advantage_051215_508_final.pdf

Hunt, D. Harold. (August 17, 2017). "This Old Loft Downtown: Living in Small Town Texas." Texas A&M Real Estate Center. Retrieved August 1, 2020. https://www.recenter.tamu.edu/articles/tierra-grande/This-Old-Loft

"Introduction." (2020). One Holyoke CDC. Retrieved July 13, 2020. https://www.oneholyoke.org/about-us/introduction/

James, Geoffrey. (2020). "33 Encouraging Quotes for Times of Crisis." Crisis.com. Retrieved August 7, 2020. https://www.inc.com/geoffrey-james/33-encouraging-quotes-for-times-of-crisis.html

Johnson, Shauna (January 10, 2019). "Huntington's Open to All Campaign Marks Milestone." *Metro News*. Retrieved August 22, 2020. https://wvmetronews.com/2019/01/10/huntingtons-open-to-all-campaign-marks-milestone/

Karas, David. (January 6, 2019). "One Man's Mission to Revitalize Small Town America." *The Christian Science Monitor*. Retrieved July 25, 2020. https://www.csmonitor.com/World/Making-a-Difference/2019/0106/One-man-s-mission-to-revitalize-small-town-America

Kendler, Courtney. (October 22, 2015). "Diversity: Can It Be Saved in Small-Town America?" Michigan State University School of Journalism. Retrieved August 22, 2020. https://news.jrn.msu.edu/2015/10/diversity-can-it-be-saved-in-small-town-america/

Lange, Alexandra. (September 30, 2019). "Who's Afraid of the Pedestrian Mall?" Curbed.com. Retrieved August 17, 2020. https://www.curbed.com/2019/9/30/20885226/best-pedestrian-mall-design#:~:text=Fulton%20Mall's%20success%20offers%20clues,shoppers%20who%20are%20already%20there.

Lee, Anna. (July 16, 2020). "After 20 Years Mice on Main Continue to Delight and Enthrall." *Greenville Journal*. Retrieved August 5, 2020. https://greenvillejournal.com/arts-culture/after-20-years-mice-on-main-greenville-continue-to-delight-and-entrall/

"The Life of Eno." (2019) Eno Center for Transportation. https://www.enotrans.org/the-life-of-eno

Little Free Library. (2020). Retrieved August 4, 2020. https://littlefreelibrary.org/

Madori-Davis, Dominic. (May 19, 2020). "Wealthy New Yorkers fled the city when the coronavirus outbreak started. New data shows where they went—and which neighborhoods emptied out the most." *New York Times*. Retrieved August 26, 2020. https://www.businessinsider.com/where-wealthy-nyc-residents-went-during-coronavirus-outbreak-nyt-report-2020-5

*The Main Street Movement*. (2020). Main Street America. Retrieved July 10, 2020. https://www.mainstreet.org/mainstreetamerica/themovement

Malone, Bonnie. (April 28, 2015). "How Sisters Became Sisters." *The Nugget Newspaper*. Retrieved July 29, 2020. https://nuggetnews.com/Content/Current-News/Current-News/Article/How-Sisters-Became-Sisters/5/5/23509

Masalo, Dismas. (February 2002). "Community, Identity & the Cultural Space." Cairn.info. https://www.cairn.info/revue-rue-descartes-2002-2-page-19.htm#

Maxwell, J. (May 5, 2003). "Good Leaders Learn How to Trust Intuition, Not Just Logic." *Maximum Leadership*. July 27, 2020. https://www.bizjournals.com/pittsburgh/stories/2003/05/05/smallb2.html

McCray, Becky. (April 2, 2013). "How to Market a Small Town." *Small Biz Survival*. Retrieved July 28, 2020. https://smallbizsurvival.com/2013/03/how-to-market-a-community.html

McCrea, Nick. (April 9, 2013). "With Closure of Biddeford Incinerator, What Will Maine Do with Its Trash?" *Bangor Daily News*. Retrieved July 25, 2020. https://bangordailynews.com/2013/04/09/news/bangor/shuttered-incinerator-raises-concerns-about-how-maine-will-handle-trash-in-the-future/

McFall, Caitlin. (August 5, 2020). "Cuomo Begs Wealthy New Yorkers to Come Back to Save the City: 'I'll buy you a drink.'" Fox News. Retrieved August 26, 2020. https://www.foxnews.com/us/cuomo-begs-wealthy-new-yorkers-to-come-back-to-save-the-city-ill-buy-you-a-drink

McMahon, Edward T. (October 2018). "The Secrets of Successful Communities." New Hampshire Municipal Association. Retrieved July 22, 2020. https://www.nhmunicipal.org/town-city-article/secrets-successful-small-communities

McPherson, Grant. (February 1, 2018). "Saco Hires PR Firm. Former Logo Up in the Air." *Biddeford-Saco-OOB Courier*. Retrieved August 1, 2020. https://chambermaster.blob.core.windows.net/userfiles/UserFiles/chambers/3069/File/SacohiresPRfirm.pdf

Meschberger, Alesa. (April 1, 2019). "Progress 2019: Downtown Garden City Sees Variety of New Business Openings." *The Garden City Telegram*. Retrieved August 1, 2020. https://www.gctelegram.com/news/20190401/progress-2019-dowtown-garden-city-sees-variety-of-new-business-openings

Milliken, Maureen. (May 12, 2020). "Rockland to Close Main Street to Traffic to Spur Shopping." *MaineBiz*. Retrieved August 18, 2020. https://www.mainebiz.biz/article/rockland-to-close-main-street-to-traffic-to-spur-shopping

Moon, Troy. (May 10, 2018.) "Pensacola's Fiesta of Five Flags." *Pensacola News Journal*. Retrieved July 15, 2020. https://www.pnj.com/story/news/2018/05/10/pensacola-fiesta-five-flag-2018-events-celebrate-citys-history/594117002/

"New Pocket Park Opens Downtown." (July 14, 2020). *The Cheyenne Post*. Retrieved July 22, 2020. https://www.thecheyennepost.com/news/new-pocket-park-opens-downtown/article_ec9e3974-c5f6-11ea-90be-4b0082100303.html

Noe, M. (2015). "Brady Street Business Owners Say Two Way Traffic Is Providing a Boost." https://www.wqad.com/article/news/local/drone/8-in-the-air/brady-street-business-owners-say-two-way-traffic-is-providing-a-boost/526-128ba320-9a08-4d05-b274-e0106fc599b1

O'Brien, Shannon. (November 5, 2019). "Proposed Downtown Olathe Apartments Stir Controversy, Questions About Old Settlers' Future." Fox4kc.com. Retrieved July 26, 2020. https://fox4kc.com/news/proposed-downtown-olathe-apartments-stir-controversy-questions-about-old-settlers-future/

Ocejo, R.E., Ervin B. Kosta, and A. Mann. (March 13, 2020). "Centering Small Cities for Urban Sociology in the 21st Century." *City & Community*. Retrieved September 2, 2020. https://onlinelibrary.wiley.com/doi/full/10.1111/cico.12484

"The Old Mill District." (2020). Visit Bend. Retrieved August 2, 2020. https://www.visitbend.com/about-bend-oregon/moving-bend-oregon/neighborhoods/the-old-mill-district/

"One Small Town, Over 100 Free Libraries." (2020). Little Free Library. Retrieved August 4, 2020. https://littlefreelibrary.org/one-small-town-over-100-little-libraries/

Pafundi, Jason, and Dennis Hoey. (January 25, 2018). "Flooding Puts Areas of Augusta, Hallowell Under Icy Water." *Kennebec Journal*. Retrieved August 6, 2020. https://www.sunjournal.com/2018/01/15/flooding-puts-areas-of-augusta-hallowell-under-icy-water/

Pant, Paula. (June 15, 2020). "Benefits of Living and Working in a Small Town." *The Balance*. Retrieved September 1, 2020. https://www.thebalance.com/benefits-of-living-and-working-in-a-small-town-453785

Peltonen, Mari. (February 3, 2020). "A Specialist in Urban Study Aesthetics Wants to Turn the City Into a Living Room For All." https://www.helsinki.fi/en/news/sustainability-news/a-specialist-in-urban-aesthetics-wants-to-turn-the-city-into-a-living-room-for-all

Pendleton, Craig. (September 2012). "Craig's Column." *Biddeford-Saco Chamber News*. Retrieved July 31, 2020. https://myemail.constantcontact.com/September-News-.html?soid=1109032175955&aid=Va-r2Ag6RLc

Pinkerton, J. (April 25, 2019). "The Kansas City Metro Posts Solid Growth." KCEconomy.com. Retrieved July 26, 2020. https://kceconomy.org/2019/04/25/the-kansas-city-metro-posts-solid-population-growth/#:~:text=The%20Kansas%20City%20metro%20area,The%20Dallas%2DFt

Pollard, D. (August 21, 2013). "A Model of Identity and Community." Resilience.org. https://www.resilience.org/stories/2013-08-21/a-model-of-identity-and-community/

"Portland Crafts Slogan to Put City on the Map". (April 4, 2013). *Portland Press Herald*. Retrieved August 1, 2020. https://www.pressherald.com/2013/04/30/portland-crafts-slogan-to-put-city-on-the-map_2013-05-01/#

Powell-Brown, Ann (2003). "Can You Be a Teacher of Literacy If You Don't Love to Read?" *Journal of Adolescent & Adult Literacy*, Vol. 47 No. 4: 284–288.

"Psychology Behind Developing Brand Loyalty." (2020). USC Dornsife. Retrieved July 28, 2020. https://appliedpsychologydegree.usc.edu/blog/psychology-behind-developing-brand-loyalty/

Quinn, Patrick. (April 13, 2013). "After Devastating Tornado, Town Reborn Green." *USA Today*. Retrieved August 8, 2020. https://www.usatoday.com/story/news/greenhouse/2013/04/13/greensburg-kansas/2078901/

Quinn, Paul, et al., 2008. "Preference for Attractive Faces in Human Infants Extends Beyond Conspecifics." HHS Public Access. https://www.ncbi.nlm.nih.gov/pmc/articles/PMC2566458/

Rice, Wayne T. (January 25, 2019). "Day After Sebring Shooting, City Copes with Tragedy, Struggles to Make Sense of 5 Deaths." *Florida Today*. Retrieved August 9, 2020. https://www.floridatoday.com/story/news/2019/01/25/sebring-shooting-sun-trust-bank/2677401002/

Riggs, W. and B. Appleyard. (2016). "The Economic Impact of One to Two-way Street Conversions: Advancing a Context Sensitive Framework." https://spa.sdsu.edu/documents/Economic_Impact.pdf.

Ritter, Sarah. (November 11, 2019). "This Joco Downtown Could Get "First Big Redevelopment.' Will It Force Businesses Out?" *The Kansas City Star*. Retrieved July 27, 2020. https://www.kansascity.com/news/local/article237114019.html

"Rural Emergency Preparedness and Response." (January 25, 2019). Rural Health Info Hub. Retrieved August 5, 2020. https://www.ruralhealthinfo.org/topics/emergency-preparedness-and-response

Ryan, Jim. (2015). "How the Mice on Main Came to Main Street." Mice on Main. Retrieved August 5, 2020. http://www.miceonmain.com/historyofmiceonmain.html

"Section 7: The Urban Experience." (2014). The People Place and Space Reader. Retrieved September 2, 2020. https://peopleplacespace.org/toc/section-7/

Shen, Maxine. (August 18, 2020). "Cuomo Blames POLICE for Crime Wave: New York governor says cops must address 'lack of trust' in communities as Big Apple shootings surge 82% and threatens to pull funding for NYPD if reforms are not in place next year." *Daily Mail*. Retrieved August 26, 2020. https://www.dailymail.co.uk/news/article-8637797/New-York-Gov-Cuomo-blasts-lawlessness-state-NYC-lack-trust-fuels-urgent-crisis.html

Short, Aaron. (January 2, 2020). "Americans Are Poised to Drive Less in 2020: This could be the year when Americans start making fewer car trips." Streets-Blog USA. Retrieved August 4, 2020. https://usa.streetsblog.org/2020/01/02/are-americans-poised-to-drive-less-in-2020

Smith, Noah. (September 13, 2018). "Diversity Is an American Strength, Not Weakness." Bloomberg. Retrieved August 22, 2020. https://www.bloom

bergquint.com/view/diversity-is-an-american-strength-not-weakness

Steuteville, R. (2019). "Cities benefit from restoring two-way traffic: Two-way streets prove safer, more walkable, and more supportive of business than one-way streets for Midwestern cities." https://www.cnu.org/publicsquare/2019/07/09/cities-benefit-one-way-two-way-conversions

Stromberg, Joseph. (June 27, 2014). "Why Free Parking is Bad for Everyone." Vox.com. Retrieved August 15, 2020. https://www.vox.com/2014/6/27/5849280/why-free-parking-is-bad-for-everyone

Sturt, D., and T. Nordstrom. (July 3, 2019). "6 Dangers of Having Great Leadership Intuition." *Forbes*. Retrieved July 24, 2020. https://www.forbes.com/sites/davidsturt/2019/07/03/6-dangers-of-having-great-leadership-intuition/#7648be362ed2

Suttie, J. (April 26, 2019). "Why Trees Can Make You Happier: Research suggest that being around trees is good for our mental and social well-being." *Greater Good Magazine*. Retrieved July 20, 2020. https://greatergood.berkeley.edu/article/item/why_trees_can_make_you_happier

Thompson, Kevin D. (August 28, 2016). "Little Free Libraries Will Soon Be Popping Up in Lake Worth." *Palm Beach Post*. Retrieved August 5, 2020. https://www.palmbeachpost.com/article/20151016/NEWS/812020894

"Trees to Return Downtown." (May 16, 2007). *Duluth News Tribune*. Retrieved July 21, 2020. https://www.duluthnewstribune.com/news/2248734-trees-return-downtown

"Two-Way Street Networks: More Efficient than Previously Thought?" (2012). http://www.accessmagazine.org/fall-2012/two-way-street-networks-efficient-previously-thought/

VanAuken, B. (September 12, 2014). "Evaluating City Mottos, Taglines, and Slogans." Branding Strategy Insider. Retrieved July 29, 2020. https://www.brandingstrategyinsider.com/evaluating-city-mottos-taglines-and-slogans/#.XxIf7RdKjIU

Walker, W. et al. (2015). "Downtown Streets: Are We Strangling Ourselves on One Way Networks?" https://nacto.org/wp-content/uploads/2015/04/Are-We-Strangling-ourselves-on-one-way-networks_Walker.pdf

Wayland, S. (2012). "A Business Case for Conversion from One-Way to Two-Way Streets." https://raisethehammer.org/article/1605/a_business_case_for_conversion_from_one-way_to_two-way_streets

Wellner, B. (2015). "Harrison Street Closes: Brady Now Two way." *Quad City Times*. https://qctimes.com/news/local/harrison-street-closes-brady-now-two-way/article_35da94e4-17da-5de7-8ceb-8d17b81d11c2.html,

"What Is a Fallacy?" (2020). Palomar. Retrieved August 11, 2020. https://www2.palomar.edu/users/bthompson/What%20is%20a%20Fallacy.html

"Wheeling Heritage." (2020). Main Street America. Retrieved July 11, 2020. https://www.mainstreet.org/mainstreetamerica/mainstreetawards/gamsa/new-item/wheeling

"Wheeling Heritage Wins Prestigious 2019 Great American Main Street Award." (2019). West Virginia Department of Commerce. Retrieved July 12, 2020. https://commerce.wv.gov/wheeling-heritage-wins-prestigious-2019-great-american-main-street-award/

"Who We Are." (2020). Main Street America. Retrieved July 10, 2020. https://www.mainstreet.org/about-us

"Why Does Food Bring People Together?" (2016). Labelle Assiette Blog. Retrieved August 22, 2020. https://labelleassiette.co.uk/blog/food-bring-people-together/

Williamson-Baker, Sarah, and Sarah Gaskill. (June 15, 2017). "How One Small Town in North Carolina Celebrates Cultural Diversity." National League of Cities. Retrieved August 22, 2020. https://www.nlc.org/article/how-one-small-town-in-north-carolina-celebrates-cultural-diversity

Yakas, Ben. (July 22, 2020). "Report: DiBlasio's Open Streets Plan Falls Short of What NYC Needs." Gothamist.com. Retrieved August 18, 2020. https://gothamist.com/news/report-de-blasios-open-streets-plan-falls-short-what-nyc-needs

# Index

Americorps VISTA  28–29
Augusta, Maine  9, 10, 15, 30–31, 34, 41–43, 44, 45, 59, 61, 63–64, 68, 73, 75, 80, 86–89, 90–92, 93, 103–104, 108–110, 111, 114, 123–127, 128, 134–137, 144–146, 150, 152–153, 196
Augusta Downtown Alliance  9, 17, 30–31, 44, 56, 59–60, 73, 75, 79, 87–88, 94, 100, 108–110, 135–136, 141, 144, 153, 154, 156–161, 162–163

Baby Boomers  7, 9, 116, 128, 130
Baltimore, Maryland  83
Beastie Boys  4
beauty premium  47–48
Bend, Oregon  121–123, 128
Berlin, New Hampshire  183
Biddeford, Maine  27, 69–70, 106–108, 111
Bloomington, Indiana  4
Boise, Idaho  6
Boston, Massachusetts  3
Bozeman, Montana  6
Brooks, Roger  97–100, 102, 108
Brooks Resources  104–106
Buffalo, New York  3
bump outs  90

Central Bend Development Program  122
Charleston, West Virginia  6
Cheyenne, Wyoming  57–58
Cheyenne Downtown Development Authority  57–58
Chicago, Illinois  3, 11
Cleveland, Ohio  3, 11
Coeur d'Alene, Idaho  36
Commerce, Texas  117
community development corporation  27, 32
Community Heart & Soul  24–27, 32, 69–70
Conch Republic  38–40
Covid-19  1–2, 57–58, 115, 150, 175, 184
Cuomo, Andrew  1–2

Damasio, Antonio  65, 67
*Daily News*  1
Davenport, Iowa  85–86

Denison, Texas  117
Denton, Texas  117, 118
Detroit, Michigan  3
*Downeast Magazine*  10
Downtown Fresno Partnership  174
Downtown Second Story Residential Program  119–121
Duluth, Iowa  55

Edmonds, Washington  56
Eno, William Phelps  79

Fleury, Larry  43–45
Floyd, George  183–184
Flint, Michigan  97
*Forbes*  66–67
forest bathing  54
Four Point Approach  22
Frey, Glenn  4

Garden City, Kansas  119–121, 128
Gardiner, New York  15
Gen X  7, 9, 130, 131
Gen Z  4, 9, 131, 184
Good, Karen  35–36
Grand Forks, North Dakota  90
Great Recession  4, 173
Greater Downtown Council  55
Greensburg, Kansas  153–154
greenscapes  49, 53–55, 62
Greenville, South Carolina  139–142
GrowSmart Maine  178–181
Gruen, Victor  173–174

Hallowell, Maine  15
Hayden, Dolores  34
Hershey, Pennsylvania  97
Holt, Michigan  186–187
Holyoke, Massachusetts  27–28
Horbovetz, Arian  170–171
Hough, Sue  2–3
Huntington, West Virginia  187–190

Indianapolis, Indiana  11
Iowa Gambling Task  65

219

## Index

Kalamazoo, Michigan 173
Key West, Florida 38–40, 45
Klein, Gary 67

Laberge Group 166–167
Lake Worth, Florida 137–139
LeBlanc, Andrew 125–127
Leckey, David 69–70
Lewiston, Maine 193–195
little free libraries 13–140
Los Angeles, California 3, 33
Lost Generation 130
Louisville, Kentucky 83
Luke, Keith 90–92

Madison, Wisconsin 6
Main Street 21–24, 26, 27, 32, 82
Main Street Van Wert 58–59
Marfa 142–144
Marshalltown, Iowa 149
McLaughlin, Shawn 161–163
McMahon, Edward T. 13–14, 22
Mellencamp, John 4–5
Miami, Florida 3
Mice on Main 139–142
millennials 4, 7, 9, 116, 117, 128, 130–131, 184, 185
Milwaukee, Wisconsin 3, 138
Morrisville, North Carolina 190–192
Muncie, Indiana 11

Nampa, Idaho 28–29
National Trust 21–22
Nevada City, California 167–169
New Albany, Indiana 84–85
New London, Connecticut 172–173
New London Development Corporation 172–173
New Orleans, Louisiana 3
New York, New York 1–5, 33, 175, 183
Newburyport, Massachusetts 12

Olathe, Kansas 71–72
Old Mill District 122–123
Old Settlers Festival 72
open streets 175
Orlando, Florida 33, 155
Orton Family foundation 69–70
Owen County, Kentucky 36–38
Owenton, Kentucky 36–38, 46

pandemic 1–2, 4, 6, 7, 92, 150, 175, 184
Paris, Texas 117
Parkhurst, Soo 195–198
Parkhurst, Tobias 73–75, 89, 126
Parkland, Florida 155
Patkus, Jesse 59–61

pedestrian malls 90, 173–175, 176
Pensacola, Florida 40–41
Pfizer 172–173
Philadelphia, Pennsylvania 33
Pittsburgh, Pennsylvania 3
pocket parks 57–58
Pouliot, Heather 108–110
Pouliot, Matt 29–31
Prada 142–144
Providence, Rhode Island 3

Redfin 4, 6
Rockland, Maine 175–178
Roodman, Cynthia 144–146
roundabouts 89
Rutland, Massachusetts 35–36

Saco, Maine 106–108
Sacramento, California 6
St. Josephs, Minnesota 190, 192–193
St. Louis, Missouri 3
San Diego, California 3
San Francisco, California 3, 6
San Jose, California 3
San Marcos, Texas 49–53, 117
Seattle, Washington 6
Sebring, Florida 154–155
Seven Steps of Crisis Management 150–152
Shoup, Donald 167–168
Sisters, Oregon 104–106
Skowhegan, Maine 106
Smith, Bill 104–106
Smith, Dylan 117
Smith, Nancy 178–181
soundscaping 49, 58–59, 62
Speck, Jeff 84–85, 87
streetscapes 49, 62
suburbs 8–9
Sulphur Springs, Texas 117

Tacoma, Washington 6
tax increment financing 119
Toccoa, Georgia 7–8
townscapes 49, 62
trickle down(town) economics 112, 127
Tucson, Arizona 3
Tuscaloosa, Alabama 152
Tyler, Texas 117

Van Auken, Brad 101–102
Van Wert, Ohio 58–59

Waco, Texas 117
Warner, W. Lloyd 12
Waterville, Maine 106
Wheeling, West Virginia 23–24

www.ingramcontent.com/pod-product-compliance
Lightning Source LLC
Chambersburg PA
CBHW032041300426
44117CB00009B/1145